D0071279

SPACES OF IDENTITY

With Germany reunited and Europe no longer divided by the Iron Curtain, where does 'Europe' end? Against which Other (besides America) is Europe to be defined, if not against Communism? How is the emergence of a new vision of Japan disrupting cultural dynamics through which Europe, America and the Orient have traditionally understood their mutual relations?

The book has a double focus throughout. At a theoretical level the prime concern is with the question of identity under the conditions of a postmodern geography – specifically with the complex and contradictory nature of cultural identities and with the role of communications technologies in the reconfiguration of contemporary cultural (and often diasporic) identities. These issues are addressed in the context of the contemporary politics of the relations between Europe and its most significant Others – America, Islam and the Orient – against whom Europe's own identity has been and is now being defined. The key questions have become those of power, boundary-marking and exclusion processes, both nationally and internationally. If identity is crucially about difference, the politics of identity necessarily raises questions of authenticity, of roots, tradition and heritage which, in turn, lead into questions of race and ethnicity.

Spaces of Identity is a stimulating account of the complex and contradictory nature of contemporary cultural identities, and important reading for all concerned with the threads from which the pattern of our contemporary identities are being woven.

David Morley is Reader in Communication Studies at Goldsmiths' College, London. **Kevin Robins** is Reader in Cultural Geography and a Researcher at the Centre for Urban and Regional Development Studies, University of Newcastle upon Tyne.

SPACES OF IDENTITY

Global Media, Electronic Landscapes and Cultural Boundaries

David Morley and Kevin Robins

London and New York

First published in 1995
by Routledge
11 New Fetter Lane, London EC4P 4EE

Simultaneously published in the USA and Canada
by Routledge
29 West 35th Street, New York, NY 10001

Set in 10/12 Times
by Florencetype Ltd, Stoodleigh, Devon
Printed and bound in Great Britain by
Mackays of Chatham PLC, Chatham, Kent

British Library Cataloguing in Publication Data
A catalogue record for this book is available from the British Library

Library of Congress Cataloguing in Publication Data
A catalogue record for this book has been requested

ISBN 0-415-09596-4 (hbk)
ISBN 0-415-09597-2 (pbk)

CONTENTS

WAITING FOR THE BARBARIANS

What are we waiting for all crowded in the forum?
    The Barbarians are to arrive today.
Within the Senate-house why is there such inaction?
The Senators making no laws what are they sitting there for?
    Because the Barbarians arrive today.
    What laws now should the Senators be making?
    When the Barbarians come they'll make the laws.

Why did our Emperor get up so early in the morning?
And at the greatest city gate why is he sitting there now,
Upon his throne, officially, why is he wearing his crown?
    Because the Barbarians arrive today.
    The Emperor is waiting to receive
    Their Leader. And in fact he has prepared
    To give him an address. On it he has
    Written him down all sorts of names and titles.

Why have our two Consuls gone out, both of them, and the Praetors,
Today with their red togas on, with their embroidered togas?
Why are they wearing bracelets, and all those amethysts too,
And all those rings on their fingers with splendid flashing
        emeralds?
Why should they be carrying today their precious walkingsticks,
With silver knobs and golden tops so wonderfully carved?
    Because the Barbarians will arrive today;
    Things of this sort dazzle the Barbarians.

And why are the fine orators not come here as usual
To get their speeches off, to say what they have to say?
    Because the Barbarians will be here today;
    And they are bored with eloquence and speechmaking.
Why should this uneasiness begin all of a sudden,
And confusion. How serious people's faces have become.
Why are all the streets and squares emptying so quickly,
And everybody turning home again so full of thought?
    Because night has fallen and the Barbarians have not come.
    And some people have arrived from the frontier;
    They said there are no Barbarians any more.

    And now what will become of us without Barbarians?—
    Those people were some sort of a solution.

C. P. Cavafy
(From *Poems* by C. P. Cavafy, trans.
John Mavrogordato, Hogarth Press,
1971, printed with permission)

INTRODUCTION

There is a double focus throughout this book. It is concerned with the complex and contradictory nature of contemporary cultural identities, and with the role of communications media in the reconfiguration of those identities. Substantively, these issues are addressed in the context of the relationships between Europe and the significant Others – America, Islam, Japan and the Orient – against which its own identity has been, and is now being, defined.

THE RESTRUCTURING OF THE GLOBAL MEDIA

Significant transformations are now occurring in the information and communications media as a consequence of new technological forms of delivery. We are seeing the restructuring of information and image spaces and the production of a new communications geography, characterised by global networks and an international space of information flows; by an increasing crisis of the national sphere; and by new forms of regional and local activity. Our senses of space and place are all being significantly reconfigured.

Patterns of movement and flows of people, culture, goods and information mean that it is now not so much physical boundaries – the geographical distances, the seas or mountain ranges – that define a community or nation's 'natural limits'. Increasingly we must think in terms of communications and transport networks and of the symbolic boundaries of language and culture – the 'spaces of transmission' defined by satellite footprints or radio signals – as providing the crucial, and permeable, boundaries of our age.

We emphasise two key, and seemingly divergent, aspects of the new spatial dynamics, each of which is bound to have an important bearing on European communications politics and upon the development of European identities. On the one hand, technological and market shifts are leading to the emergence of global image industries and world markets; we are witnessing the 'deterritorialisation' of audiovisual production and the

1

elaboration of transnational systems of delivery. On the other hand, however, there have been significant developments towards local production and local distribution networks. Thus, cable and microwave technologies facilitate the fragmentation of mass markets and the targeting of particular audience segments by large media and advertising corporations. There has also been a development towards local and regional production complexes; they are fragile and precarious, but they offer some promise for local economies and local cultures. This tension between globalism and localism is, of course, occurring at the same time as the national focus for broadcasting is arguably becoming less significant and as the public service framework of national media systems is being undermined. The issue is not one of global media or local media, but of how global and local are articulated. Is it possible to develop decentralised media industries and what Kenneth Frampton refers to as a genuinely 'critical regionalism' or a local regional culture that sees itself not introspectively but as an inflexion of global culture and that favours diversity, plurality, discontinuity? These issues take us beyond the impasse of debates around public service broadcasting, with their national perspectives. The significant issues relate to the relationship between supra-national and sub-national spheres. One possibility is global homogeneity. Another, which takes advantage of the progressive aspects of current developments, offers the possibility of reinventing and rearticulating international and local cultures and identities.

THE MAKING OF CONTEMPORARY EUROPE

The European Union has become increasingly conscious of the potential role of the new communications technologies in laying the material supports of (possible) pan-European markets and audiences, and in defining a sense of what it means, in this day and age, to be a 'European'. Its policy increasingly recognises that culture is at the heart of the European project (or, more crudely put, that questions of culture lie beneath the 'bottom line' of the potential profits of pan-European markets). The EU has identified the audiovisual and other communications industries as key instruments in the creation of a sense of European cultural identity. The problem lies in the vast discrepancy between the rather idealistic and over-simplified concept of 'Europe' which recent policy has sought to promote, and the realities of contemporary tribalisms, within and without this 'Europe', whether or not they have yet resulted in the horrors of 'ethnic cleansing'. If we are to understand the current and future role of the communications industries in Europe, we must understand the context in which they are being developed.

The creation of a pan-European market in the audiovisual sector is motivated largely by the ambition to use this as a foundation for competition in global media markets. The European Commission has sought to harness these developments in order to promote what it calls a 'European audiovisual space'. Through a range of initiatives – the MEDIA programme, European Cinema and Television Year (1988), the RACE and Audiovisual EUREKA programmes – it has sought to lay the foundations for a post-national audiovisual territory. Legislative and regulatory liberalisation and harmonisation have had as their goal an era of 'television without frontiers'. This 'Europe without frontiers' means 'the elimination of all barriers to the buying and selling of audiovisual products and to their transmission and reception in the Community'. On this basis, it is argued, European media interests can then become 'global players' alongside American and Japanese conglomerates.

But it is not simply a matter of economic and technological self-assertion. The European broadcasting agenda also has a significant cultural dimension. The question of new media markets is closely associated with improving mutual knowledge among European peoples and increasing their consciousness of the life and destiny they have in common. The European Commission has encouraged programme-makers to appeal to a large European audience because such broadcasts can help to develop the sense of belonging to a Community composed of countries which are different, yet partake of a deep solidarity. This assertion of a common cultural identity is clearly assuming a strategic importance for the present attempt to restore European self-confidence.

But this is not without its problems. Not everyone feels attracted to this kind of Euro-identity, and many are, at the very least, uncertain about what the claims to 'unity in diversity' of European culture might actually mean. The idea of a Europe without frontiers and the experience of transborder media flows can actually work to create anxieties and a sense of cultural disorientation. One response to these upheavals has been to find refuge in more localised senses of place and identity; we have seen the flourishing of cultural regionalism and small nationalisms (Basques, Scots, Bretons and so on). Euro-identity also does little to make room for the large numbers of migrant and diasporic populations now living in the continent. What does the idea of Europe add up to when so many within feel that they are excluded? European identity, for all its apparent self-confidence, remains a vulnerable and anxious phenomenon, and is increasingly articulated with regressive forms of pan-European white racism.

If there are internal tensions, there are also external challenges to the coherence of European identity. Developments which might be seen either as on the periphery of Europe (or as beyond Europe) pose considerable challenges. Developments to the east and south of Europe raise questions about other territories and identities – Balkan, Central European, Baltic, North African, Arab, Islamic, Mediterranean – and of their implications for Europe. Will these developments undermine the small (north-western) vision of Europe? Or might they potentially expand and enrich it?

3

To what extent do these areas seek to develop better relations with Europe? To what extent are they being pulled towards alternative points of reference? What range of identities might be possible within the European 'cultural space'? How might they cohere around elements of both local and cosmopolitan culture? What new boundaries and divisions might develop between social, cultural and ethnic groupings? What is the relation between the previously dominant Western European culture and the newly stirring nationalist cultures of Eastern Europe? Just as the territories outside the European Community must consider their relationship to this cultural and economic space, so must Europe come to terms with what this 'beyond Europe' means for it.

In addition to questions about the changing relations of place and identity in the emerging postmodern geography of Europe, we also address the articulation of these structural developments with the everyday processes of consumption, through which these larger structures are lived and experienced. We address the potential impact of the new communications technologies from the point of view of their domestic users and audiences. The question here is how, for example, new patterns of supply of television programming will be filtered and mediated by the process of domestic consumption, in the everyday practices and domestic rituals through which contemporary electronic communities are reconstituted on a daily basis.

In recent years, the relation of geographically and electronically based communities has received considerable attention. Certainly, the role of broadcasting in the constitution and maintenance of communities through time and space has been increasingly recognised, as has its role in the constitution of national identities. Some have gone so far as to suggest that, in thinking about the question of national and other cultural identities, we might usefully begin with the question of how communication systems are involved in their construction and maintenance. Other commentators have pointed to the role of new communications technologies in mediating social experience in more complex and differentiated ways – whether in terms of the effect of video time-shift in disrupting the 'simultaneity' of social experience presumed by established models of broadcasting, or in terms of the development of various forms of 'narrowcasting' (i.e. programming aimed at specific target audiences) and of local and specialised media production for differentiated audiences.

We explore the issues raised by the development of new forms of localised and fragmented media production and consumption as they interact with questions of national, cultural and ethnic identity. The chapters in this book address the role of broadcasting in supplying a sense of identity – a symbolic or fictional 'homeland' – in an era in which the fragmentation of the established forms of broadcasting (and of their audiences) is but a part of a wider process of fragmentation of public

4

space and the public sphere. Our argument is that the burden of catering to the various forms of 'nostalgia' – for a sense of community, tradition, identity and belonging – falls increasingly on the electronic media at a time when they are, in fact, beginning to operate in new ways, often addressing geographically dispersed segments of different national or other communities.

We are also concerned specifically with questions of memory in the construction of definitions of Europe and European culture. It is in this context that we address the centrality of the metaphor of 'Heimat' or 'homeland', taking as a particular instance the debates opened up in Germany by Edgar Reitz's *Heimat*, with its focus on the opposition Heimat:Fremde (homeland:foreignness). We take the 'German story' to be both a symbolic condensation of many of the most problematic themes of the European past, and a central issue in the contemporary *Realpolitik* of Europe.

In considering the possibilities and the limits of European integration, we are confronted, from the outset, with questions of collective and cultural identity. Europe is experiencing a process of economic and social transformation which is weakening older institutions and structures. The geography of Europe – economic, political and cultural – is being refashioned in the context of an ever more apparent global–local nexus. In this process, there is great scope and potential for elaborating new forms of bonding: new senses of community; new attachments and allegiances; new identities and subjectivities. The question is how 'Europe' is to be reimagined. The danger is that an oppressive European tradition and history will re-establish itself, and that Europe will remain fixed in the 'geographical disposition' that has historically governed the relation between its sovereign identity and the world of the Other. The danger is that empire will reassert itself in new ways. It is in this context that we must consider the significance of new information and communications technologies. In what ways might they contribute to a new geographical disposition and new senses of community? How might they facilitate dialogue between communities of common interest and communities of difference? It cannot simply be assumed that 'television without frontiers' is self-evidently beneficial and integrative. There are frontiers that have nothing to do with trade and markets, and it is with these imagined and imaginary frontiers that we have, ultimately, to come to terms.

EUROPE AND ITS OTHERS

Europe is not just a geographical site, it is also an idea: an idea inextricably linked with the myths of Western civilisation and grievously shaped by the haunting encounters with its colonial Others. These essays are concerned with the European cultural agenda, its ideals, its repressions and its pathologies. We are concerned with historical continuities and discontinuities in European development, with historical traditions as they are invented and reinvented, and with the cultural heritage associated with European/Western civilisation. Inevitably, this means that we are also concerned with the various forms of alterity against which Europe has historically defined its own identity. It is important to note that, within European culture, the construction of 'Otherness' has its own history (cf. McGrane, 1989). Thus, as Atkinson notes,

> In Renaissance discourse, the relevant moral and intellectual frame-work was religious. The non-European alien was coded in terms of the 'pagan', 'heathen', and the demonic. For the Enlightenment, the key feature of the Other was 'ignorance' and 'superstition'. In the nineteenth century, when modern anthropology was born, the 'primitive' was coded in terms of 'development' and evolutionary time.

> (Atkinson, 1992: 40)

In the years since its initial (1978) publication, Edward Said's path-breaking study of *Orientalism* has transformed our understanding of the relations between the 'West and the Rest' (cf. Hall, 1992a). A number of the later chapters in this book take up these concerns. Thus, in our discussion of 'Techno-orientalism' (chapter 8), we take as our starting point the recent wave of cultural paranoia concerning Japan and the Orient, which has been observable both in the USA (witness the concern with Japanese takeovers in Hollywood) and in Europe (witness European outbursts about the imperialist schemes of Japanese business for the domination of the West). It seems that, in this context, the franchise on the story of the future is perceived to be passing into Oriental hands (a recurrent theme in contemporary popular culture, from *Blade Runner* through *Black Rain* to the *Ninja Turtles*, and in political journalism – in Europe and in America). The traditional equation of the West with modernity and of the Orient with the exotic (but underdeveloped) past is thrown into crisis in this new scenario, as the dynamic hub of the world economy is increasingly perceived to have moved from the Atlantic to the Pacific Rim. What concerns us here is the way in which the Orient (and Japan in particular) is increasingly perceived as a problem for the West, and the ways in which a powerful set of discursive correspondences are presently being established between Japan, the Orient and the Other. More specifically, we explore why, at this historical moment, this particular Other is coming to occupy such a threatening position in the imagination of the West.

If, within Europe, 1992 was an important date in the timetable for the construction of the European Single Market, it was also a date with another significance. It also commemorated the 500th anniversary of the

6

Spanish 'discovery' of the New World, marking the date of Columbus' famous voyage, and the date of the Spanish reconquest of Granada and of the expulsion of the Moors and the Jews from Spain. As Stuart Hall (ibid.) notes, what we see here is a double movement, in which Spain both expels its 'internal Others' (the Moors, the Jews) and discovers the 'external Others' of the New World. We explore the parallels between the history of these imperial conquests and contemporary structures of cultural imperialism, drawing on the work of writers such as de Certeau (1988), Greenblatt (1992) and Todorov (1992), concerning the question of power and representation (see chapter 10). The historical questions they raise – about who speaks of whom, who is empowered to tell what kind of stories about which Others, and who is spoken of, but silent – find close parallels, we argue, in contemporary structures of control over flows of information and entertainment (cf. Schiller 1969, 1992).

At the same time, we are also concerned to question models of cultural imperialism which presume the existence of pure, internally homogeneous and authentic cultures, which are then seen to be, belatedly, subverted or corrupted by foreign influences. If we are concerned to understand the powers of cultural imperialism, our conceptual models of the absorption and indigenisation of 'foreign' influences will need to be more subtle than those of traditional models of media effects (cf. Morley, 1992: ch. 1). We would agree with Arjun Appadurai (1988: 39) that 'natives . . . , people confined to and by the places to which they belong, groups unsullied by contact with a larger world, have probably never existed', and likewise with James Clifford (1992) about the importance of developing a model of 'travelling cultures', whose essence is not conceived as rooted in geographical place. Chow's (1993) ironic question, 'Where have all the natives gone?', is well-posed, in its challenge to simplistic models of Third World 'native' cultures.

If one of our concerns is with the impact of Western media on 'the Rest', then another, correlative question concerns the impact of representations of Others on Western audiences. Today, many of us in the West have only to sit on a couch and press a button to behold the exotic Other; the global news media have made us all into armchair anthropologists or ethnographers, nightly witnesses to the strange customs of Others. One of our particular concerns is with the potentially regressive dimensions of this continual 'screening' of the Other. 'They' are made present to 'us', but how? Susan Sontag (1979) refers to simultaneous processes of exposure and insulation, in the face of this barrage of visual imagery. In our analysis of Western media coverage of crises, such as those in the Gulf War and in Bosnia, we explore the potential of certain forms of psychoanalytic theory, in enabling us to grasp better the processes through which the television screen, while presenting us with information on these events, may simultaneously function as a filter or distancing mechanism,

7

allowing us also to 'screen out' the more disturbing aspects of the events we feel compelled to 'witness' through these media. We again take up the potential of psychoanalytic concepts for the development of media theory, examining the 'psycho-geography' of anxiety and fear in the new Europe, in relation to our analysis of the dangers of nationalism.

In the face of what Kobena Mercer (1990) has called the 'sheer diffi-culty of living with difference', we see, all around us, in contemporary Europe, a resurgence of various forms of nationalism and calls for a return to the pure (if mythic) certainties of the 'old traditions' and to the homo-geneity of an identity on which they are presumed to have been based – what Salman Rushdie (1982) has characterised as a return to the 'absolutism of the pure'. It is in this context that we explore the con-temporary resurgence of the 'heritage' industry in Britain, as both a regres-sive 'little Englandism', and a nostalgic attempt to revivify pure and indigenous regional cultures in reaction against what are perceived as threatening forms of cultural hybridity.

It will no longer do to equate 'history' with the genealogy of the West and its imperial conquests. To do so, as Levinas (1983) has noted, is to indulge in a narcissistic form of self-centred 'egology' – a form of onto-logical imperialism, in which all of human history is seen from the view-point of (and as reaching its apogee in) Europe and the West. This process itself (hopefully) reached its own apogee with the publication of Francis Fukuyama's 'The End of History' in 1989, with its uncritical celebration of US dominance in the 'New World Order', as the logical and necessary culmination of history itself (see pages 200–6 for a discussion of Fukuyama's work). In our view, what is at stake here is not so much the end of history as the end of ethno-centrism. As Cornell West argues, post-modernity itself may perhaps be best understood as a 'set of responses to the decentring of Europe – of living in a world that no longer rests upon [that] European hegemony which began in 1492' (1991: 6).

It is in this context that we would wish the chapters that follow to be read. They have been written, singly and jointly, as part of a collabora-tive project stretching from 1987 to 1994. Given the extent of that collaboration, we have felt that it would be inappropriate to attempt to distinguish our respective individual and joint authorships here, even though some earlier versions of some of the chapters have previously appeared separately, as essays under our individual names. Certain themes recur across the different chapters – the most important of which we have attempted to identify in this introduction. While we have attempted to edit out the most obvious overlaps between chapters, given the nature of the key concerns, to which we have returned at different stages of our collaboration, and in different contexts, the reader will, in places, encounter, if not repetition, then certainly recurrent themes. Again, much has changed, in the seven years since the first of these pieces was written, but while we have edited each piece so as to eradicate the most obviously outdated observations, we have left the basic structure of our arguments intact – to do more than this would have risked arriving at a point at which everything had to be rewritten from scratch. We can only hope that even the earliest pieces here will still stand the weight of contemporary scrutiny. We offer them as a rough transcript of an ongoing dialogue in which each of us, at least, has learned much, as we have brought our different intellectual histories and concerns together, in the pursuit of these questions of common interest.

All translations in the text are our own, unless stated otherwise.

1

GLOBALISATION AS IDENTITY CRISIS

The new global media landscape

For business purposes . . . the boundaries that separate one nation
from another are no more real than the equator. They are merely
convenient demarcations of ethnic, linguistic and cultural entities.
They do not define business requirements or consumer trends.

(IBM, 1990)

FROM NATIONAL TO GLOBAL MEDIA

Until very recently, what has prevailed in Britain, as elsewhere in Europe,
has been the system of public service broadcasting, involving the provision
of mixed programming – with strict controls on the amount of foreign
material shown – on national channels available to all. The principle that
governed the regulation of broadcasting was that of 'public interest'.
Broadcasting should contribute to the public and political life of the nation;
in the words of the BBC's first Director-General, John Reith, it should
serve as 'the integrator of democracy' (quoted in Cardiff and Scannell,
1987: 159). Broadcasting should also help to construct a sense of national
unity. In the earliest days of the BBC, the medium of radio was consciously
employed 'to forge a link between the dispersed and disparate listeners
and the symbolic heartland of national life' (ibid.: 157). In the post-war
years, it was television that became the central mechanism for constructing this collective life and culture of the nation. In succession, radio and
television have 'brought into being a culture in common to whole populations and a shared public life of a quite new kind' (Scannell, 1989: 138).
Historically, then, broadcasting has assumed a dual role, serving as the
political public sphere of the nation state, and as the focus for national
cultural identification. (Even in the very different context of the United
States, where commercial broadcasting was the norm from the beginning,
national concerns were paramount; the 'national networks' of CBS, NBC
and ABC served as the focus for national life, interests and activities.) We
can say that, on either side of the Atlantic, broadcasting has been one of

10

the key institutions through which listeners and viewers have come to imagine themselves as members of the national community.

Now, however, things are changing, and changing decisively. During the 1980s, as a consequence of the complex interplay of regulatory, economic and technological change, dramatic upheavals took place in the media industries, laying the basis for what must be seen as a new media order. What was most significant was the decisive shift in regulatory principles: from regulation in the public interest to a new regulatory regime – sometimes erroneously described as 'deregulation' – driven by economic and entrepreneurial imperatives. Within this changed context, viewers are no longer addressed in political terms, that is as the citizens of a national community, but rather as economic entities, as parts of a consumer market (Robins and Webster, 1990). The political and social concerns of the public service era – with democracy and public life, with national culture and identity – have come to be regarded as factors inhibiting the development of new media markets. In the new media order, the overriding objective is to dismantle such 'barriers to trade'. No longer constrained by, or responsible to, a public philosophy, media corporations and businesses are now simply required to respond to consumer demand and to maximise consumer choice.

Driven now by the logic of profit and competition, the overriding objective of the new media corporations is to get their product to the largest number of consumers. There is, then, an expansionist tendency at work, pushing ceaselessly towards the construction of enlarged audiovisual spaces and markets. The imperative is to break down the old boundaries and frontiers of national communities, which now present themselves as arbitrary and irrational obstacles to this reorganisation of business strategies. Audiovisual geographies are thus becoming detached from the symbolic spaces of national culture, and realigned on the basis of the more 'universal' principles of international consumer culture. The free and unimpeded circulation of programmes – television without frontiers – is the great ideal in the new order. It is an ideal whose logic is driving ultimately towards the creation of global programming and global markets – and already we are seeing the rise to power of global corporations intent on turning ideal into reality. The new media order is set to become a global order.

In considering these questions, let us begin with what we would call the mythology of global media. A fine example of this is the 'Worldview address', delivered to the 1990 Edinburgh International Television Festival by the late Steven Ross (1990), then head of the world's largest media corporation, Time Warner. According to Ross, Time Warner stands for 'complete freedom of information', that is for the 'free flow of ideas, products and technologies in the spirit of fair competition'. National frontiers he sees as a relic of the past: 'the new reality of international media is driven more by market opportunity than by national identity'.

11

We are, says Ross, 'on the path to a truly free and open competition that will be dictated by consumers' tastes and desires'. It is a world order in which the consumer is truly sovereign.

The world that Time Warner is anxious to construct will be 'a better world' (for Time Warner and for the consumers of its products). 'The competitive market place of ideas and experience can only bring the world closer together', Ross maintains. 'With new technologies, we can bring services and ideas that will help draw even the most remote areas of the world into the international media community'. A world 'closer together', it is assumed, will be a more democratic one. Thinking of recent events in Eastern Europe, Ross associates the free flow of communications with the overthrow of totalitarian societies. 'Who', he asks, 'could have imagined the satellite, the fax machine, CNN, television – and even records and movies – as tools of democratic revolution?' From this point of view, media corporations are now at the cutting edge of the new world order. 'It is up to us', says Ross, 'the producers and distributors of ideas, to facilitate this movement and to participate in it with an acute awareness of our responsibility as citizens of one world . . . . We can help to see to it that all peoples of all races, religions, and nationalities have equality and respect'.

For Ross, the global media corporations of the 1990s are now finally and truly realising what McLuhan predicted in the 1960s. In the eyes of Ross communication is a good thing and the more freely it flows, the better it is; experiences shared on a global scale, through the new communications media, will help us to transcend the differences between different cultures and societies, and to work towards 'genuine mutual trust and understanding'. The message is simple and uplifting: it is the story of progress towards freedom and democracy on a world scale, and of the responsibility of companies like Time Warner to 'actively lead the way toward making the world a better place'.

Steven Ross offers us one way of interpreting the significance of globalisation in the media industries. And, indeed, there is something attractive about his 'worldview', with its appeal to international democracy and the 'interconnection of cultures'. Nonetheless, it is all too easy to see how in reality the 'free circulation' of media products might be about corporate power and profits, rather more than about a 'better world'. What we are being asked to buy is very much an idealised image of a new media order, an image which bears little relation to the real order that is presently taking shape around us.

THE NEW MEDIA ORDER

Herbert Schiller's interpretation of the new media order differs considerably from that offered by Steven Ross. 'The actual sources of what is being called globalisation are not to be found in a newly achieved harmony of interests in the international arena', Schiller argues. What he sees is 'transnational corporate cultural domination'; a world in which 'private giant economic enterprises pursue – sometimes competitively, sometimes co-operatively – historical capitalist objectives of profit making and capital accumulation, in continuously changing market and geopolitical conditions' (Schiller, 1991: 20–1). What is emphasised here is the historical continuity, and consistency, in corporate motivations. What is recognised and acknowledged is that, in the 1990s, the context of this drive for market and competitive position has been significantly transformed. The struggle for power and profits is now being waged at the global scale (Aksoy and Robins, 1992).

What we are seeing is the construction of the media order through the entrepreneurial devices of a comparatively small number of global players, the likes of Time Warner, Sony, Matsushita, Rupert Murdoch's News Corporation and the Walt Disney Company (see table 1). For viewers, the new media order has become apparent through the emergence of new commercial channels, such as BSkyB, CNN, MTV or the Cartoon Network. What we are seeing is the development of a new media market characterised by new services, new delivery systems and new forms of payment. In place of the mixed-programming channels of the 'traditional' broadcasters, we now have the proliferation of generic channels (sport, news, music, movies). It is estimated that the 59 channels licensed to operate in the UK in 1992 will increase to around 130 by 2002 (Booz-Allen Hamilton, 1993: 9). In the United States, there are soon likely to be more than two hundred channels. It is, of course, the global media players that are investing in these channels (and the UK is only one small part in their global jigsaw).

Global corporations are presently manoeuvring for world supremacy. There are three basic options open to media corporations: 'The first is to be a studio and produce products. The second is to be a wholesale distributor of products, as MTV, CBS, and HBO are. The third is to be a hardware delivery system, whether that hardware is a cable wire or a Walkman' (Auletta, 1993b: 81). The objective for the real global players is to operate across two or even all three of these activities. It is this ambition that motivated the takeovers of Hollywood studios (Universal by Matsushita, Columbia/TriStar by Sony, Fox by Rupert Murdoch). As Steven Ross (1990) observes, 'mass is critical, if it is combined with vertical integration and the resulting combination is intelligently managed'. The issue for media corporations now is to decide what scale of integration they need to achieve, and are capable of managing, in order to build globally.

But there is more to it than just integration within the media sector. What we are beginning to see is a much more fundamental process of transformation, in which entertainment and information businesses are

13

Table 1 The world's top 20 audiovisual (AV) companies by turnover

Rank 1991	1990				
1	1	Time Warner	USA	11,517.0	12,021.0
2	2	Sony Corporation	Japan	24,977.7	28,372.1
3	13	Matsushita Electric Industrial	Japan	45,578.4	55,303.2
4	3	Capital Cities/ABC	USA	5,386.0	5,382.0
5	4	NHK	Japan	3,743.4	4,029.0
6	5	ARD	Germany	3,557.8	3,580.2
7	10	Philips (Polygram)	Netherlands	30,624.0	30,478.7
8	8	Fininvest	Italy	6,310.8	8,138.0
9	9	Fujisankei*	Japan	5,127.0	6,000.0
10	11	Bertelsmann	Germany	8,972.6	9,613.7
11	7	General Electric/NBC	USA	58,414.0	60,236.0
12	6	CBS	USA	3,260.0	3,035.0
13	15	News Corporation	Australia	8,248.0	8,590.6
14	14	RAI	Italy	2,502.6	2,732.6
15	16	Walt Disney Company	USA	5,843.7	6,182.4
16	12	BBC	UK	2,687.4	2,743.3
17	18	Thorn EMI	UK	6,352.5	6,343.0
18	17	Paramount	USA	3,869.0	3,895.4
19	19	Nintendo	Japan	3,114.7	3,767.4
20	23	Tokyo Broadcasting System	Japan	1,343.4	1,586.4

*estimate

Source: IDATE (Institut de l'Audiovisuel et des Télécommunications en Europe), Montpellier, 1991.

converging with the telecommunications industry. A sign of things to come was the projected, but ultimately unsuccessful, merger, in 1993, of the telecommunications company Bell with the largest US cable company, TCI. The new company would have become the world's largest media corporation. It was described, by Bell Atlantic's chairman, as 'a perfect information age marriage' and 'a model for communications in the next century' (Dickson, 1993). The new 'multi-media' giant would have provided not only conventional cable television, but also telecommunications services, computer games and software, home banking and shopping, video on demand, and other interactive services. The aim is still to develop information and communications 'super-highways' that will move us beyond the era of mass media and into that of personalised media and individual choice.

But it will be personalised media and individual choice, of course, on the basis of what is available and for sale. Global corporations are securing control over programming (production, archives), over distribution and over transmission systems. The flow of images and products is both more intensive and more extensive than in the past. What should also be emphasised is how much American cultural domination remains a fundamental part of this new order, though now American or American-style output is also the staple fare of non-US interests too (Schiller, 1991). As a writer in the *Financial Times* recently observed, 'soon hardly anywhere on earth will be entirely safe from at least the potential of tuning in to cheerful American voices revealing the latest news or introducing the oldest films' (Snoddy, 1993).

What corporate manoeuvres and machinations are seeking to bring into existence is a global media space and market. In the mid-1980s, Saatchi & Saatchi were talking about 'world cultural convergence', and arguing that 'convergences in demography, behaviour and shared cultural elements are creating a more favourable climate for acceptance of a single product and positioning across a wide range of geography'. Television programmes such as *Dallas*, or films such as *Star Wars* or *E.T.* were seen to 'have crossed many national boundaries to achieve world awareness for their plots, characters, etc.' (Winram, 1984: 21). Theodore Levitt, whose influential book, *The Marketing Imagination*, helped to shape the Saatchi outlook, was, at the same time, pointing to the increasing standardisation and homogenisation of markets across the world. 'The global corporation', he argued, 'looks to the nations of the world not for how they are different but for how they are alike . . . it seeks constantly in every way to standardise everything into a common global mode' (Levitt, 1983: 28). Of course, if it is profitable to do so, global companies will respond to the demands of particular segments of the market. In so doing, however, 'they will search for opportunities to sell to similar segments throughout the globe to achieve the scale economies that keep their costs competitive' (ibid.: 26). The strategy is to 'treat these market segments as global, not local, markets' (Winram, 1984: 19).

There appears to be the same logic at work in the 1990s. American movies – such as *The Flintstones* and *Jurassic Park* – are still breaking box-office records across the world (hence the keen struggle to acquire Hollywood studios and archives). Satellite and cable channels are also making headway in marketing standardised product worldwide. MTV, recently invited into Lithuania to help promote democracy, and CNN, now on twelve satellites beaming 'global village' news the world over, seem to have come close to finding the answer to global marketing. The new 'super-highways', still in their early stages of development, seem set to push processes of standardisation further. But they are also likely to add more complexity, delivering 'personalised' and 'individualised' services to specialised and 'niche' markets. Such strategies, it should be emphasised, 'are not denials or contradictions of global homogenisation, but rather its confirmation . . . globalisation does not mean the end of segments. It means, instead, their expansion to worldwide proportions' (Levitt, 1983: 30–1).

So much for the logic of corporate ambition. The question that we must now consider is how this logic unfolds as it encounters and negotiates the real world, the world of already existing and established markets and cultures. Cable News Network (CNN), launched in 1980 by the American entrepreneur Ted Turner, has achieved its phenomenal success through the worldwide distribution of a single, English-language news service. Increasingly, however, the channel is confronting the accusation that it is too American in its corporate identity. CNN's global presence is interpreted as an expression of American cultural domination, and this clearly raises problems as to its credibility as a global news-provider. Back at company headquarters, this also translates into a fundamental dilemma over market strategy and position. CNN's present news service has been successful in reaching the world's business and political elites, but it has not significantly penetrated mass markets, where local affiliations and attachments are far stronger. To reach such viewers 'CNN would have to dramatically change its vision of a single, English-speaking global network', and 'to effect that change Turner would need to seek partners and would need to localise' (Auletta, 1993a: 30). CNN is having to recognise that the pursuit of further success will entail the production of different editions, in different languages, in different parts of the world. To this end, collaboration with local partners will be essential. In the context of growing competition – from, among others, Sky News, BBC World Service Television and Reuters – CNN must learn to reconcile global ambitions with local complexities.

The case of Star TV provides another good example of the necessary accommodation between global and local dynamics. As part of their strategy for global hegemony, media corporations have sectioned the world into large geo-economic regions. Star, a Hong Kong-based company which began broadcasting in August 1991, has effectively constructed the Asia region; stretching from Turkey to Japan, from Mongolia to Indonesia, it encompasses thirty-eight countries (though only thirteen receive Star signals at present). The station combines pan-Asian programmes and advertising with a certain amount of material targeted at 'spot markets', such as India or Taiwan. It also sought to balance Asian programming (Indian or Chinese pop music and films, for example) with 'Western' channels (MTV, BBC World Service Television, Prime Sports), many of which are highly popular and welcomed as forces of internationalisation and 'modernisation' (Poole, 1993). Acknowledgement of its success across this vast region came in July 1993 when Rupert Murdoch's News Corporation paid US$525 million for a controlling share of Star TV. For Murdoch, the Asian region was part of his 'global dream', and he will clearly seek to market his Sky channels there. But he also recognises the enormous cultural and linguistic differences within the region, and is planning to create separate services for India and China, and possibly also for Indonesia (Snoddy, 1993). Given the diversity and complexity of this market, and the enormous political (China, Indonesia) and religious

(Malaysia) sensitivities, Murdoch's 'local' partners are crucial to the future success of Star. Success will depend on finding the right balance between market integration and market diversity.

In his 'Worldview address', Steven Ross (1990) acknowledged that global media must 'be sensitive to the cultural environment and needs of every locale in which we operate'. Anxious to avert charges of cultural homogenisation and domination, global corporations are concerned to develop local credentials and credibility (though in this context, of course, 'local' may amount to a multi-national region).

CULTURE AND POLITICS IN THE NEW MEDIA ORDER

During the 1980s, we saw considerable efforts by the European Community, on behalf of European media corporations, to construct a 'European audiovisual area'. In this context, we can identify some of the tensions and problems arising out of the globalisation process. The clear objective of the European Community has been to bring into existence the European equivalents of Sony and Time Warner. It has sought to make the painful transition from the old public service era, in which broadcasters provided a diverse and balanced range of programmes for citizen-viewers, to a new regime in which the imperative is to maximise the competitive position of European media businesses committed to satisfying the needs of consumers in global markets. It is the logic of industrial concentration and integration, working towards the creation of a few media giants. It is also the logic of globalisation, pushing towards the greater standardisation and homogenisation of output, and detaching media cultures from the particularities of place and context.

And yet there is also another, and contrary, force at work, challenging the imperatives of globalisation. As an antidote to the internationalisation of programming, and as compensation for the standardisation and loss of identity that is associated with global networks, we have seen a resurgent interest in regionalism within Europe, appealing to the kind of situated meaning and emotional belonging that appear to have been eroded by the logic of globalisation. This new regionalism puts value on the diversity and difference of identities in Europe, and seeks to sustain and conserve the variety of cultural heritages, regional and national. Broadcasting has been seen as a major resource in the pursuit of this objective, and in the 1980s we saw a growing interest in promoting media industries and activities within the regions and small nations of Europe. In most cases, principles of local public interest have been mobilised against the interests of transnational market forces. In lobbying for support from the European Community, the argument has been put that 'in the particular case of regional TV programming in the European vernacular languages, the criteria should not be based on audience ratings and percentages of the language-speaking population, nor on strict, economic cost-effectiveness' (Garitaonandia, 1993: 291). Since the late 1980s, a certain level of support has been elicited from the EC, particularly through its MEDIA programme, which provides loans and support for small producers across the continent. Within the Community there has been increasing sensitivity towards cultural differences and commitment to the preservation of cultural identities in Europe.

Here again we have an example of the global–local nexus. 'Local' in this case, however, means something quite different from what it means in the corporate lexicon. In this context, it relates to the distinctive identities and interests of local and regional communities. In these global times, there are those who desire to 're-territorialise' the media, that is to re-establish a relationship between media and territory. They are determined that the media should contribute to sustaining both the distinctiveness and the integrity of local and regional cultures, against the threatening forces of 'de-territorialisation' and homogenisation. 'Local' in this sense constitutes a challenge to the strategies of global corporate interests.

If the processes of globalisation provoke fear and resentment, these tend, for the most part, to become attached to the perceived threat of American culture and 'Americanisation'. American mass culture has, for a very long time, been seen as a force that is eroding and dissolving European culture and tradition. The cultural domination of Hollywood has appeared to jeopardise the very survival of Europe's cultural industries. The culture of the continent is seen to be 'in thrall to American money – and ultimately American values'; put simply, from this perspective, 'Hollywood is the enemy' (Malcolm, 1990). The American share of the European cinema market is now 75 per cent (whilst the non-American share of US box-office takings stands at only 2 per cent). In consequence, quotas have been imposed on non-European (in effect American) programming, with the dual aim of protecting cultural sovereignty and enhancing the competitive position of domestic producers. This was a key issue in the last round of GATT negotiations (1993/4). Whilst the United States was calling, in the name of free trade and the free circulation of ideas, for the scrapping of quota restrictions, European interests were resolved to preserve them in order, as they saw it, to defend the cultural specificity and integrity of European civilisation. In France, there has been considerable hostility to Britain, for its having afforded Ted Turner access to European audiences. According to one critic, 'Turner is only the avant-garde of the big US companies who are sitting back to see how Europe reacts. If he gets in, Disney and Time Warner will follow' (Powell, 1993). The European stance is seen as a battle for freedom of expression: 'We want the Americans to let us survive. Ours is a struggle for the diversity of European culture, so that our children will be able to hear French and German and Italian spoken in films' (ibid.). Again, the emphasis is on particularity and difference, in the face of what seems to threaten their dissolution.

In and across the new spaces of global media, there is a complex interaction between economic and cultural dynamics. But where is politics in all this? Public service broadcasting acted as the focus, not only for national culture, but also for political and democratic life. Questions of identity and questions of citizenship were bound together. What is presently happening to public service systems now raises very real questions about the future of political culture. There are acute difficulties in the way of constructing mechanisms for effective publicity and debate across a transnational space. The European Community has so far failed to develop an adequate political culture or a basis for European citizenship. Questions of identity and of citizenship have become dissociated, and the very real current danger is that, within the European audiovisual space, the compensations of cultural identification will be made to prevail over the political objectives of public communication and debate. And, of course, this 'democratic deficit' is not only an issue of concern in the European zone of the world's new media order.

GLOBALISATION AND THE EUROPEAN IDENTITY CRISIS

The questions are, first, how Europe is to come to terms with the forces of globalisation that are reshaping the contemporary world system and, second, what kind of identity can Europeans imagine for themselves in the new world order? The available allegiances seem to come in three scales. The most commodious is the sense of being a European, of belonging to a common European home. It was this sense of European communitarian identity that the '1992' campaign sought to encourage and popularise. As argued earlier, this might well be seen as an attempt to engineer a cultural unity as the basis for a market large enough to facilitate European competition against Japan and the United States, in a triadic world economic system. What were mobilised to this end, however, were the old and familiar motifs of European tradition and heritage. And what was invoked was what T. S. Eliot (1948) celebrated as 'the spiritual organism of Europe', a common descent rooted in Greece and Rome and two thousand years of Christianity.

More manageable in scale, and still highly appealing, is the sense of national identity, which, over the past two thousand years or so, has existed, more or less comfortably, in compromise with the idea of Europe. 'When we speak of "European Culture"', Eliot declared, 'we mean the identities which we can discover in the various national cultures . . . .

19

There can be no European culture if these countries are reduced to identity' (ibid.: 120–1). As the spectre of nationalism again spreads across Europe, we can see the strength of the claim to difference and distinctiveness. If there was for a moment the belief that 1992 marked the beginning of the end for the European nation state, the period since then has shown that state nationalism remains a powerful way of belonging. In the wake of German reunification, we have seen the reassertion of French and British differences, sovereignties and interests. More frighteningly, this period has also shown the continuing attraction of ethno-nationalism as a way of belonging, with movements like Jean-Marie Le Pen's Front National in France working towards the 're-ethnicisation' of national identity. Their aim is 'to reinvent the authentic national community and to oppose it to the open society, which is then stigmatised as globalised and "cosmopolitan"' (Taguieff, 1992: 35). In this worst case, national difference demands national purity.

A third kind of allegiance in this new Europe is through small and local identities. This scale of attachment finds expression in the idea of a Europe of regions, cantons and small nations. Against more abstract or universalist claims, this marks a preference for a particularistic sense of community. The rich pluralism of regional traditions, languages, dialects and cultures is held up as the basis for a more meaningful experience of community. Like Eliot's idea of a regional 'constellation of cultures', this new regionalism, too, works against the forces of uniformity that are seen as threatening the very idea of European culture. It urges local attachments against the anonymous standardisation of global culture; it reasserts local independence against the abstract and bureaucratic power of transnational agencies. The appeal of this Europe of the 'Heimats' – Basque, Lombard, Breton, Corsican and others – is to a more 'authentic' way of belonging.

These identities represent different ways of responding to Europe's exposure to the forces of globalisation and global realignment. We should not see them as simple alternatives: to be European now is to be implicated in all three – continental, national and regional – and being European is about managing some amalgam of these different scales of identity. How this is done will, of course, vary. Change may cause some to take refuge in regressive and protective identities, but it may provoke others to create a more ecumenical and cosmopolitan identity. If small nationalism is often about the search for roots, it can also be used to promote democracy against national and European bureaucracies. And if 'Europe' seems to offer an enlarged, post-national way of belonging, it can also easily turn into a fortress identity and a superstate mentality. How these different possibilities will be negotiated, be it defensively or progressively, remains to be seen. The conundrum, what identity, or identities, for Europeans is still to be resolved.

But how much is really possible? What are the real chances that Europe might flourish in a new world order? We ask these questions because globalisation seems more about a threat than about opening up new horizons; because it actually seems to expose a crisis of identity for Europe. Europe and its nations are no longer what they once were, no longer at the centre of the world, no longer the source of universal values. 'Europe, the mighty, the leader of the world, no longer exists; Europe the source of inspiration for all higher cultures has been exhausted' (Heller and Feher, 1988: 156). Whereas Europe once stood for civilisation and progress, now it is about retrenchment and containment. Whereas once its project was about universalism, now it is about recovering a sense of European particularism (or particularisms). And now it is about 'the Europeanisation, not of the rest of the world, but . . . of Europe itself' (Sontag, 1989: 80). Magris poses the issue most dramatically: 'It may be that Europe is finished, a negligible province in a history decided elsewhere, in the press-button rooms of other empires' (1990: 265). Europe has to survive the loss of its myth, and it has to come to terms with a world in which its position has been relativised. What would it take to achieve this?

NEGATIVE IDENTITY AND UNITY

This is less a matter of what identity for Europe, than of what kind of identity. Geoffrey Barraclough has described how the idea of Europe has always been constructed around a negative conception of unity and community. 'Among the ambiguities which have befogged the question of European unity in the past', he argues, 'there is, first of all, the tendency, very marked since the time of the First Crusade, to think of it only in terms of hostility towards and reaction against something else. It might be the Greeks or the Arabs, or the Turks; more than once it has been England; today [1963] it is the Soviet Union' (1963: 53). In the new Europe, the same exclusionary principles continue to operate, and European identity is still constructed against those – without and within – who appear to be non-European or anti-European. Today it is perhaps the Japanese, the Muslims and the poor who are most seen to threaten the European ideal. The Japanese because, as the first 'non-white' culture to become part of modernity, it is they who have now become the source of inspiration for other cultures. The Muslims and the poor – the fifty million inside and all the travellers from North Africa, Turkey, Romania, Bangladesh or wherever – because they are seen as the forces of anarchy and disorder. Europe is 'Europe' against these Others.

In the history of the European nation states, the sense of national unity has been closely linked to the integrity and sovereignty of the national territory. In the new European Community the matter of territorial integrity remains paramount. With the lifting of economic barriers within

21

the Community to create the single market, the issue of security of Europe's external boundaries becomes all the more fundamental. If, for most of this century, the Soviet empire marked a 'natural' boundary to the east, the end of the Cold War has terminated this convenient state of affairs. Once again 'the Eastern question' is opened up, and with it 'the Southern question'. Indeed, with the dramatic return of 'the Balkan question' to the headlines of the European media, we seem to confront less the 'end of history' (Fukuyama, 1992) than the 'return of history'. Along its eastern and southern edges, Europe is now having to re-negotiate its territorial limits as an economic and political entity. As J. G. A. Pocock argues, 'Europe is again an empire concerned for the security of its *limites*'. It is in a position where 'it must decide whether to extend or refuse its political power over violent and unstable cultures along its borders but not yet within its system: Serbs and Croats, if one chances to be Austrian, Kurds and Iraqis if Turkey is admitted to be part of "Europe"' (1991: 10).

Who can be assimilated? And who must be excluded? Pocock sees the 'new barbarians' as those populations who do not achieve the sophistication without which the global market has little for them and less need of them (ibid.: 10). But it is not simply a question of economic, or even political, criteria for inclusion. What is happening along these eastern and southern edges is also about suturing the cultural identity of Europe. This desire for clarity, this need to know precisely where Europe ends, is about the construction of a symbolic geography that will separate the insiders from the outsiders (the Others). Implicit in these words is the suggestion that the next Iron Curtain should divide Europe from, and insulate it against, the Islamic Other.

This agenda is clearly about something more than just territorial integrity. What seems to be at stake is something like the psychic coherence and identity of Europe. Like its unity, European identity is also constructed around a negative principle. What is at work is a general principle which Cornelius Castoriadis describes as 'the apparent incapacity to constitute oneself as oneself without excluding the other – *and* the apparent inability to exclude the other without devaluing and, ultimately, hating him' (1990: 29). What is at issue is how this principle has functioned historically in the constitution of a European identity. How – through a history of colonialism, evangelism and orientalism – an Other has been created and excluded, and how, against this hated Other, a sense of continental European identity has been made possible. It is the opposition of 'whiteness' to 'non-whiteness', according to Scott Malcomson, that has been central to distinguishing Europeans from non-Europeans or anti-Europeans. Faced with one another, Europeans were Germans, Britons or Swedes, but 'faced with other skin colours and religions, Europeans saw themselves as white, Christian, civilised and Enlightened' (1991: 10). What has been constructed has been a pan-European ethnicity. The 'spiritual organism' of Europe has been constructed around this 'ethnicity'. This crisis of identity in contemporary Europe is the crisis of this pan-European ethnic myth.

It is, however, not only a matter of ethnicity but also of religion, or perhaps of the way in which questions of geography, ethnicity and religion have become historically intertwined. Thus, the Iranian Ambassador to the Vatican observes how it is almost impossible to disentangle the image of the West from that of Christianity:

> Christianity does not exist only in the West. Even when we point to one particular Christianity, we cannot say that it equals the 'West'. But . . . Westerners, when they confront 'outsiders', even though they might not be religious themselves, see themselves as carriers of this religion . . . this Christian heritage. Therefore, the Westerners' self-image of themselves, in their encounters with 'outsiders', is almost always Christian, though they may not themselves be Christian. [If] it is difficult to say that Christianity is always Western, it is still largely true to say that the West is always Christian.
>
> (interviewed in *Conversations: Islam and Christianity*,
> Channel 4, 26 February 1994)

THE HIDDEN FACE OF OUR IDENTITY

What kind of identity for Europe? The language of official Euro-culture is significant: it is the language of cohesion, community, unity, integration, security. What is invoked, though never avowed, is the possibility of a new European order defined by a clear sense of its own coherence, and integrity. European identity is imagined in terms of an idealised wholeness and plenitude. And identity, as such, is imagined in terms of boundedness and containment (cf. Massey, 1992). Conceived in this sense, it is always – eternally and inherently – fated to anxiety; its desired coherence and integrity must always be conserved and sustained against the forces of disintegration and dissolution at work in the world. In the continuous struggle against such imagined forces, the logic of enclosure and fortification of identity is consolidated.

It is through the history of European nationalism that this kind of protective 'identitarian' thinking has been most fully articulated and realised. The construction of nation states involved the elimination of complexity, the extrusion or marginalisation of elements that compromised the 'clarity' of national attachment. This process was about the purification of space and of identity. The nation state does not easily tolerate difference. As Georges Corm argues: 'Homogeneity – religious, national, political and territorial, involving natural frontiers – has been

23

the basis of European modernity, constructed around the nation state' (1989: 58). Monolithic and inward-looking, the unitary state seemed to be the realisation of a desire for coherence and integrity of identity.

Rather than realising this desire, of course, we might suspect that it was the *Realpolitik* of nation-building that created the conditions of possibility for this desire – this kind of desire – ever to be imagined. It was in the course of this historical process that such a reduced and self-enclosed way of being and of belonging came to seem both natural and ideal. We must regret that it is this kind of diminished identity-thinking, albeit at a higher order, that is now informing the present attempts to forge a sense of European identity. The idea of a unitary continent appears to correspond best with what we have come to expect of identity, with what should make European citizens feel most comfortable.

What we must remember, however, is that historically 'European' has been more than this. We should recall that it has, in its past, required more complexity and a greater openness from its citizens. Corm draws our attention to the transnational empires of the Habsburgs and the Ottomans. The identity of imperial populations was rich, he argues, because of the complex circulations and permutations of ethnic, religious and linguistic groups, across large geographical regions of the empire. You could be Slav and Muslim, Slav and Catholic, as well as Slav and Orthodox; you could be Orthodox and Slav, but also Orthodox and Greek or Arabic; you could speak local languages like Serbo-Croat or Albanian, but also the official and elite languages of the empire; you could be Orthodox amongst Catholics and Muslims and Jews of all varieties. 'Not that it was idyllic or perfect', Corm observes, 'but at least, where it prevailed, difference was never experienced as a scandal or as a defect of identity' (ibid.: 50–1). Pluralism and complexity of identity was a resource and a source of enrichment.

This might sound like an exercise in nostalgia for fallen empires, but that is not what is intended. The point is, rather, to draw attention to the fact that identity has been, and can be, experienced in ways that are richer than those offered by the nation state. They are richer because they are more difficult, because they involve negotiation with, and, more importantly, commitment to, what is different. That this in itself is worthwhile is, of course, a value judgement. Is it conceivable that Europe might again make this choice for real complexity? Perhaps the better, and more serious, question is what will happen because it will not?

It is in fact no diversion, at this moment in Europe's history, to be reminded of those old and cosmopolitan empires with their fluid populations. As we confront economic and political integration on a planetary scale, it is inevitable that we shall see greater flows and greater mobility of populations across Europe. Contrary to the belief that the partitioning of the continent into national territories and communities would inhibit

24

the redistribution of populations, what we are seeing is the inability of boundaries and frontiers to manage Europe's travellers on the move. Globalisation means that those we consider as Other or alien – the 'new barbarians' – will be increasingly in our midst. How shall we come to terms with their presence inside the citadel of Europe? Europe has been exposed to the forces of globalisation, but it is not open to them. The dubious achievement of European nationalism has been to make sure that difference is experienced as a scandal and a defect of identity. Thus, while we are unable to avoid 'strangers', we do not have the resources to live anything but uneasily with them.

Yet the stranger, the foreigner, is not only among us, but also inside us. He is, says Julia Kristeva, 'the hidden face of our identity' (1991: 20). What is hidden, or repressed, creates in us a sense of existential unease and foreboding. What has been alienated in the construction of our identities comes back to haunt our imagination and disturb our peace of mind. In our fearful anticipations, says Kristeva, the stranger looms as a 'powerful persecutor against whom a "we" solidifies in order to take revenge. . . . Must we not stick together, remain among ourselves, expel the intruder, or at least keep him in "his" place?' (ibid.). Keeping 'him' at bay is what keeps 'us' together. Kristeva proposes an alternative basis of identity for the new cosmopolis: 'Living with the other, with the foreigner, confronts us with the possibility or not of *being an other*. It is not simply – humanistically – a matter of our being able to accept the other, but of *being in his place*, and this means to imagine and make oneself for oneself' (ibid.: 13, our emphasis). This is, inevitably, an unsettling proposition. As Ricoeur notes:

> when we discover that there are several cultures, instead of just one, and consequently, at the time we acknowledge the end of a sort of cultural monopoly, be it illusory or real, we are threatened . . . [by] our own discovery. Suddenly, it becomes possible that there are just *Others*, that we ourselves are an 'other' among Others.
>
> (1965: 278)

Difference as a resource and as a source of enrichment. That this should seem such a utopian possibility says much about where we are, and where we are not, with European identity at the present moment.

2

REIMAGINED COMMUNITIES?
New media, new possibilities

Very much remains to be done by way of detailed discussions and proposals, but we cannot in any case live much longer with the confusions of the existing 'international' economy and the existing 'nation state'. If we cannot find and communicate social forms of more substance than these, we shall be condemned to endure the accelerating pace of false and frenetic nationalisms and of reckless and uncontrollable global transnationalism.

(Raymond Williams, 1983)

In the present period, we are seeing processes of political economic restructuring and transformation which involve changes in the historical system of accumulation and social organisation. At the heart of these historical developments is a process of spatial restructuring and reconfiguration. This process is the major concern of the following discussion. It involves at once a transformation of the spatial matrix of society and of the subjective experience of, and orientation to, space and spatiality. Consideration requires a social theory that is informed by the geographical imagination.

Our particular concern is with the media industries, which are implicated in these socio-spatial processes in quite significant and distinctive ways. We want to explore the nature of current transformations, the breaks and continuities, and to assess the implications of the changing configuration of 'image spaces'. Through the prism of geographical analysis it becomes possible to take up some key questions concerning the relationship between economic and cultural aspects of these transformations, to explore the articulations of economic spaces and cultural spaces. Following this line of enquiry, issues around the politics of communication converge with the politics of space and place. Questions of communication are also about the nature and scope of community. In a world of 'false and frenetic nationalisms and of reckless and uncontrollable global transnationalism', the struggle for meaningful communities and 'actual social identities' is more and more difficult: 'we have to explore new forms of variable societies, in which over the whole range of social purposes different sizes

26

of society are defined for different kinds of issue and decision' (Williams, 1983: 198–9).

BEYOND FORDISM?

What is the broader context within which the transformation of media industries and markets is taking place? One of the most suggestive ways of looking at the present period of upheaval has been that developed by the Regulation School of political economists (see *inter alia*, Aglietta, 1979; Billaudot and Gauron, 1985; Boyer, 1986a, 1986b; Lipietz, 1987) with their analyses of the decline of the social system they call Fordism. Within this perspective, Fordism is understood in terms of the articulation of a par-ticular 'regime of accumulation', centred around mass production and mass consumption, with an appropriate 'mode of regulation'. 'Social reg-ulation' is a matter of both the organisational and institutional structures, including the apparatuses of the (Keynesian) state, but also the norms, habits, and internalised rules governing the lifeworld – the 'architecture of socialisation' (Billaudot and Gauron, 1985: 22) – which ensure social reproduction and the absorption of conflicts and tensions, always provi-sionally, over a certain period of time. What is being argued is that Fordism as a mode of capitalist development and as a historically specific coher-ence of accumulation and regulation, has now reached its limits. The inher-ent control problems of Fordism – for example, rising wages and declining productivity, overcapacity and market saturation, competition from low-wage countries, increasing costs for public services – have brought the system into crisis. This crisis, moreover, is structural (rather than simply cyclical), and it is a matter of political, social and cultural crisis as much as of economic decline and stagnation. In so far as the resources of Fordism/Keynesianism have become exhausted, the future of capitalist development demands a fundamental and innovative restructuring of accumulation and regulation.

If the historical nature of Fordism and the dynamics of its crisis are becoming clear enough, the question of its successor regime of accumu-lation is more problematic and contentious. What lies beyond Fordism? There are many accounts of post-Fordism, increasingly congealing into a new orthodoxy of optimism, which identify a new social coherence centred around what is often referred to as an emergent regime of flexible accu-mulation. So-called flexible specialisation is manifest in new forms of decentralised production and in the design and product mix aimed at niche markets; demassified enterprises (in which production is no longer concentrated in large factories on a single site) abandon economies of scale in favour of economies of scope; and workers supposedly assume new skills and responsibilities and a new sense of autonomy. This perspective finds its apogee in the work of Michael Piore and Charles

27

Sabel (1984) and other celebrants of the 'Third Italy' and the 'Emilian model' (a somewhat idealistic model of the potential for regional economic development, based on decentralised networks of small, artisan-based companies, using new computer technologies, as occurred in the Emilia-Romagna district in Italy, during the 1970s). These authors see the transcendence of Fordism in terms of a kind of return to feudalism, with the growth of a new class of artisans and the emergence of localised industrial districts. Whilst there are certain important insights here – to which we shall return below – there are also strongly ideological elements informing this new myth of flexibility. Post-Fordism is, in effect, imagined as anti-Fordism: it is quite simply the inverse of, and antithesis to, the rigid and massified system of Fordism.

This kind of idealised and teleological account is clearly unsatisfactory. Any real-world transition beyond Fordism will inevitably be a great deal more complex, unruly and uncertain. It cannot be a matter of an evolutionary movement from one distinct social system to another; rather, it is a process that promises to be fraught with turbulence and disruption. Projected futures cannot simply and effortlessly dissolve away the solidity of inherited social structures, infrastructures and relations. The process of transformation is complex and uneven, and it is genuinely difficult to establish whether the present period marks the emergence of a post-Fordist society, whether it should be characterised as neo-Fordist, or whether, in fact, it remains a period of late Fordism. On what basis is, say, flexible specialisation classified as a distinguishing feature of post-Fordism? The basis of definition and periodisation is, in fact, not at all self-evident. In a complex process of change, we have to ask by what criteria we might identify the components of a new phase of accumulation, and also how we do so without falling into the trap of teleologism. We must be clear that, in so far as the direction of change will be a matter of struggle and contestation, neither the emergence nor the nature of any society beyond Fordism is predetermined or inevitable.

The present discussion is concerned with one major area of change centring around the nature and meaning of space. What transformations are taking place in the social production of space, place and spatiality, and what new political logics does this set in motion? Our contention is that space is of paramount importance in this period of transition and restructuring:

> the current crisis is *accentuating spatiality* and revealing more clearly than ever before the spatial and locational strategies of capitalist accumulation and the necessity for labour and all segments of society 'peripheralised' by capitalist development and restructuring to create spatially conscious counterstrategies at all geographical scales, in all territorial locales.
>
> (Soja, 1985: 188, our emphasis)

Idealising visions of post-Fordism pick up on this new salience of space, but they do so only very partially. What they perceive is the transmutation of a centralised space economy into new forms of decentralisation and dissemination; they emphasise the increasing importance of localised industrial districts and zones like those described by the economist Alfred Marshall early this century. Reality is more complex and contradictory, however. If the growing significance of neo-Marshallian local economic districts is indeed an identifiable trend, then there are also apparently countervailing tendencies towards a global network economy. Manuel Castells has powerfully described how what he calls the information mode of development, based upon new communications systems and information technologies, is bringing about 'the transformation of spatial *places* into *flows* and *channels* – what amounts to the *delocalisation of the processes of production and consumption*' (1983: 5, our emphasis). Castells argues that corporate information networks are underpinning the expansion and integration of the capitalist world system, realising the possibility of a world assembly line, and opening up truly global markets. 'The new space of a world capitalist system', he writes, 'is a space of variable geometry, formed by locations hierarchically ordered in a continuously changing network of flows' (ibid.: 7). What we are moving towards is a fundamentally delocalised world order articulated around a small number of 'concentrated centres for production of knowledge and storage of information as well as centres for emission of images and information' (ibid.: 6), nerve centres in the cybernetic grids, command and control headquarters of the world financial and industrial system. The consequence, Castells believes, is 'the formation of a new historical relationship between space and society' (ibid.: 3).

The elaboration of a new spatial order is a consequence, then, of two contrary dynamics. Such complexity, has, of course, always characterised the production of space under capitalism. The historical sequence of capitalist spatialities, which has always manifested itself through the geography of uneven territorial development, has been a consequence of the interplay between centripetal and centrifugal forces, between centralisation and decentralisation, agglomeration and dispersal, homogenisation and differentiation. David Harvey (1985) has identified a fundamental developmental logic underpinning this contradictory process. Capital has always sought to overcome spatial barriers and to improve the 'continuity of flow'. It remains the case, however, that spatial constraints always exist and persist in so far as 'capital and labour must be brought together at a particular point in space for production to proceed' (ibid.: 145). Mobility and fixity are integrally and necessarily related: 'The ability of both capital and labour power to move . . . from place to place depends upon the creation of fixed, secure, and largely immobile social and physical infrastructures. The ability to overcome space is predicated on the production

29

of space' (ibid.: 149). There are, then, forces working towards the simultaneous transcendence and disruption of immobility and coherence; both are moments of the same total process of spatial development.

How, then, is this spatial logic working itself out in the present period? On the basis of new information and communications technologies, capital can now be described as hypermobile and hyperflexible, tending towards deterritorialisation and delocalisation. But this is not the only characteristic tendency in the present period. Even if capital significantly reduces the friction of geography, it cannot escape its dependence on spatial fixity. Space and place cannot be annihilated. As Scott Lash and John Urry argue, 'the effect of heightened spatial indifference has profound effects upon particular places and upon the forms of life that can be sustained within them – contemporary developments may well be heightening the salience of such localities' (1987: 86). The increasing mobility of corporations is associated with the possibility of fractionalising and subdividing operations and situating them in different places, and, in the process, taking advantage of small variations in the nature of different localities. The spatial matrix of contemporary capitalism is one that, in fact, combines and articulates tendencies towards both globalisation and localisation. These new forms of spatial deployment very much reflect the changing organisational structure of accumulation, and, particularly, new patterns of combined corporate integration and disintegration. One developmental logic of capitalist corporations is towards both horizontal and vertical integration, extending the monopolistic logic of concentration that characterised the Fordist regime of accumulation, and this on an increasingly global scale. This continuing integrative process is complemented, however, by certain tendencies towards vertical disintegration, towards the fragmentation of organisational elements into separate and specialised yet functionally interlinked units. This is generally a matter of externalising non-strategic, or, perhaps, unpredictable and variable functions and labour processes – and thereby externalising uncertainty and risk – on the basis of subcontracting or market links.

These emerging organisational transformations take place in and through space and have significant implications for territorial development. Vertical disintegration results in the formation of a localised nexus of small units, often centred around one or a few dominant large companies, and involved in close contractor/subcontractor relationships, continuous information exchange and, thus, spatial proximity. The consequence of the new dynamics of flexible specialisation, with its tendencies towards spatial agglomeration, has been to give a new centrality to local economies (Courlet and Judet, 1986). It is at the level of locality that important new economic and social developments are being worked out. It is precisely this aspect of organisational-territorial transformation that the idealising champions of post-Fordist industrial districts have identified as decisive. They do so in a rather one-sided way, however, disarticulating the local form from its global framework. Territorial complexes of quasi-integrated organisations are extremely vulnerable to external disruptions inflicted by globally mobile and footloose corporations: 'The evolution of flexibility within corporations . . . means that places are created and used up more quickly for the purposes of production or consumption' (Thrift, 1987: 211).

In a context in which 'regions "implode" into localities and nations "explode" into a complex global space' (Albertsen, 1986: 4–5), we have, then, an increasingly direct relationship between the local and the global. And as part of this process, it should be emphasised, the role and significance of the nation state has become ever more problematical and questionable though no less ambitious. For Manuel Castells, the prospects are bleak: 'On the one hand, the space of power is being transformed into flows. On the other hand, the space of meaning is being reduced to microterritories of new tribal communities' (1983: 4). He envisages a new 'space of collective alienation', one in which there is a 'disconnection between people and spatial form', 'the outer experience is cut off from the inner experience' (ibid.: 7). Castells' prognosis should not be taken lightly. But does the present situation contain other, progressive and hopeful possibilities?

IMAGE SPACES

These processes of socio-spatial transformation are the essential context for understanding the nature and significance of developments in the media industries. In this section and the next we want to look at the developing relationship between globalisation and localisation specifically in terms of the logics at work in the audiovisual industries. We want to reorientate the politics of communication towards a politics of space and place. What is the nature of emerging new image markets and image spaces, and what significance do these have for 'imaginary space' (Garnier, 1987), the sense of space and the sense of place? The context for the restructuring of image spaces is the very clear crisis of public service regulation, with its focus on the national arena and national culture. It is a complex process. Thus, whilst it is increasingly clear that technological and economic transformations are surpassing the regulatory capacities of the nation state, there is, at the ideological level, still an obsessive and regressive 'desire to reproduce the nation that has died and the moral and social certainties which have vanished with it . . . to fudge and forge a false unity based on faded images of the nation' (MacCabe, 1988: 29). National ambitions and endeavours will not simply disappear. In this context, none the less, what scope is there for intervention between the global and the local? Castells (1983: 16) again fears the worst: 'the

31

coexistence both of the monopoly of messages by the big networks and of the increasingly narrow codes of local microcultures around their parochial cable TVs'. Is the prospect necessarily and inevitably one of increasing privatism, localism, and 'cultural tribalism' within an electronic global village?

To begin to answer this question, we must look at the new media industries in terms of the complex dynamics of restructuring that we have already discussed in more general terms, particularly the interplay between globalisation and localisation. What is most apparent and remarkable is the accelerating formation of global communications empires, such as those of Murdoch, Berlusconi or Bertelsmann. Internationalisation is not, of course, a new phenomenon but it is now entering a new stage, and the 'maintenance of national sovereignty and identity [is] becoming increasingly difficult as the unities of economic and cultural production and consumption become increasingly transnational' (Collins, Garnham and Locksley, 1988: 55). We are seeing the emergence of truly global, decentred, corporations in which diverse media products (film and television, press and publishing, music and video) are being combined into overarching communications empires. Co-financed and co-produced products are made on a global assembly line and are aimed at world markets. Out of a context of collapsing public service traditions, and the consequent deregulation of national broadcasting systems, these mega-corporations are shaping a global space of image flows.

This process of globalisation is very much a function of increasing corporate integration. Various forms of horizontal alignment are apparent, at both national and international levels, with new alliances between broadcasters, film and television producers, publishers, record producers and so on. As a Logica report (1987: 131) makes very clear, it is 'the emergence of new media groups on a vertically integrated scale [that] is the single most important factor in the nature and spread of commercial TV development in Europe'. The progression of Rupert Murdoch, through Fox Broadcasting, 20th Century Fox and Sky Channel, towards the achievement of integrated control over production, distribution and broadcasting is simply the most obvious example. Logica (ibid.: 268–70) identifies the main functions in the chain of television production as those of originator, programmer, broadcaster, carrier and network operator, and it argues that new media groups are aiming to achieve vertical integration over some or all of the above roles. Total integration is, in fact, likely to be less significant, and less attainable, than the strategic integration of particular functions, and Logica identifies those of carrier/broadcaster, broadcaster/programmer and programmer/originator as critical to the consolidation of power blocs in the communications industries.

The tendency towards vertical integration is not, then, absolute and encompassing; it is also associated with processes of partial vertical disintegration. Thus, in the case of the American motion picture industry, Michael Storper and Susan Christopherson (1987) suggest that whilst the major studios control and dominate finance, product definition, distribution and marketing, there has been a move towards the externalisation of production and the use of small independent producers. This process of deverticalisation (in which the historical process of vertical integration is reversed) is associated with the externalisation of risk and with the attempt to exploit maximum variety of creative resources. One significant consequence has been a distinctive new pattern of location: independent producers have become spatially concentrated 'because the specialised nature of their services and the constant change in product requires nonroutine, frequent market transactions with other firms, such as production companies and major studios' (Christopherson and Storper, 1986: 316). The instability of casualised employment relations and the importance of contact networks generate significant agglomeration tendencies at a local level.

There are many who see this trend towards vertical disintegration and territorial localisation as heralding a benign post-Fordist era of flexible specialisation and cultural industrial districts. It is important, however, to emphasise that vertical disintegration applies primarily to the production sector. As Nicholas Garnham argues: 'It is cultural distribution, not cultural production, that is the key locus of power and profit. It is access to distributions which is the key to cultural plurality' (1986: 31–2). It is also important to emphasise that the logics of integration and disintegration are not contradictory, but, rather, quite complementary. Whilst disintegration and localisation are important, however, integration and globalisation remain the dominant forces (Aksoy and Robins, 1992).

The evolution of localised media production has become a significant issue in Europe, too, assuming distinct and particular forms in specific national and regional contexts (Robins and Cornford, 1994). The case of Britain offers a good example of partial vertical disintegration and, particularly, of its ambiguous and contradictory political implications. Whereas previously the functions of production, editorial and repertoire, and distribution, had been integrated in British broadcasting, with the opening of Channel 4 in 1982 there was a move towards their disaggregation. As with the American film industry, the key innovation was the externalisation of programme-making, which had as its consequence the growth and consolidation of a small-business sector of independent producers. Many of these companies, often involved in politically radical projects, located their activities away from the metropolitan centre, forming into small and localised agglomerations in regional cities (such as Cardiff, Newcastle, Bristol, Leeds, Manchester, Birmingham). These developments succoured real hopes and anticipations for the deconcentration, decentralisation and democratisation of the audiovisual industries.

Subsequently, a second wave of deverticalisation emerged, in the context of the government's decision, following the recommendations of the Peacock Report (1986), that the BBC and ITV companies should sub-contract 25 per cent of their programmes to independent producers. This new wave of transformation, however, severely undercut idealising expectations and projections. It was increasingly clear that externalisation and subcontracting of production was creating, not 'independent' and autonomous programme-makers, but a casualised, segmented and precarious work-force. The creation of an external work-force was above all part of a strategy to break the 'restrictive practices' of the broadcasting unions. 'Flexible working deals', such as those imposed by Tyne Tees, London Weekend Television, TV-AM and Thames Television, were aimed at asserting discipline and control over employees and thereby, of course, strengthening profitability and comparative advantage. Flexibility translates into power: through new contractual relations with internal employees and through the power of market relations with external subcontractors. So-called flexible specialisation combines organisational and functional disintegration or disaggregation with the continued integration of control and co-ordination (Cornford and Robins, 1995, forthcoming).

What, we must now ask, are the political implications of these combined processes of integration and disintegration, globalisation and localisation? What is, in fact, emerging is a certain displacement of national frameworks in favour of perspectives and agendas appropriate to both supra-national and sub-national dynamics. In this process, new questions are being thrown up about the interrelation of economic and market spaces on the one hand, and arenas of cultural consumption and collective identity on the other.

The global politics of communication centres around the international 'war of images' and the struggle between 'image superpowers' (Frèches, 1986). This 'war of position' between transnational corporations is reflected very strongly in the concerns of the European Commission. In a world swamped by television images, the key questions are 'Where will these pictures come from? Who will capture the market – and the employment – for producing and transmitting them?' (Commission of the European Communities, 1986: 3). If US dominance is to be challenged, it is argued, then the construction of a pan-European industry and market is imperative: the common market 'must create conditions for economies of scale to allow European industries to produce in greater quantities, at the lowest possible price, and to recoup their investment costs' (Commission of the European Communities, 1988a: 3). Technical progress is now 'making a mockery of frontiers' and the 'day of purely national audiences, markets and channels is gone': the logic of development must be towards a 'European audiovisual area' (Commission of the European

Communities, 1986: 3). In default of this, it is feared that European audio-visual markets are likely to be dominated by the output of American, Japanese or Brazilian corporations.

This strategy is very much aimed at supporting, and integrating, large European corporations. Open skies and network flows are seen as fundamental to the creation of a single large market that will underpin a European industrial and economic renaissance. In this context, 'television without frontiers' (Commission of the European Communities, 1984) is also very much implicated in opening up global advertising markets and spaces. As yet, 'the restrictions and constraints on television advertising across Europe mean that the television set is still relatively unexploited as an advertising medium' (Tydeman and Kelm, 1986: 63). The future of the image industries is very much embedded in that of global advertising; a European audiovisual area is intended to support and facilitate freedom of commercial speech in Europe (Hondius, 1985).

This pan-European space of accumulation is also projected as a space of culture and identity: 'the creation of a large market establishes a European area based on common cultural roots as well as social and economic realities' (Commission of the European Communities, 1987: 3). It is a matter of 'maintaining and promoting the cultural identity of Europe', of 'improving mutual knowledge among our peoples and increasing their consciousness of the life and destiny they have in common' (Commission of the European Communities, 1988b: 3, 11). A transnational politics of culture is worked out in terms of the articulation of European affiliations and allegiances as against, particularly, an Atlanticist cultural identity. But there are problems with what such a 'people's Europe' might be. What is the meaning of this 'sense of belonging to a community composed of countries which are different yet partake of a deep solidarity' (ibid.: 4)? Is it possible to translate a multinational administrative unity into any meaningful identity and solidarity? Perhaps it is the differences, what the Commission (1986: 8) recognises as 'richness' and 'cultural diversity', which are more significant in the creation of positive attachments and identities? What must be recognised is that there are forces also working against cultural homogenisation and transnationalism. In the context of centripetal tendencies brought about by the globalisation of communications, there are also centrifugal tendencies to protect and preserve native languages and cultures (Gifreu, 1986). The 'globalisation of social transactions', experienced as an 'internationalisation process' which is gradually robbing Europe of its originality and demobilising its citizens so that European cultural differences are disintegrating (Bassand, 1988: 72), also conspires to produce localised and particularised communities and identities.

Working both against and within a supra-national politics of communication and culture, there is a growing sub-national agenda focused around local and urban cultural identities. Local media are seen as 'regional building tools not only in traditional cultural terms (regional awareness, cultural identity, linguistic crystallisation), but also in terms of economy (provision of jobs, sensitisation of the public to communication technologies, dynamisation of local markets, etc.)' (Crookes and Vittet-Philippe, 1986: 4). As Torsten Hägerstrand argues, in the context of a system society, in which many activities have 'released themselves from the bonds and fetters of place', and in which the media 'have contributed very little to the local and regional content of world-pictures', there arise countervailing tendencies to explore the 'possibility space' of local media, to establish localised arenas for public debate and cultural expression, to elaborate, in fact, meaningful local public spheres (Hägerstrand, 1986: 10, 16, 18).

The British case is again instructive. Tendencies in the organisation of the audiovisual industries towards partial disintegration and the externalisation of production, in a society historically characterised by a national framework of centralised and metropolitan cultural influence, became in the 1980s associated with the elaboration of significant local cultural initiatives. In a number of urban and local contexts, the image industries have been at the forefront of local economic and cultural development strategies. Glasgow ('European City of Culture'), Sheffield, Birmingham, Liverpool, Newcastle, Bradford, Cardiff ('Media City') were prominent in launching initiatives. Following the model of the Greater London Council in the early 1980s, these strategies moved towards the elaboration of localised cultural industrial districts, along neo-Marshallian lines. In many cases, this question of local industrial and cultural public spheres raised questions about public space, and issues of the quality of working and leisure time became translated into policies for the urban fabric and the design of the built environment.

It was not simply a story of economic and cultural radicalisation, however: the local sphere is a contested terrain. Neither was the culture of locality a concern only of progressive local authorities. It was also high on the agenda of communications conglomerates seeking to combine global marketing with the targeting of local and regional consumers. The cultural industries are not just about programme-making, but also and crucially about distribution, and so long as the new conduits of distribution, such as cable and microwave systems, are closed to democratic access, then aspirations for cultural radicalism will remain an empty ideal.

Local initiatives have also been shaped by external political intervention: local autonomy and accountability have been undermined by centrally imposed development strategies. Whilst 'the official story from the centre has been one of rolling back the state and freedom from bureaucratic control', it is in fact the case that 'the "market freedom" supposedly represented by Free Enterprise Zones and Urban Development Corporations is supported by an almost unprecedented level of state subsidy and support' (Duncan and Goodwin, 1988: 272). What we have in the combined strategies of the development corporations for industry, leisure and the urban fabric is an opportunist inflection and incorporation of that earlier localist politics. The arts and cultural industries have been drawn into the heart of this entrepreneurial initiative. Cable is envisaged as a means 'to tackle multifarious difficulties being faced in inner city areas and to achieve successful regeneration' (Cable Authority, 1987). And, according to the Arts Council, the arts

> arc essential ingredients in the mix of cultural, environmental and recreational amenities which reinforce economic growth and development. They attract tourism and the jobs it brings. More importantly, they can serve as the main catalyst for the wholesale regeneration of an area. They provide focal points for community pride and identity.
>
> (1988: 2)

The new culture of enterprise enlists the enterprise of culture to manufacture differentiated urban or local identities. These are centred around the creation of an image, a fabricated and inauthentic identity, a false aura, usually achieved through 'the recuperation of "history" (real, imagined, or simply re-created as pastiche) and of "community" (again, real, imagined, or simply packaged for sale by producers)' (Harvey, 1987: 274). The context for this is the increased pressure on cities and localities to adopt an entrepreneurial stance in order to attract mobile global capital. The marketing of local identities and images is a function of intensified inter-urban competition, and success 'is often short-lived or rendered moot by competing or alternative innovations arising elsewhere' (ibid.: 278). Under such conditions, local economies are precarious and local identities and cultures may be false and fragile.

REIMAGINED COMMUNITIES?

So far, we have approached recent developments in the media industries in terms of broader political economic transformations, associated with the dual tendency towards globalisation and localisation of image spaces. We want now to approach these same processes from a different perspective, to look at the media in terms of cultural transformations. As Fredric Jameson argues, 'the locus of our new reality and the cultural politics by which it must be confronted is that of space' (Stephanson, 1987: 40). This concerns spatial processes and structures, but also the subjective side of space, orientation within space and experience of space. And it is also a matter of both global space and local space: 'what is wanted is . . . a new relationship between a global cultural style and the specificity and demands of a concrete local or national situation' (ibid.). How do we position ourselves within the new global cultural space? How do we reconcile our cognitive existence in hyperspace, in the virtual space of electronic networks, with our bodily existence in localised space? Can we reposition ourself in local space without falling into nostalgic sentiments of community and *Gemeinschaft*? In Raymond Williams' (1983) terms, what new forms of identity and of bonding are possible and appropriate?

Contemporary cultural theory has been concerned with the disorientating experience of global space, and fundamental to this concern is the impact of global-image space. Richard Kearney (1988a: 1–2) describes a world in which the image reigns supreme, a 'Civilisation of the Image' in which 'reality has become a pale reflection of the image . . . . The real and the imaginary have become almost impossible to distinguish'. With 'the omnipresence of self destructing images which simulate each other in a limitless interplay of mirrors', argues Kearney, 'the psychic world is as colonised as the physical world by the whole image industry' (ibid.: 1, 5). This globalisation of image flows and spaces is fundamentally transforming spatiality and sense of space and place. Fredric Jameson (see Stephanson, 1987: 33) refers to the 'existential bewilderment in this new postmodern space', a 'culture in which one cannot position itself'.

This aspect of 'postmodernisation' is most apparent in the writings of Jean Baudrillard. In the society of the image, he argues, the individual is 'now only a pure screen, a switching centre for all the networks of influence' (Baudrillard, 1985b: 133). With the television image, 'our own body and the whole surrounding universe become a control screen': 'the simple presence of the television changes the rest of the habitat into a kind of archaic envelope, a vestige of human relations whose very survival remains perplexing . . . as soon as behaviour is crystallised on certain screens and operational terminals, what's left appears only as a large useless body, deserted and condemned' (ibid.: 129). This is the world of screen and network, the 'smooth operational surface of communication'; it is a world of 'absolute proximity, the total instantaneity of things, the feeling of no defence, no retreat' (ibid.: 133).

This hyperspace is very much the cultural echo of that logic of transnational networks and communicating flows which Manuel Castells sees as characterising the globalisation and cybernation of accumulation. However, whilst Castells (1983: 4) sees the consequence of this as 'the destruction of human experience, therefore of communication, and therefore of society', Baudrillard (1985b: 132) comes to celebrate 'a state of fascination and vertigo linked to this obscene delirium of communication'. He is seduced by the new communications networks, by the information and image flows, and by the decentred and disorientated identities associated with them. This new space of flows is shaped and controlled by transnational capital: it is the space of IBM and AT&T, of Murdoch and

Berlusconi. It is their evolving network marketplace of commodity flows and advertising spectacle that generates Baudrillard's 'ecstasy of communication'. It is their screens and networks and simulations and cybernetic systems that produce his awe before the technological sublime.

This does, of course, engage with important developments in the late twentieth century. We should not devalue this moment of truth; it may even be exhilarating to know it. But the point must be to push it further. As Richard Kearney (1988a: 380) argues, 'it is not sufficient to merely know that the technological colonisation of images is a symptom of a globally computered network of "third stage" multinational capital'. Knowing this, we must ask a more difficult question: 'Where are we find a place of critical distance where we may begin to imagine alternative projects of social existence capable of counteracting the paralysis which the "technological sublime" induces in us?'

What is significant about this kind of postmodernist culture and theory is its preoccupation with mediation: image, simulation, network, screen, spectacle. Marike Finlay (quoted in Young, 1989: 86) suggests that postmodernism is 'a psychotic defence against the loss of referential identity'. Technological mediation is associated with estrangement from the real. In philosophical terms, this psychotic derealisation is an ultimate consequence of the logic of scientific and administrative rationality, the totalising ambitions of abstract and formal reason. In more social terms, it is a 'culturally generalised psychosis' appropriate to a rationalised, bureaucratic and technocratic society of indirect relationships and large-scale system integration, now on a global scale; a society in which space-transcending information and communications technologies allow 'the creation of organisations sufficiently complex and "impersonal" that they are readily reified', and conceived 'not as products of human action but as autonomous systems' (Calhoun, 1988: 5).

Rationalisation in both its bureaucratic and psychotic forms is characterised by what Michael Rustin (1987: 31) calls abstract universalism, with its 'denial of the particular location of human lives in place and time', its placeless and non-referential sense of identity. Rustin argues that cultural and political intervention needs, rather, to take account of social texture, density, difference. What is needed is 'a new particularism', a 'recognition that collective identities are formed through the common occupancy of space, and constituted in relations of particularist kinds' (ibid.: 34). This is about the reclamation or reimagination of a sense of referential identity, the revaluation of concrete and particular experience. In Richard Rorty's terms, it is about solidarity, as opposed to objectivity, as a way of placing one's life in a larger context. According to the Enlightenment ideal of objectivity, the individual 'distances himself [sic] from the actual persons around him . . . by attaching himself to something which can be described without reference to any particular human beings' (Rorty,

1985: 3). The desire for solidarity, on the other hand, is referential and contextualised: the individual tells the story of his or her contribution to a community, be it 'the actual historical one in which they live, or another actual one, distant in time or place, or a quite imaginary one'. This process of bonding can occur in the context of attachment to bounded territorial locations, though it should not be thought that this is about an ambition to return to the parochial world of *Gemeinschaft*. Solidarity and collectivity should also have aspirations directed beyond the locality. In terms of the global-image space, Richard Kearney calls for 'a practice of imagination capable of responding to the postmodern call of the other reaching towards us from the mediated gaze':

> On the far side of the self-reflecting looking glass, beyond the play of masks and mirrors, there are human beings who suffer and struggle, live and die, hope and despair. Even in those televisual images which transmit events from the furthest corners of our globe, we are being addressed, potentially at least, by living others . . . . Are not those of us who witness such images . . . obliged to respond not just to surface reflections on a screen but to the call of human beings they communicate?
>
> (1988a: 387–8)

What does this mean for European identities? Refuge in some simple and coherent national, and nationalist, identity cannot be easily sustained. In a European context, at least, the 'imagined communities' of nationalism are increasingly problematical. Whilst a protracted and fierce rearguard action will, no doubt, be waged in the embittered defence of nations, and nationhood, it is clear that socio-spatial transformations in the late twentieth century call for new orientations and new forms of bonding. The most obvious response to these new conditions has, of course, been the attempt to build a European Community: 'a common market', a 'citizens' Europe', a 'Europe of Culture'. The attempt to cope with simultaneous fragmentation and globalisation here produces a political compromise whereby national cultures are subsumed and preserved in a spurious, administrative-bureaucratic internationalism. Defined as it is against the American and Japanese 'threats', this really amounts to a kind of supra-nationalism (and perhaps super-nationalism?).

But what, then, are the conditions and requirements for genuinely reimagined communities? As Raymond Williams argues in *Towards 2000* (1983), we must explore new forms of variable societies and variable identities. Postmodern culture must be elaborated out of differential and plural identities, rather than collapsing into some false cohesion and unity. It must be about positions and positioning in local and global space: about contexts of bodily existence and about existence in mediated space. At one level, it is about bounded and localised spatial arenas which bring individuals into direct social contact, about revaluing public places and recreating a civic culture. But it must be recognised, as Craig Calhoun (1988: 27–8) argues, that 'however desirable decentralised communities might be, they are at most complements to system integration and not alternatives to it'. It is necessary to improve the way large-scale systems work, and this means learning how to use the mass media and the new communications technologies to create 'a new forum for public discourse'.

Much of this discussion has emphasised the stifling power of global-image corporations. However, emergent transformations in the space of accumulation and in the spatial disposition of cultural forms, do open up some new possibilities for reimagined solidarities. The recent growth in decentralised programme-making opens up at least the possibility of local media spaces. It is possible to envisage 'an amplification of the internal flows of communication in regions and localities' that might 'establish platforms for public debate and distinctive cultural expression' (Hägerstrand, 1986: 18). Public discourse, grounded in a spatial framework, could be elaborated in a local public sphere. In this context, media culture must be seen as part of a much broader strategy for local development through the stimulation of cultural innovation, identity and difference (Bassand et al., 1986). Whilst such localism could, of course, degenerate into introverted and nostalgic historicism and heritage fixation, local attachment can be seen in more radical and innovative terms. New conditions of mobility make local attachment not a matter of ascribed and determined identity but increasingly a question of choice, decision and variability. Local cultures are, moreover, permeated and suffused by external influences. As Kenneth Frampton argues, local cultures can only be constituted now as locally inflected manifestations of global culture. What is called for, in his view, is a strategy of Critical Regionalism 'to mediate the impact of universal civilisation with elements derived indirectly from the peculiarities of a particular phase' (Frampton, 1985: 21). A critical regional or local culture must necessarily be in dialogue with global culture.

But contemporary cultural identities must also be about internationalism in a direct sense, about our positions in transnational spaces. At one level, this can be a matter of supra-national language and cultural communities: for example, 'francophone identities' (Jouanny, 1988) or, more radically, a 'latin audiovisual space' (Mattelart, Delcourt and Mattelart, 1984). But it must also transcend a Eurocentric perspective to achieve other forms of dialogue and collectivity. Fundamental here are solidarities with Third World cultures: those outside Europe, but also Third World communities, in all their diversity, now installed within European territories. European identity can no longer be, simply and unproblematically, a matter of Western intellectual and cultural traditions. As a consequence of its belligerent, imperialistic and colonialist history, Europe now contains a rich diversity of cultures and identities. The question is whether ethnic (and also gendered) differences are disavowed and repressed, or whether they can be accepted – and accepted, moreover, in their difference.

3

CULTURE, COMMUNITY AND IDENTITY

Communications technologies and the reconfiguration of Europe

> As Europe is my own imagination
> – many shall see her,
> many shall not –
> though it's only the old familiar world
> and not some abstract mystical dream.
>   Allen Ginsberg

Richard Collins notes the remark made by a French independent producer, speaking at a trade forum in Toronto, that nowadays 'Television is in colour, in stereo and in English' (1988: 1). In a similar vein the Latin American novelist Manuel Puig recalls that viewing Hollywood films in Argentina led him to conclude 'at one point in my childhood . . . that reality was spoken in English and came sub-titled'. We might also recall that, when asked for his opinion of European civilisation, Mahatma Gandhi is reported to have replied only that he thought that 'it would be a very good idea'.

Contemporary technological developments, and particularly the emergence of satellite television, have given a new urgency to the question of information flows. Thus Collins (1988: 6) has noted the greater difficulty, for national states, of policing the circulation of electronic products, precisely because they assume no material form (unlike films or books, with which a customs post can deal more easily). Similarly, Philip Schlesinger (1986: 126) has noted that satellite broadcasting threatens to undermine the very basis of present policies for the policing of national space. Collins has pointed to the possibility of satellite television presaging the generalisation of the 'Canadian experience' of subservience to American cultural interests (1988: 13) and has observed that satellite television may indeed be seen to herald what he calls the 'Canadianisation of European television' (ibid.: 20). Thus, these new technologies, it has been argued, have worryingly negative consequences for established national (and indeed continental) identities, and, at the same time, have potentially unpoliceable and thus 'disturbing' effects, not only in dissaggregating established audiences/communities, but also in creating new ones across national boundaries. Against these fears, various writers have also noted the limitations on the exportability of American culture, both in the sense of the limitations imposed in principle (by language/culture) on the export of information products as opposed to material goods, and in the empirical sense that European fears about being swamped by American culture can arguably be contradicted, to some extent, by empirical evidence of continuing audience preferences for 'home' products (cf. Mills, 1985).

THE CONSTRUCTION OF CULTURAL IDENTITIES

Until relatively recently, debates surrounding the questions of cultural identity and cultural imperialism functioned with a largely uninterrogated model of what 'cultural identities' are. On the whole, the question has tended to be posed (with varying degrees of technological determinism) as one concerning the potential impact of a 'new technology' (e.g. satellite broadcasting) on a set of pre-given objects, national (or cultural) identities. Formulations (and assumptions) of this type seem to have underlain many of the European Community's debates (and policies) surrounding these issues. Thus, it has often been assumed, for instance, that the integrity and continued existence of communities and their political institutions depends crucially on their communications sovereignty, and that if a community consumes 'too much' (unspecified) exogeneous information 'the legitimacy of the native political institutions will come under threat and the community will ultimately cease to exist' (Banks and Collins, 1989: 2). It is in this light that we can perhaps best understand much recent European Community policy which, in response to the perceived threat of 'cocacolonisation', has been concerned to promote and develop a sense of European identity, in which unity is the goal and information/culture (which is perceived to have 'homogenising' effects, cf. Schlesinger, 1987: 220) is the means to achieve it. Or, as Jean Monnet put it, 'if we were beginning the European Community all over again, we should begin with culture' (quoted in ibid.: 222).

From this perspective, debates such as those over the potential 'denationalisation' of Italy (as Italy is seen to incur the danger of becoming an area of pure consumption, because of the weakness of its production base, cf. Schlesinger, 1986: 137) acquire a different significance. Schlesinger argues that 'collective identity and its constitution is a problem, not something that may be presumed to exist as a prior condition of political agency' (1987: 240). From this angle, culture has to be seen as a site of perpetual contestation (both inter- and intra-nationally) and we cannot view the 'achievement' of a national culture as some kind of one-off task which, having been 'completed' could equally be 'undone'. Rather it is, necessarily, a continuous, and continuously problematic process (cf. Gramsci, 1971, on hegemony as a continuous movement between unstable equilibria). In a similar vein, Donald has argued that we might usefully focus on

> the apparatuses of discourse, technologies and institutions (print capitalism, education, mass media and so forth) which produced what is generally recognised as 'the national culture' . . . the nation is an effect of these cultural technologies, not their origin. A nation does not express itself through its culture: it is cultural apparatuses that produce 'the nation'. What is produced is not an identity or a single consciousness . . . but (hierarchically organised) values, dispositions and differences. This cultural and social heterogeneity is given a certain fixity by the articulating principle of 'the nation'. The 'national' defines the culture's unity by differentiating it from other cultures, by marking its boundaries; a fictional unity, of course, because the 'us' on the inside is itself always differentiated.
>
> (1988: 32)

IDENTITY AS DIFFERENCE: CONSTITUTIVE RELATIONS

In his classic study of linguistics, Saussure (1974) argues that, within the realm of language, there are only differences, with no positive terms. Thus, when he analyses the problem of identity in language (when two linguistic units are to count as instances of the same category) he concludes that identity is wholly a function of differences within a system. Thus, as he argues, we must approach the problem from the fundamental recognition that the 'units' of language which we wish to understand are 'purely differential and defined not by their positive content but negatively, by their relations with the other terms of the system. Their most precise characteristic is in being what the others are not' (Saussure, 1974: 117).

We wish to argue that this same principle should be applied in the analysis of cultural identities. Rather than analysing cultural or (national) identities one by one and then, subsequently (as an optional move) thinking about how they are related to each other (through relations of alliance or opposition, domination or subordination), we must grasp how these 'identities', in Saussurean terms, are only constituted in and through their relations to one another. Thus, to make the argument more concrete, it is inappropriate to start by trying to define 'European culture', for example, and then subsequently analysing its relations to other cultural identities. Rather, from this perspective, 'European culture' is seen to be constituted precisely through its distinctions from and oppositions to American culture, Asian culture, Islamic culture, etc. Thus, difference is constitutive of identity. Again Schlesinger offers a useful formulation. As

45

he puts it:

> identity is as much about exclusion as it is about inclusion, and the
> critical factor for defining the ethnic group therefore becomes the
> social *boundary* which defines the group with respect to other groups
> . . . not the cultural reality within those borders.
>
> (1987: 235)

Viewed in this way, collective identity is based on the (selective) processes
of memory (cf. Wright, 1985), so that a given group recognises itself
through its memory of a common past. Thus, we can develop a dynamic
view of identity, focusing on the ability of social groups continually to
recompose and redefine their boundaries (Schlesinger, 1987: 230).

From this perspective, then, national identity is a specific form of collective identity:

> All identities are constituted within a system of social relations and
> require the reciprocal recognition of others. Identity . . . is not to
> be considered a 'thing' but rather a 'system of relations and repre-
> sentations' . . . the maintenance of an agent's identity is . . . a
> continual process of recomposition rather than a given one, in which
> the two constitutive dimensions of self-identification and affirmation
> of difference are continually locked . . . identity is seen as a
> dynamic, *emergent* aspect of collective action.
>
> (ibid.: 236–7)

The argument, so far, has been pitched at the level of socio-cultural
analysis. However, there is another dimension to the problem, which is
well developed by Donald in his analysis of the constitution of English
culture, where he also addresses the psychic processes involved in the
constitution and maintenance of identity and difference. In pursuit of this
argument, Donald asks why there are so many grotesque foreign villains
(e.g. Fu Manchu, Dr No, etc.) in popular fiction, and why the problem of
identity is so often played out by its projection onto 'dangerous women'
in popular films (e.g. *film noir*). His point is that these popular fictions
speak to fundamental psychic processes, and attention to them can help
us to make sense of what he calls the 'paranoid strand in popular culture,
the clinging to familiar polarities and the horror of difference' (Donald,
1988: 44). As he puts it:

> Manifest in racism, its violent misogyny, and its phobias about alien
> cultures, alien ideologies and 'enemies within', is the terror that
> without the known boundaries, everything will collapse in undiffer-
> entiated, miasmic chaos, that identity will disintegrate, and the 'I'
> will be suffocated or swamped.
>
> (ibid.)

46

This is the fear at the heart of the question of 'identity', whether posed at the level of the individual or of the nation. Driven by such fears, as the Mattelarts have noted, the defence of a given 'cultural identity' easily slips into the most hackneyed nationalism, or even racism, and the nationalist affirmation of the superiority of one group over another (cf. Mattelart, Delcourt and Mattelart, 1984). The question is not abstract: it is a matter of the relative power of different groups to define national identity, and their abilities to mobilise their definitions through their control of cultural institutions. Here we enter the terrain of what Hobsbawm and Ranger (1983) have referred to as the 'invention of tradition'. Tradition is not a matter of a fixed or given set of beliefs or practices which are handed down or accepted passively. Rather, as Wright (1985) has argued, tradition is very much a matter of present-day politics, and of the way in which powerful institutions function to select particular values from the past, and to mobilise them in contemporary practices (cf. Mrs Thatcher's call for the return to 'Victorian values' and Mr Major's 'back to basics' campaign in the UK). Through such mechanisms of cultural reproduction, a particular version of the 'collective memory', and thus a particular sense of national identity, is produced.

However, while this stress on the cultural construction of identities (and on the role of media in that process) is of great value, it is none the less worthwhile to take hold of Schudson's (1994) critique of what he would see as the 'idealist' version of such arguments. Schudson argues that, while we must attend to the role of culture in the integration of social groups, it does not follow that cultural integration is either the sole, or a sufficient, or even a necessary condition of social cohesion. In making this argument Schudson parallels Lockwood's (1954) criticisms of the role ascribed to culture in structural functionalism (cf. Lockwood's distinction between 'social integration' and 'system integration' and his argument that these two can vary independently of each other). Schudson here also echoes the criticisms of Abercombie *et al.* (1984) of the overblown claims sometimes made on behalf of the role of the 'media' in the reproduction of ideology as the sole (or principal) explanation of social order.

As Schudson notes, human societies are often held together by several different mechanisms of integration – based on territory, or on kinship links through the economic links of exchange and the market, or through political structures. It is not only that culture is not necessarily the central integrative mechanism in many societies and that it is 'economic and political integration, rather than cultural forces' which have 'borne the primary responsibility for the integration of the masses into modern states', but as Schudson also notes, 'culture . . . even if coherent and unified in its own terms, does not necessarily call forth integration at the level of societal action' (1994: 164): it can perfectly well be a divisive factor.

47

All of this is only necessary by way of caution in the face of recent tendencies perhaps to over-privilege cultural forms and modes of integration above their political or economic counterparts. Thus Schudson goes on to observe that

> it may be better to suggest not that there are several forces that help societies to cohere but that there are several different ways in which a society is integrated. Societies may be coherent *orders*, meaning that political control is effectively exercised. They may be coherently *co-ordinated*, meaning that people of different . . . values manage through various . . . . mechanisms to interact peacefully. And they may be coherent *communities*, with shared allegiance to a common set of values.
>
> (ibid.: 65)

Schudson's stress, however, is on the *may*, in each of these sentences: for our purposes, it is the last of his cautions – against the presumption that a 'society' necessarily constitutes a 'community' – that is of most relevance.

A PARTICULAR CASE

Various commentators (see, *inter alia*, Ascherson, 1988; Glenny, 1988; Schlesinger, 1989) have pointed to the re-emergence of nationalist movements in recent years (not least in Eastern Europe, as the constraints of Soviet hegemony loosened and then crumbled) and also to the politically contradictory character of these demands for national autonomy. Clearly the issues at stake here are pertinent right across Western (cf. also the Basque and Breton movements) and Eastern Europe. However, being English, we shall attempt to pursue the point by means of an analysis which focuses on a cultural process with which we are more familiar and in which we are, necessarily, implicated more directly.

As Stuart Hood (1988) has argued, 'cultural nationalism assumes that nations are monolithic and denies the importance of subcultures based on regionalism and class within the political unity of the nation'. His fundamental point concerns the way in which the cultural identity of Britain has been constructed so as to deny the relations of power that exist between England, Scotland, Wales and Northern Ireland, as the constituent parts of the United Kingdom. Britain's cultural identity is, in fact, formulated around the cultural identity of its dominant English part. At root, this is an expression of a 'dangerous tradition of envious, fearful nationalism' which is both jingoistic and xenophobic (and indeed racist) and which 'looks for and finds outlets for its fears and rages in attacks on those who are different' (ibid.: 30–1).

Both Hood and Raphael Samuel (1988) have argued that the key cultural process in play in recent British politics is one in which a romantically sanitised version of the British past has been busily recreated: a quite reactionary vision of pastoral England/Albion. Samuel describes this process as the creation of a 'born again cultural nationalism', which operates across a number of fields. Thus, he points to the boom in the conservation/heritage movement; the re-evaluation of English landscape painting; educational reforms aimed at returning to 'traditional standards' in English and history, as core components of the educational curriculum; in the realm of architecture and design, a return to the use of 'traditional materials', as Habitat has replaced its Scandinavian pine with 'traditional English kitchen furniture', and Covent Garden's new shopping piazza has been recreated as a (Dickensian) walk down England's memory lane, past 'shoppes' offering 'traditional fare' in a picturesque nightmare of time undone. Samuel cuttingly defines this overall tendency as operating within the context of a defence of national tradition against European intellectual history . . . 'a kind of [upper – DM/KR] class revenge for the modernisations [read Europeanisation – DM/KR] of the 1960s' (ibid.: lvi).

Clearly, there is more at stake here than the question of whether one likes 'traditional paisley patterns'. What else is at stake is the question of race, because the 'England' being reconstructed in this way is being conceptualised around a tradition which is unproblematically white – which Britain's contemporary population is not. In his study of British racism, *'There Ain't No Black in the Union Jack'*, Paul Gilroy (1986) puts the point simply, characterising all of this as a 'morbid celebration of England and Englishness from which blacks are systematically excluded' (Gilroy, quoted in Donald, 1988: 31).

In taking up this argument, Stuart Hall rightly points out that 'ethnicity, in the form of a culturally-contrasted sense of Englishness and a particularly closed, exclusive and regressive form of English national identity, is one of the core characteristics of British racism today' (Hall, 1988: 29). He argues for the need to 'decouple ethnicity . . . from its equivalence with nationalism, imperialism, racism and the state, which are the points of attachment around which a distinctive British, (or more accurately English) ethnicity has been constructed' and for the need 'to develop a new cultural politics and a new conception of ethnicity . . . which engages rather than suppresses difference' (ibid.).

The point is, of course, by no means exclusive to the British context. Indeed it may well be, as Sivanandan (1988) argues, that we shall in the near future see a gradual shift from national and ethnocentric forms of racism to Eurocentric or pan-European forms of racism. Yasmin Alibhai (1989) has noted that there is 'a respectable xenophobia mushrooming all over the continent that is pushing some of the collective dreams for 1992 to cluster around a concept of Europe which is white, racist and much more powerful than any post-war individual state'. National identities are being transformed into a 'white continentalism'. European unity is being defined against 'alien' culture and around a self-image of European superiority. This she sees in Mrs Thatcher's invocation of a 'common experience' rooted in the colonial history of the European nation states. In her infamous speech in Bruges, in 1989, the then British Prime Minister could confidently and unashamedly declare 'the story of how Europeans explored and colonised and – yes, without apology – civilised much of the world [to be] an extraordinary tale of talent, skill and courage'. As Alibhai concludes, all this 'raises a central and neglected question: where do non-white Europeans fall within such a vision?'

As a consequence of its belligerent, imperialistic and colonialist history, Europe now contains a rich diversity of cultures and identities. The question is whether ethnic (and also gendered) differences are disavowed and repressed, or whether they can be accepted – and accepted, moreover, in their difference.

EUROPE VERSUS AMERICA

'Europe can no longer be understood by starting out from Europe itself', writes Jean Baudrillard (1988a). European identity must come to terms with its 'imaginary America' and with the 'spectre of Americanisation'. America plays a complicated part in the constitution of European cultural identity. In one respect it is 'anti-Europe'; it is mobilised as the paradigm of the traditionless, the land of the material, not the cultural. But it is also Europe's alter ego, an exaggerated reflection of what Europe fears it will become, or perhaps what Europe is already. A country with no past and therefore no real culture, America has become 'a paradigm for the future threatening every advanced industrial democracy in the world' (Hebdige, 1988b: 52–3). In this process, the great Satan of American anti-culture is counterposed to the comfortable values and traditions by which Europeans have understood and identified themselves, not only as 'Europeans' but also as 'cultured' and 'civilised'. In this section we explore the dynamics of the debate about American culture in Europe, from the point of view of the structuralist perspective outlined earlier. Among other things we shall argue that anti-Americanism usually has a suppressed class content, which means that it also functions as a defence of dominant class definitions of the 'national' culture in question.

It is worth noting that all of this has a very long pedigree. If President Mitterand's 'nightmare' of the day when a European can be defined as someone who watches American soap opera on a Japanese television was a phenomenon of the late 1980s, we can find much the same sentiment being expressed in the British context in 1945 by Lord Keynes, then Chairman of the Arts Council:

How satisfactory it would be if different parts of the citizenry would again walk their several ways as they once did. Let every part of Merry England be merry in its own way. Death to Hollywood!

(quoted in Donald, 1988: 32)

Even the most contemporary versions of the argument seem to have an oddly dated tone – as Meaghan Morris (1987) has remarked, Baudrillard's *America* reads rather like a new edition of De Tocqueville.

It is, of course, a problem which is more complex than 'Europe versus America'. For one thing, 'American films, best selling books and such, were "European" long before any European media' (Wendelbo, 1986: 15). The information industries of tomorrow, on either side of the Atlantic, are already Euro-American in composition (cf. the importance of the US-owned McCann Erikson advertising agency in Europe and, conversely, the entry in the late 1980s of the Saatchi & Saatchi agency into the US market). This is the background to the 'cry to maintain a national character, against the mongrel commercialisation of a fake Europe which is half-American anyway' (Walker, 1988a).

All these commentaries reveal that in recent years the European Commission has sought to revitalise in its media policies a sense of European identity associated with the heritage of 'Western Civilisation' (or, as Kenneth Clark (ex-) nominated it, in his well-known television series, *Civilisation*). What is being ideologically mobilised is the gravity of Graeco-Roman cultural tradition. What is being invoked is a common history and destiny grounded in the presumption of the moral, political, aesthetic and scientific superiority of the European continent. The present push for economic, political and cultural unity 'is an attempt to refurbish the old image of princess Europa as wealthy, free and powerful' (Keane, 1989: 30).

The vanity of that approach is well caught in Baudrillard's observations:

Once a nation and a culture have been centralised by a solid histori-cal process, they experience insurmountable difficulties when they attempt either to create viable sub-units or to integrate themselves into some coherent larger entity. . . . Hence the difficulties currently being encountered in the attempt to find a European spirit and culture, a European dynamism. Inability to produce a federal event (Europe), a local event (decentralisation), a racial event (multi-racialism). Too entangled by our history, we can only produce an apologetic centralism (a Clochemerle pluralism) and an apologetic mixing (our soft racism).

(1988a: 83)

In developing our understanding of the 'impact' of American media and cultural forms in Europe, we should, of course, also remember Armand Mattelart's warning that the

51

idea of a monolithic, triumphant imperialism, wiping out all diversity and homogenising all cultures is absurd. . . . The idea that imperialism invades different sectors of a society in a uniform way must be abandoned. What must be substituted is the demand for an analysis that illuminates the particular milieux that favour [or hinder – DM/KR] this penetration.

(1979: 61)

This is not simply an academic perspective: the same recognition of the continuing pertinence of 'national differences' has informed the recognition of many American companies that they will need to develop 'national variants' of their products (and adverts) for different national markets within Europe, rather than relying on 'Eurobrands'. In a similar way, Collins (1988) has noted the retreat of many of the entrepreneurial enthusiasts of 'European' satellite television, away from their original pan-European ambitions, towards a revised perspective which accepts the limitations and divisions of separate language/cultural markets in Europe.

Here the experience of the Howard Johnson hotel/restaurant chain in the early 1970s seems to be repeated. In 1972 their chairman announced their withdrawal from the overall Euro-market, saying

we are too Americanised to make it in Europe . . . our company is now drawing up plans for a new chain of more European-style motels . . . looking for market areas where the cultural differences between America and Europe are less marked and will pose less problems, e.g. business travel and hotels.

(quoted in Bigsby, 1975)

So on some things, at least, the marxists and the businessmen can agree. However, the problems at issue here are in fact more complex still. The comments from the chairman of Howard Johnson find an interesting parallel in Collins' analysis of the differential 'cultural discount' (cf. Hoskins and Mirus, 1988) for various types of products, in a range of markets, where cultural differences function to 'discount' or limit the range of the 'exportability' of a given product. But 'cultural discount' is no simple matter of geographical proximity. Collins goes on to quote a *World Film News* survey from the 1930s, which reported that film exhibitors in working-class areas of Scotland were

on the whole satisfied with the more vigorous American films . . . [but] practically unanimous in regarding the majority of British films as unsuitable for their audiences. British films, one Scottish exhibitor writes, should rather be called English films, in a particularly parochial sense; they are more 'foreign' to his audience than the products of Hollywood, over 6000 miles away.

(quoted in Collins, 1988: 7)

DALLAS WITH TAILFINS: THE VULGAR POLITICS OF TASTE

We have argued earlier that when the defence of cultural identity gets confused with the defence of a fixed past, it runs the risk of playing a strictly conservative role, quite apart from the difficulties of establishing any definition of the authentic/national culture being 'defended', which inevitably will contain elements which were originally foreign.

Throughout the 1980s, *Dallas* functioned as the most obvious 'hate symbol' of this kind of 'cultural emasculation', as immortalised in ex-Director-General of the BBC Alastair Milne's fear that the deregulation of British television would lead to the 'threat of wall-to-wall *Dallas*'. As Ien Ang put it, the international popularity of *Dallas* was frequently offered as knock-down 'evidence of the threat posed by US style commercial culture to all authentic national cultures and identities' (Ang, 1985: 2). We wish to suggest that these debates need to be seen in the context of the long gestation of anti-Americanism in European culture, and that, specifically, the present debate about the impact of commercial American television programmes in a Europe which comprises many countries that are still dominated by a very traditional form of public service programming, can usefully be informed by consideration of the anti-American rhetoric of the debates surrounding the introduction of commercial television in Britain in the 1950s.

Up to that time, the BBC held sole monopoly of British television. That monopoly was originally granted at a time when the British cultural elite saw its position undermined by the seemingly unstoppable flow of American popular culture, Hollywood, Tin Pan Alley, 'cheap American fiction', etc. The role of the BBC was to maintain (under Lord Reith's stewardship) national standards in the face of this threat to the Great English Cultural Tradition (see Mulgan and Worpole, 1985). The problem was that, as soon as ITV was launched in the 1950s, offering new cultural forms based on elements of working-class and regional cultures (melodramas, irreverent presenters, non-standard accents, etc.), the working-class audience deserted the BBC in droves. As Mulgan and Worpole put it, 'the BBC . . . by its refusal to engage with anything other than the cultural tradition of the Southern upper class, left a vast, vacant, cultural space which the early entrepreneurs of ITV were only too happy to fill' (ibid.).

The cultural significance of this development was the focus of considerable debate in the UK during the 1980s (summarised in articles by Connell, 1983 and Garnham, 1983). In that context, Connell argued that the key factor was that the commercial channel, ITV, 'led the way in making connections with and expressing popular structures of feeling and taste. By its very logic, a commercial TV station is bound to attempt to

53

meet the tastes and needs of its audience' (Connell, 1983). The BBC quickly learnt that, if it was to survive, it had to emulate ITV's success in this respect, which it was only able to do by likewise producing more material which directly connected with working-class patterns of taste and cultural preferences (with new types of programmes, drawing on elements from the tradition of the music hall, and featuring presenters and performers with regional and various 'non-U' accents).

Traditionally, the left and its anti-American allies have explained the dominance of American programmes in the international television market by reference to the considerable economic advantages accruing to American producers, as a result of the huge scale of their domestic market. These advantages are, of course, considerable, but what if there is also something intrinsic to the products which constitutes the basis of their appeal to working-class audiences in other countries? In his investigation of literary tastes among the British working class, Worpole (1983) interviewed a number of men who recall their pleasures in discovering American detective fiction writing in the 1930s. Here is an ex-docker explaining why, for him, this American literature had a greater appeal than the writers of the English literary tradition.

> I read the English writers, H G Wells, Arnold Bennett . . . but they weren't my kind of people. You always had the edge of class there . . . what intrigued me about the American writers was they were talking the way we talked.
>
> (ibid.: 30)

We shall return to the point at the end of this section: for the moment let us only note the importance of the vernacular language in constituting the appeal of these American forms of popular culture. The idea that English or European 'high culture' is in danger of being swamped by a relentless deluge of 'Americana' is hardly new. Dick Hebdige (1988b) traces these fears back to at least the 1930s, when writers as different as the conservative Evelyn Waugh and the socialist George Orwell were united by a fascinated loathing for modern architecture, holiday camps, advertising, fast food, plastics and (later) chewing gum. To both Waugh and Orwell, these were the images of the 'soft', enervating, 'easy life' which threatened to smother British cultural identity. By the 1950s, the battle lines in this debate were drawn: 'real culture', quality and taste on one side, the ersatz blandishment of soft disposable commodities, stream-lined cars, rock and roll, crime and promiscuity on the other. As Hebdige says, when anything American was sighted, it tended to be interpreted (at least by those working in the context of education or professional cultural criticism) as the 'beginning of the end'. Hebdige describes how the images of crime, disaffected youth, urban crisis and spiritual drift became 'anchored together around popular American commodities, fixing a chain of associations which has become thoroughly sedimented in British common-sense' (ibid.: 57). Thus, in particular, American (fast) food became a standard metaphor for declining standards. The very notion of the 'Americanisation' of television thus now stands for a whole series of associations to do with commercialisation, banality and the destruction of traditional values.

The debate which Hebdige opened up goes back to Richard Hoggart's work on *The Uses of Literacy* (1958). Hoggart's book is a detailed appreciation of traditional working-class community life, coupled with a critique of the homogenising impact of American culture on working-class life, which he saw as being destroyed by the 'hollow brightness', the 'shiny barbarism' and 'spiritual decay' of imported American culture, which was leading to an aesthetic breakdown, in which traditional values were undermined and replaced by a 'Candy Floss World' of easy thrills and cheap fiction.

This lamentation of the deleterious effects of Americanisation was, and continues to be, advanced from the left just as much as from the right of the political spectrum. However, Hebdige's central point is that these 'vulgar' American products, streamlined, plastic and glamorous, were precisely those which appealed to substantial sections of the British working class (cf. our earlier comments on the popularity of ITV with its working-class audience). While, from the paternalistic point of view of the upholders of 'traditional British values', these American-imported products constituted a 'chromium hoard bearing down on us', for a popular audience, Hebdige argues, they constituted a space in which oppositional meanings (in relation to dominant traditions of British culture) could be negotiated and expressed.

In passing, we would also like to add one more twist to the story. The images which Orwell and Hoggart use to characterise the damaging effects of American popular culture have a recurring theme: the emasculation or 'feminisation' of the authentic muscle and masculinity of the British industrial working class, which they saw as under attack from an excess of Americana, characterised essentially by passivity, leisure and domesticity, warm baths, sun-bathing and the easy life; expressed perhaps most graphically in Hoggart's image of American culture 'unbending the springs of action' among British working-class people. When the discussion of American programming is combined with that of programming in the genre of soap opera, principally understood as a feminine form in itself, we are clearly (from Hoggart's or Orwell's position) dealing with the lowest of the low, or, as Charlotte Brunsdon (1986) has characterised it, what is seen as 'the trashiest trash' (cf. Huyssen, 1988).

As Bigsby put it some time ago, in a world where the 'modern' experience has often been equated with an 'Imaginary America' (cf. Webster, 1989):

Opposition to popular culture and complaints about Americanisation have often amounted to little more than laments over a changing world . . . where 'Americanisation' frequently means little more than the incidence of change, and change, especially in new cultural forms, provokes established patterns of negative reaction. The new is characterised as brash, crude, unsubtle, mindless and (as Matthew Arnold insisted) destructive of taste and tradition. 'America' is thus mobilised as the paradigm of the traditionless, the land of the *material* counterposed to the '*cultural*'.

(Bigsby, 1975: 6, our emphasis)

In her contribution to the British debate surrounding American popular culture, Cora Kaplan usefully points towards an approach which is sensitive to the different meanings which the same products can have in different national contexts, thus moving us away from the unhelpfully 'essentialist' terms in which many of these debates have, thus far, been couched. She notes that in their 'home' context, in the 1950s and 1960s

American thrillers/westerns etc were seen as somehow 'essentially' rightwing in some ideological sense . . . [however] in Britain the genres and narratives of American popular culture acted as a kind of wedge, forcing into the open, by contrast . . . a recognition of the class-bound complacency of the 'Great Tradition' of British Culture.

(quoted in Webster, 1988: 179)

As Hebdige argues, in Britain the debate and popular culture, during the key period of the 1950s and 1960s, concentrated on the question of the design or style of 'modern' American products, and especially their 'streamlining', which was seen as vulgar (in bad taste) by reference to the established canons of European design. These 'streamlined' products (notably American cars) which were so (regretfully) popular among working-class consumers, were decried as decadent, decorative and excessive. These things were seen as 'vulgar', in the strict sense of the 'vulgate': of, pertaining to the common people. These American products were scorned by the British cultural elite as being 'the jazz of the drawing board . . . products of a short-term, low-rent, chromium utopia'. And worst of all was the ever-popular Cadillac, whose tailfins were described as representing the 'Vietnam of product design' (Hebdige, 1988b: 65–6).

The problem for the critics was, of course, that the popularity of these products, while it might be decried and regretted, could not be wished away. By breaking away from traditional, class-based notions of 'good taste', the products did make genuine connections with the actual tastes and desires of large numbers of working-class people. For these consumers, the products represented powerful symbols of a massive improvement in

56

the material quality of their lives. For them 'America' was a very positive symbol (cf. Frith, 1983) functioning largely by opposition to what they perceived as the dead hand of traditional English culture, as defined by the cultural elite.

We argued earlier that identity is always as much a matter of difference as it is of similarities, and that what is significant is an understanding of who is being differentiated from whom. For Europeans, 'America' has long provided the negative pole against which 'we' have defined ourselves, the image of what 'we' are not, or that which 'we' do not wish to imagine ourselves to be, or that which it is feared 'we' are about to become. But the terms of this debate have now acquired a certain historical fixity, which is relatively autonomous of their material basis (cf. Althusser, 1972). Because now, as Ang and Morley put it:

> While the European nations still wrangle over their respective attempts to protect their cultural sovereignty from this 'American invasion' the terms are shifting yet again, as we approach the point at which Spanish becomes the first language of all the Americas and as the United States begins to face the consequences of having become the world's largest debtor nation. As the pivot of the world economy swings from the Atlantic to the Pacific basin, a fundamental modification in the balance of economic power is taking place, whose impacts have begun to make themselves felt in the cultural sphere as well. Sony's purchase of CBS presages what may yet turn out to be a fundamental re-alignment of international cultural forces, and the old cultural ramparts along Europe's Atlantic coast may well turn out to be facing in quite the wrong direction. In fact, European nations may now face the prospect of a different form of marginalisation from the world stage, a prospect that throws the threat of 'Americanisation' into quite a new perspective.

> (1989: 140)

If 'vulgar' American products – streamlined, plastic and glamorous – have long been attractive to European audiences, perhaps the problem is not really about a brash and material American culture, but rather about a fake, 'antique' Europe? Perhaps America is now within, now part of a European cultural repertoire, part of European identity. Durham (1993) reverses the issue, and raises the interesting question as to where 'America' is: his view is that 'The US is not here, within these specific [North American – DM/KR] lands. It is in Europe. It is Europe's ghost . . . ' (ibid.: 249). At the same time, he urges Europeans to see their 'permanent settler colonies' (e.g. the USA, Canada and Australia) as 'your best efforts, as the most logical extension of your culture . . . your standard, your proper measure, not an aberration you can disclaim' (ibid.: 144). Ricoeur (1992) points out that according to Karl Jaspers, 'Europe' is best

57

understood as extending from San Francisco to Vladivostok. Conversely, Ang (1992) argues precisely that the current 'problem for Europe . . . is to learn how to marginalise itself, to see its present in its historical particularity and its limitedness' (ibid.: 28).

EUROPE: A QUESTION OF GEOGRAPHY?

In discussing the question of European geographies (cf. Mackinder, 1904) it is as well to remember that it has never been entirely clear what is that entity called 'Europe': the very definition of the term itself is a matter of history and politics. Once we depart from the terrain of physical geography, the questions, naturally, become even more complex. Banks and Collins argue that

> European economic, political and cultural realms are not congruent . . . the single market of the EEC is not congruent with the cultural unities of Europe: three of Europe's four German speaking states are outside the EEC (though the largest is in it). The EEC's two Anglophone states have the experience – unique among European states – of being subordinate members of their world language (and cultural) community and, have therefore a 'culture' that finds Paris more foreign than Boston, Hamburg further away than Melbourne.
>
> (1989: 10)

Again, basic cultural issues are already at stake in these definitions. As Collins asks, 'what will become of European culture should Turkey, an Islamic (albeit a modernised and secularised) state, join the community?' (1988: 17).

We argued earlier that the debate about European culture has largely been stimulated by a fear that heavy viewing of television programmes from other (principally American) cultures would, over time, erode the cultures, values and traditions of the nations of Europe. Operating in response to this fear, current European initiatives can thus be seen as an attempt to intervene so as to (re)create a distinctive European culture – an enterprise which Collins describes as culminating in the 'absurd spectacle of a retreat to the Middle Ages for a coherent vision of European identity' (ibid.: 22), a retreat perhaps to the (distinctly pre-electronic) moment in which, as Donald argues, 'the literary forms of the European languages provided the medium for the definition and diffusion of national vernaculars, in opposition to the transnational jargon of Latin and subnational regional dialects' (Donald, 1988: 33). The cultural politics at stake here are of a quite contradictory character.

It may be that what is most apparent and remarkable in the present context is the accelerating formation of global communications empires, such as those of Murdoch, Berlusconi, Bertelsmann, Sony, Disney,

Paramount and so on. Internationalisation is not, of course, a new phenomenon; it has always been a constitutive aspect of capitalist development. But it is now entering a new stage, and the maintenance of national sovereignty and identity is becoming increasingly difficult, as the unities of economic and cultural production and consumption become increasingly transnational. It is now increasingly apparent, as Raymond Williams argued, that in the development of modern industrial societies, 'the nation-state in its classical European forms is at once too large and too small for the range of real social purposes' (1983: 197). In this new situation, we also need to focus on the new dialectic of local and global. In a world which seems to be increasingly dominated by a global cultural repertoire, new communities and identities are constantly being built and rebuilt. In many cases, it is a case of a fake and bogus sense of community:

> The more cosmopolitan capitalism becomes, the more it seems to wear a homespun look: the more nomadic its operations, the more it advertises its local affiliations. . . . Geographically, the population may be becoming more mobile; imaginatively, it cleaves to a spirit of place. The pastoral version of the national myth – the idea that the 'real England' is in the countryside – has never been more widely popular. . . . The language of patriotism may be unfashionable but the appetite for roots – even make-believe ones, is unappeasable.
>
> (Samuel, 1988: 30)

But localism can also be a more positive force, an attempt to elaborate a creative local response to the invasive influence of global capital. If localities are increasingly nodes in the emerging global networks, then local consciousness and action may throw up new 'possibilities for more efficacious, and self-conscious, participation in world affairs by people in local communities' (Alger, 1988: 322).

The politics of space and place are then crucial. The key question is whether national and nationalist identities can be transcended in favour of more meaningful identities, or whether they will simply transform in regressive and alienating ways. Some commentators foresee a prospect of increasing privatism, localism and 'cultural tribalism' within an electronic 'global village'. For Manuel Castells, the prospects are bleak. He foresees a process whereby the 'space of power' is transformed into image flows over which we have less and less control, while the 'space of meaning' is reduced to the 'microterritories' of new tribal communities (Castells, 1983: 16).

Similarly, in their analysis of technologies and decentralisation, Mattelart and Piemme argue that small is not necessarily beautiful:

> At a time when the sphere of capital is being globalised, the bourgeoisie thinks worldwide, while encouraging the petite-bourgeoisie

to think local. . . . The local seems to signify a return to the concrete, at the same time as the concrete it rediscovers takes us . . . further away from the possibility of understanding a vaster reality, from which the concrete takes its meaning . . . the local is of real interest only where it permits . . . a better grasp . . . of the dialectic between the abstract/universal and the concrete/experienced.

(1983: 415)

As broadcasting nations, the countries of Europe are, of course, not only different but also, in various senses, at odds with one another. We might emphasise the advantageous position of the anglophone states within the European Community (given the position of English as the *lingua franca* of the region). Thus, Britain is a significant exporter of television material to the rest of Europe, and it is in a quite different relation to American programming than is the rest of Europe, by simple virtue of the shared and hegemonic language. Philip Schlesinger (1986) notes both how the 'Big Four' (Britain, France, Germany and Italy) dominate all television exchanges within the European Broadcasting Union, and how the EBU itself exports three times as much to the East European International Radio and TV organisations (OIRT) as it imports. There are, of course, historical issues at stake as well. As Walker (1988a) noted in his account of the significance of 1992, there are those within Europe who might well see 1992 as the 'the last campaign, the third battle of the Ardennes, at which the Anglo-Saxons are finally defeated . . . and Britain takes its (humble) place within the Fourth (Deutschmark) Reich'. There are certainly those who foresee that 'a dynamic Europe should be built around the Franco-German duo' (Pierre Bérégovoy, French Finance Minister, quoted in ibid.). As with the definition of national cultural identities, so too is the shaping of a European culture and identity centred around the relative power of different parties.

We must, of course, beware of taking for granted a particular set of assumptions, deriving from the Cold War period, that when we say 'Europe', what we really mean is Europe west of the Iron Curtain. Recent talk of *Mitteleuropa* and the Soviet call for a definition of our 'common European home' must necessarily be taken into account in our debates. There are also those who would want to make claims for the status of Budapest and Prague as the true centres, historically, of European culture (cf. Kundera, 1984). We must also take into account both the changing nature of power relations within Eastern Europe and also the changing relations between the 'two Europes'. Manuel Escudero, co-ordinator of the Spanish Socialist Party's 'Programme 2000', has predicted that 'the people of Eastern Europe [will] play the same kind of role for the EEC that the southern Europeans played in the 1960s and 1970s' (quoted in Walker, 1988a). More melodramatically, Neil

Ascherson (1988) offers a scenario in which 'Europe in 2018 will consist of a Western superstate, whose floors are scrubbed by Romanians and Poles, and a periphery of beggarly Bantustans'.

DEGREES OF EXPORTABILITY

Within this broader context, let us now consider the central issue of the transnationalisation of culture. This is a process in which the 'vertical' organisation of people within national communities is, to varying degrees, and in varying contexts, being supplanted by their organisation into 'hori-zontal' communities – people are connected electronically rather that by geographical proximity. In his analysis of the increasing significance of cross-border transmissions in creating electronic communities, Claus-Dieter Rath argues that 'frontiers of a national, regional or cultural kind no longer count: what counts much more is the boundary of the territory of transmission . . . which increasingly bears little relationship to the geographical territory of any given nation state' (1985: 202).

If we wish to avoid a form of technological determinism we should not, of course, presume that any of these technological developments will be uniform in their effects. In our view, the key questions concern the ways in which a range of social and cultural divisions (matters of generation and education, for example) inflect both the take-up and the cultural impact of the new communications technologies. Commercial broadcasters and their market-research agencies are in a position, given their neces-sary sensitivity to questions of audience research, penetration rates and the like, to throw some light on these questions from an empirical point of view.

There is, for example, already evidence that, within northern Europe, it is young people who are the heaviest viewers of satellite channels. Thus, in her summary of the empirical material available on the development of an international audience within Europe, Pam Mills notes 'the heightened appeal of imported programmes to young people. Older viewers are more likely to avoid imported programmes, for language and cultural reasons. Younger viewers are, however, increasingly familiar with foreign-language material' (1985: 493). Similarly, John Clemens reported AGB Television International's work as indicating that 'the high entertainment output [of Sky and Super Channel] is attracting the young Dutch audience and may well predict the pattern of the future', and that in Belgium, 'amongst children once again . . . [consumption patterns] are biased away from the national broadcasters' (1987: 306). Again, Richard Collins notes a tendency, specifically in the sphere of musical culture, towards 'the rupturing of national cultural communities along a fault-line of age' (1989: 11).

It is, of course, not only a matter of age. In her survey quoted above, Mills summarises the overall position in Britain: 'Acceptance of foreign-language material is predictably highest among the better educated, those in the higher social groups and those living nearer the capital' (1985: 4). Rather than concern ourselves with the 'Europeanisation' or 'transnationalisation' of culture in the abstract, we need to ask more concrete questions. For which particular groups, in which types of places, is this prospect becoming a reality? And what can this tell us about the future? Martin Walker (1988a) worries about the emergence of a standardised 'Euro-business' class, clutching their inevitable Filofaxes and sporting the standard 'business Euro-uniform worn from Glasgow down to Naples'. These, presumably, are precisely the people for whom 'Europe' is becoming a tangible reality. They are also the people to whom Collins refers in his comments on the current development of the European newspaper market – those on the upper side of the fault-line of social class, across Europe – who, given their competence in English, are particularly likely to 'become differentiated from their co-linguists and integrated into a new cosmopolitan culture where the growth of "horizontal" links to similar strata elsewhere will supplant the longer established "vertical" links with [their own] national language community' (1988c: 11).

This, of course, returns us to the question of the terms in which European culture is, even if only for particular groups within our societies, being transnationalised. And those terms are, of course, literally, English – or anglophone. Our analysis of the cultural impact of any form of domination must always be differentiated, concerned to establish which groups, in which places, are receptive (or not) to it. Similarly, we now want to argue, we must pay close attention to the relative popularity or exportability of different parts of the cultural repertoire, of the (in this case, anglophone) cultural products in question. It is the anglophone, and principally American, audiovisual media that are cutting horizontally across the world audience, engaging the attention and mobilising the enthusiasm of popular audiences, and often binding them into cultural unities that are transnational. They are 'restratifying national communities and separating elite from mass or popular taste, and thus threatening the cultural hegemony enjoyed by the national cultural elites' (Collins, 1988: 10).

However, not all anglophone cultural products are equally exportable. We must ask a more specific question about which types and varieties of anglophone product are exportable to whom, under what conditions. Colin Hoskins and Rolf Mirus offer the concept of 'cultural discount' to account for the fundamental process through which 'a particular programme, rooted in one culture, and thus attractive in that environment, will have a diminished appeal elsewhere, as viewers find it difficult to identify with the style, values, beliefs, institutions and behavioural patterns of the material in question' (1988: 500). The point, however, is that cultural discount can be argued to apply differentially to various types of information

62

products as they are exported. In an attempt to offer a more differentiated analysis Collins argues that 'Cultural discount is likely to be lower
for audiovisual products than for written works, and within the audiovisual category, lower for works with little linguistic content than for works
in which speech is an important element' (1989: 8).

For this reason, the argument runs, programming with a high speech
content, because it is subject to so much misunderstanding, is unpopular
with 'foreign' viewers. Conversely, a channel such as MTV builds its
international appeal precisely on the fact that there is little problem with
language, in so far as, according to MTV's European Chief Executive
Officer, 'for the bulk of our music programming, the words are practically irrelevant' (quoted in Collins, 1988: 30). The point is supported by
Mills, who argues that 'programming that is not dependent on understanding the language – for example, an opera or ballet channel or a
pop channel – will attract widely dispersed and sometimes potentially
large audiences, but informational programming . . . will meet language
barriers' (1985: 501).

Attempts to attract a European audience with English language
programming, not unlike the attempt to create European advertising
markets, do seem to have largely foundered in the face of the linguistic
and cultural divisions in play between the different sectors of the audience. Witness the difficulties experienced by projects such as Super
Channel, which have attempted to develop pan-European programming.
We seem now to be experiencing a form of revisionism amongst the advertisers and the major satellite channels, with the retrenchment to strategies more closely adapted to the linguistic divisions across the continent
(cf. Mulgan, 1989).

By and large, everyone seems to agree on the difficulties, although
different commentators offer contradictory scenarios for the future.
Collins (1989) suggests that cultural discount will be higher for entertainment than for informational programming, while, conversely,
Clemens (1987) argues that a more likely scenario is one in which we
see a combination of privately owned pan-European channels specialising in entertainment programming with multilingual soundtracks,
alongside national state channels specialising in news and current affairs
programming.

Despite the uncertainties over the most likely course of future development, some things are clear. There is a growing realisation that the
success of American-style commercial programming in Europe is context-
dependent in a very specific sense. US imports only do well when domestic
television is not producing comparable entertainment programming.
Whenever viewers have the alternative of comparable entertainment
programming in their own language, the American programmes tend to
come off second best.

So, the question about future developments can be reformulated as one about the potential cultural impact of some types of American (or pan-European) programming on specific audience categories, in particular types of context (as defined by national programming policies). Even within that more specified context we need to be quite cautious in attributing effects (on audiences) to programmes. This is not simply because programmes do not have simple or straightforward effects on their viewers which can be easily predicted from an analysis of their content (or their production history). It is also because, precisely in order to be exportable, programmes such as *Dallas* have to operate at a very high level of abstraction, and the price of this approach to a universality of appeal is a higher level of polysemy or multi-accentuality. The research of Ang (1985) and of Liebes and Katz (1989) reminds us just how open these types of programmes are to reinterpretation by audiences outside their country of origin. Which brings us, finally, to the question of the audience.

DOMESTIC VIEWING AS NATIONAL RITUAL: FAMILY, TELEVISION, NATION

We have spent some time engaging with the debates about cultural identity, new technologies and the transnationalisation of culture in the terms in which they are customarily posed – that is, from the point of view of production economics, the changing technologies of distribution and their potential cultural effects on media audiences. We now want to reverse the terms of the argument, and to look at the question from the point of view of the domestic users and audiences of these new technologies, as they function in the context of household and family cultures. How will the new patterns of supply of programming be filtered and mediated by the process of domestic consumption? The key issues, we suggest, concern the role of these technologies in disrupting established boundaries (at national and domestic levels, simultaneously) and in rearticulating the private and public spheres in new ways. Our argument is that analysis of the processes of creation of new image spaces and cultural identities needs to be grounded in the analysis of the everyday practices and domestic rituals through which contemporary electronic communities are constituted and reconstructed (at both micro- and macro-levels) on a daily basis.

In rehearsing these issues we shall primarily be drawing on a body of work which has developed in recent years around the role of broadcast media in the construction of national communities. Clearly, given our earlier arguments about the inadequacy of the concept of the nation in relation to many current economic, political and cultural developments, we are aware that it is not only (or even primarily) national communities that are at stake here. Rather, our interest in these arguments lies in the model they may offer for understanding the role of communications technologies in the construction of a whole series of 'electronic communities' – at the local, regional, national and international levels. In each of these cases, though, we would argue that we must pay close attention to the articulation of public and private worlds, and particularly the relation of the domestic group – broadcasting's primary audience – to the wider communities of which it is a constituent part.

Eli Zaretsky notes that, historically, 'the early bourgeoisie understood the family to be the basic unit of the social order – "a little church, a little state" and the lowest rung in the ladder of social authority. They conceived of society as composed not of individuals but of families' (1976: 42). In a similar vein, Fontaine observes that in contemporary industrial societies 'households are also units in the political and economic organisation of society; as such they are part of the public domain. A legal address is an expected attribute of a citizen'. Thus, while the household enjoys privacy, which implies the right to exclude (unless the police have a warrant) and to enjoy autonomy of action, that 'privacy is as much a matter of social definition as the effect of thick walls' (Fontaine, 1988: 280). Moreover, as Jacques Donzelot (1979) argues, the family does not have a unique or unambiguous status. For certain (e.g. juridical) purposes, it is private; for others it is public. Intervention by various state welfare agencies, for example, to regulate child-rearing (or television-viewing) practices within the family, is legitimated by reference to the state's just concern with the 'proper' upbringing of future members of the national labour force. For Donzelot, the family is not simply a private institution but also the point of intersection of a whole range of medical, judicial, educational and psychiatric practices – it is by no means a wholly private realm, somehow outside (or indeed, setting the limits of) the social. In this sense the family is neither totally separate from, nor opposed to, the state; rather the 'private' itself is a (legally, juridically) constructed space, in which the state and other agencies intervene. Among these agencies are, of course, communications and information organisations.

Paddy Scannell (1988) has usefully analysed the unobtrusive ways in which broadcasting sustains the lives and routines from one day to the next, year in, year out, of whole populations. This is, in effect, to pay attention to the role of the media in the very structuring of time and in the socialisation of the private sphere. Scannell's focus is on the role of national broadcasting media as central agents of national culture, in the mobilisation of popular involvement in the calendar of national life. He analyses the way in which broadcast media constitute a cultural resource shared by millions, and the way in which, for instance, long-running popular serials provide a past in common to whole populations.

Thus, Scannell argues, modern mass democratic politics has its forum in the radically new kind of public sphere that broadcasting constitutes. In their historical analysis of the development of British broadcasting, Cardiff and Scannell (1987) focus on its crucial role in forging a link between the dispersed and disparate listeners and the symbolic heartland of national life, and on its role in promoting a sense of communal identity within its audience, at both regional and national levels. Historically, the BBC, for example, can be seen to have been centrally concerned to 'supply its isolated listeners with a sense of the community they had lost, translated from a local to a national and even global level' (ibid.: 162). Here we see precisely the concern to articulate the private and public spheres: to connect the family and the nation. As Cardiff and Scannell note, the audience has always been seen as composed of family units – as 'a vast cluster of families, rather than in terms of social classes or different taste publics' (ibid.: 161). Lord Reith himself was most concerned with the possibilities that broadcasting offered of 'making the nation one man'. Shown at its crudest level of operation, Cardiff and Scannell report from an Empire Day radio programme in 1935 in which a mother is heard explaining to her daughter: 'The British Empire, Mary, is made up of one big family'. Mary asks, 'You mean a family like ours, Mummy?', and mother replies, 'Yes, darling. But very much larger'. The pervasive symbol of unification was, from the beginning, the family, 'connoting Mother Britain and her children in the Empire, as well as the Royal Family and each little family of listeners' (ibid.: 162).

This point is not merely quaint or historical. In a close parallel, Brunsdon and Morley (1978) argue that the central image of much contemporary current affairs and 'magazine' programming is precisely the family – and the nation as composed of families. In this type of broadcasting, the nuclear family is the unspoken premise of much programme discourse: not only is the programming address to a 'family audience' but this domestic focus accounts both for the content ('human-interest stories') and the mode of presentation (the emphasis on the everyday aspects of public issues: 'so what will this new law mean for ordinary consumers?'). What is assumed to unite the audience, the 'nation of families', is their experience of domestic life. In this sense, broadcasting does much more than simply make available experiences (the Cup Final, the Proms) which were previously available only to those who could be physically present. Beyond this, the 'magic carpet' of broadcasting technologies has played a fundamental role in promoting national unity at a symbolic level, linking individuals and their families to the centres of national life, offering the audience an image of itself and of the nation as a knowable community, a wider, public world beyond the routines of a narrow existence, to which these technologies give symbolic access.

In a similar vein, in his analysis of the development of radio light entertainment, Simon Frith observes that, by bringing public events into the
home, radio did more than simply make them accessible. More importantly, 'what was on offer was access to a community . . . what was (and
is) enjoyable is the sense that you too can become significant by turning
on a switch' (1983: 120–1). And thus, while domestic listening or viewing
might be 'a very peculiar form of public participation' it offers the sense
of participation in a (domesticated) national community; the spectator
'can feel part of an imaginary totality' (Rath, 1988: 37).

From a Latin American perspective, Martin-Barbero identifies the key
role of the communications media as 'converting the masses into a people
and the people into a nation'. He notes that, in many Latin American
countries, it was above all the 'development of national broadcasting
systems which provided the people of different regions and provinces with
a first daily experience of the nation' (1988: 455). As he argues, the
construction and emergence of national identities cannot properly be
understood without reference to the role of communications technologies.
These technologies allowed people 'a space of identification'; not just an
evocation of a common memory, but rather 'the experience of encounter
and of solidarity'. Thus, the nation is to be understood not simply as an
abstraction, but as a lived experience made possible by broadcasting technologies, whose achievement was the 'transmutation of the political idea
of the nation into lived experience, into sentiment and into the quotidian'
(ibid.: 456, 461).

We can perhaps begin to identify the terms necessary to connect the
micro- and macro-levels of study and to articulate our analysis of television as an essentially domestic medium with that of larger-scale cultural
processes, such as those of the construction of national publics and cultural
identities.

How might we conceive of this articulation between the domestic and
the national? Some years ago, John Ellis referred, somewhat gnomically,
to television as 'the private life of the nation state' (1982: 5). His comment
can be seen as a parallel to the argument in Brunsdon and Morley (1978)
about the way in which British television is often concerned to construct
an image of the national 'we', an 'us' whose constituent elements are
'ordinary families'. This frequently provides the very basis of the broadcasters' claims to represent their audience – and of their implicit appeals
for various forms of audience identification with the programme presenters. In the same way, John Hartley has argued that 'television is one of
the prime sites upon which a given nation is constructed for its members'
(1978: 124), drawing, like many others, on Benedict Anderson's concept
of the nation as an 'imagined community', the construct of particular
discourses. As Anderson puts it: 'An American will never meet, or even
know the names of more than a handful of his fellow Americans. He has

no idea of what they are up to at any one time. But he has complete confidence in their steady, anonymous, simultaneous activity' (1983: 31). Wherein lies this simultaneity? One source we can look at is the regulation of simultaneous experience through broadcast schedules. Where does this confidence come from? Among other sources, Anderson points to the newspaper as a mechanism for providing imaginary links between the members of a national community. As Hartley puts it, newspapers are 'at one and the same time the ultimate fiction, since they construct the imagined community, and the basis of a mass ritual or ceremony that millions engage in every day' (1978: 124).

Herman Bausinger develops the point about the newspaper as a linking mechanism between the rituals of the domestic, the organisation of the schedules of everyday life and the construction of the 'imagined community' of the nation. He comments on the nature of the disruption caused when a morning edition of a newspaper fails to appear. His point concerns that which is missed. As he puts it:

> Is it a question . . . of the missing content of the paper? Or isn't it rather that one misses the newspaper itself? Because the newspaper is part of it (a constitutive part of the ritual of breakfast for many people), reading it proves that the breakfast time world is still in order.
>
> (Bausinger, 1984: 344)

And, of course, vice versa.

A similar point, and indeed, a stronger one, given the necessary simultaneity of broadcast television viewing, could be made in relation to the watching of evening news broadcasts for many viewers – where the fact of watching, and engaging in a joint ritual with millions of others, can be argued to be at least as important as any informational content gained from the broadcast. For our purposes, the point we would stress here is the potential usefulness of the model offered by Bausinger's analysis for focusing our analysis on the role of communications media in articulating our private and public worlds.

The further point, inevitably, involves the significance of these arguments in the context of current and prospective changes in the structure of broadcasting. The proliferation of broadcast channels, through cable and satellite television, is likely to move us towards a more fragmented social world than that of traditional national broadcast television. These new forms of communication may in fact play a significant part in deconstructing national cultures, and the interactive and 'rescheduling' potentialities of video and other new communications technologies may well disrupt our assumptions of any 'necessary simultaneity' of social experience.

There is a substantial body of evidence that broadcast television constitutes a significant cultural resource on which large numbers of people depend, to a greater or lesser extent, to supply their needs, both for information and entertainment. There is further evidence that broadcast television plays a significant role (both at a calendrical and at a quotidian level) in organising and scheduling our participation in public life, in the realms of politics and leisure activities. Satellite television is bringing about significant changes in the extent and the nature of the supply of programming (directly, through its own programme strategies, and indirectly, through the responses which existing broadcast institutions are making in order to compete with their new rivals). Given these premises, the need is clear for the cultural impact of these changes in programme supply to be closely monitored during this key period of broadcasting history, in which, in Europe and North America, established patterns of consumption may be expected to fragment in a number of directions. The key issue concerns the role of the new technologies in offering a changed (and varying) menu of cultural resources, from and by means of which we will all be constructing our senses of self-identity. In analysing those processes, we must attend closely to how cultural identities are produced, both at the macro- and micro-levels, and ask what role these various media play in the construction of our sense of ourselves – as individuals and as members of communities at various levels – whether families, regions, nations, or supra-national communities. But, above all, we must not address these issues as a set of political abstractions for they are, finally, matters of our (mediated) everyday lives.

To return to the global questions with which we began, concerning new communications technologies, changing cultural identities and the various modes of cultural imperialism, it may be that we have much to learn from those for whom the question of cultural imperialism has long been unavoidable. Confronted now by fears of domination by American and multinational corporations in the new communications industries, there is an understandable tendency to fall back into a 'Fortress Europe' posture, designed to fend off 'America', and a concern to defend indigenous national cultures against the threat of 'Brussels'. However, as Martin-Barbero (1988) puts it, this is to define our indigenous culture as a 'natural fact', a kind of pre-reality, static and without development, the 'motionless point' of departure from which modernity is measured. From this perspective,

> transformed into the touchstone of identity, the indigenous would seem to be the only thing which remains for us of the 'authentic', that secret place in which the purity of our cultural roots remains and is preserved. All the rest is contamination and loss of identity.
>
> (ibid.: 459)

The rejection of any such calls for 'authenticity' or 'purity' in the defence of 'national culture' is the precondition of our effective engagement with the ongoing processes of cultural reconfiguration in Europe.

4

EUROCULTURE
Communication, space and time

The central focus of this chapter is on questions of geography and history, and especially on their interrelationships. We are concerned with historical continuities and discontinuities in European development, with historical traditions as they are invented and reinvented, with the cultural inheritance and heritage associated with 'European Civilisation'. We are also concerned with the geographical dimensions of change in the present period: with reconfigurations of place and territory; with new forms of spatial orientation and referentiality; and with changing meanings and senses of community. And because any discussion of communication and culture must inevitably raise the question of power, this too will be at the heart of our enquiry. We must consider the relation between geographies, histories and powers – what Harold Adams Innis (1950) referred to as the 'problem of empire'.

COMMUNICATION, CULTURE AND IDENTITY

The empires of communications moguls like Rupert Murdoch and Silvio Berlusconi are undeniably potent forces in the world, and it is not really surprising that many observers attribute them with absolute powers. Thus, it is argued by Richard Peet that 'the tendency is towards the production of one world mind, one world culture, and the consequent disappearance of regional consciousness flowing from the local specificities of the human past' (1986: 169). The global media are seen as unproblematically capturing the hearts and minds of their audiences and producing an increasingly homogeneous global consciousness and culture. We are, according to Peet now in an era of 'ultra-culture' in which the world's people have been transformed into 'latent cogs in the capitalist production and consumption machine' (1982: 298).

The power and influence of transnational media conglomerates we take as given. The really significant question, for us, concerns how we think of the functioning and effectivity of this power. What is the nature of the relationship between communications, culture and identity? In the prevailing view, this relationship is conceived (with varying degrees of technological determinism) in terms of the 'impact' of new communications technologies upon culture and cultural identities. It is precisely this approach that informs Richard Peet's account of the creation of a 'world-synthetic consciousness and culture' by the global communications industries. Such a formulation is fraught with difficulties. The power of the media is assumed and never demonstrated. Such an assumption is grounded in the model of the communication process that informs this approach, what James Carey (1977) has referred to as the 'transmission view of communication'. Within this model, communications technologies are the active and determining forces, whilst culture and identity are passive and reactive. Communications technologies are the causal forces, and identities are the effect, shaped and modified by the 'impact' of the technologies. It is also the case – and this will be a major focus of the subsequent discussion – that there is no theoretical understanding of cultural identity within this perspective: cultural identity is a black box. The only real issue that is raised concerns the vulnerability of cultural identity to attack from the exogenous forces of 'foreign' communications empires. The problem then is one of resisting cultural invasion and fortifying indigenous identity. Change is seen as problematical, a matter of cultural erosion and even extinction. The great fear, apparent in the work of Peet, for example, is that positive national identities are being replaced by a global non-identity. This kind of thinking is also apparent in those strategies which, in response to the perceived threat of 'colonisation', seek to sustain and defend 'a sense of European identity' – strategies which easily succumb to a protective 'Fortress Europe' mentality.

From that perspective, cultural identity is both an unproblematical and a residual category. If we are really to understand the relation between communication, culture and identity, then we must move beyond this deterministic model of the communication process. Within this prevailing framework, cultural identities can only ever be responsive and reactive to the controlling stimulus of communications technologies. What is needed is a better formulation of the problem, one that takes cultural identity as a problematical and a central category. As Philip Schlesinger argues, in the context of a discussion of national identity:

> We now need to turn around the terms of the conventional argument: *not* to start with communication and its supposed effects on national identity and culture, but rather to begin by posing the problem of national identity itself, to ask how it might be analysed and what importance communicative practices might play in its constitution.
>
> (1987: 234)

The challenge is to understand how social and cultural identities are constituted and to consider the parameters within which cultural identities and

71

orientations might be reconstituted in the present period. Within this more fundamental agenda, we can then begin to ask questions, theoretical and political, about the power and the potential of new communications technologies.

Our concern is with collective cultural identity. Against the static and fixed conception in the dominant communications model, we need to develop an alternative which emphasises the active, dynamic and contested nature of collective identities. Collective identity involves the achievement, by individual actors or by social groups, of a certain coherence, cohesion and continuity. Such bonding will always be provisional and more or less precarious. As Alberto Melucci argues,

> Collective identity formation is a delicate process and requires continual investments. As it comes to resemble more institutionalised forms of social action, collective identity may crystallise into organisational forms, a system of rules, and patterns of leadership. In less institutionalised forms of action its character more closely resembles a process which must be continually activated in order for action to be possible.
>
> (1989: 34–5)

The cohesion of collective identity must be sustained *through time*, through a collective memory, through lived and shared traditions, through the sense of a common past and heritage. It must also be maintained *across space*, through a complex mapping of territories and frontiers, principles of inclusion and exclusion that define 'us' against 'them'. At certain moments the established and normative bases of collective identity enter into crisis. Coherence and continuity are threatened by fragmentation and discontinuity; the emotional investments that inform the sense of identity are disconnected. Symbolically, 1992 was the date that identified one such critical moment. The question is how we manage this crisis: whether it will be regressively through the reassertion of 'traditional' identities and allegiances, or whether it will be possible to imagine new forms of cohesion and collectivity.

POSTMODERN GEOGRAPHIES?

The advanced capitalist societies are in a period of profound structural transformation. For some commentators this marks a shift from industrial to post-industrial society, whilst for others it is about the transition from organised to disorganised capitalism. The most influential formulation, developed by the French Regulationists, describes it in terms of the historical trajectory from Fordism to post-Fordism. The nature of the restructuring process is a difficult matter that cannot be generally addressed here (see chapter 2). What must be emphasised, however, is that this transformation is characterised by quite contradictory developments and by a complex interweaving of change and continuity. Against those who would have us believe that the shape of post-Fordist things to come is already clear, we must argue that the course is not obvious, not determined, not yet decided. For the moment we can only say that we are in a period of crisis, in a period that seems to be moving beyond Fordism. Any future regime of accumulation is yet to be invented and remains a matter of contestation.

Our particular concern is with the geographical dynamics of this restructuring process. In their development, capitalist societies have used space as part of their strategies for growth and competition. This has involved a historical succession of spatial structures of production, each associated with 'new sets of relations between activities in different places, new spatial patterns of social organisation, new dimensions of inequality and new relations of dominance and dependence' (Massey, 1984: 8). There has been a complex interplay between the functional logic of corporate organisational structure and the territorial logic of particular places. As Ray Hudson argues, 'there is a reciprocal relationship between the restructuring of capital, changing spatial divisions of labour and the specificities of localities' (1988: 493). If there have been significant discontinuities, there have also been forms of continuity and cumulativeness in this historical process. Meanings and traditions, attachments and allegiances, accrue around the sense of place, and patterns of economic and political organisation, of power and dependency, are inscribed in the relations between particular locales (cities, regions, nations).

Whilst the final outcome of current geographical restructuring and reconfiguration remains uncertain, some key elements of the process can already be identified. What appears to be emerging is a new articulation of spatial scales – of global, national and local spheres – associated with the increasing transnationalisation of accumulation (Robins and Gillespie, 1988). The worldwide organisation and integration of corporate activities is bringing about a more immediate and direct articulation of global and local spaces. Particular localities and cities are drawn into the logic of transnational networks. Advanced forms of globalisation 'involve the strategic creation of linked production complexes, each appropriate to a diverse mix of regional and social endowments and distributed as an interregional network in accordance with a global strategic conception', and the viability of regional economies becomes 'a product of their ability to articulate a coherent organisational presence within a global milieu' (Gordon, 1989: 116). What appears to be developing through this process is a new global network and matrix of unevenly developed regions, cities and localities. And, in the context of this global–local interface, economic and political governance at the national scale becomes increasingly problematic. As David Held argues, 'the internationalisation of production finance and other economic resources is unquestionably eroding the capacity of the (nation) state to control its own economic future' (1988: 13).

The processes we are describing are not only economic, but also political and cultural, and have enormous resonances for collective organisation and identity in the late twentieth century. The fundamental principle for political attachment in capitalist societies has been through national and nationalist identities, through citizenship of the nation state. This allegiance is now being increasingly undermined – though the recent resurgence of national-populist ideologies may well be seen as a rearguard response to this tendency – and we are seeing the emergence of both enlarged (continental European) and restricted (local, regional, provincial) conceptions of citizenship (Ajzenberg, 1988). New forms of bonding, belonging and involvement are being forged out of the global–local nexus (Alger, 1988). It is, of course, much more difficult to create and sustain a sense of internationalism, and the prevailing tendency is towards a new or renewed localism. The question is whether such affiliations will be conservative, parochial and introspective, or whether it is possible to reimagine local communities in more ecumenical and cosmopolitan terms.

Some of the cultural dimensions of this global–local dynamic are reflected in the practices and theories of postmodernism. Space and place have been foregrounded as central to postmodern sensibilities and identities. According to Edward Soja, 'the contemporary period of restructuring has been accompanied by an accentuated visibility and consciousness of spatiality and spatialisation, regionalisation and regionalism' (1989: 173). In one form of postmodernism, the emphasis is on the nature and experience of the new spatiality produced by international communications and image networks. This is a global space of image, screen and surface, where real and imaginary orders become fused. The experience of this decentred hyperspace, this space of absolute proximity and instantaneity, may be one of disorientation, dislocation and fragmentation, or, alternatively, it is possible to 'make a virtue of the capacity to negotiate disorder', to accept disorientation and fragmentation as a state of authenticity (Rustin, 1989: 121). In another form of postmodernism, this overwhelming sense and experience of space is negotiated defensively by invoking the spirit of place. This strategy looks to the re-enchantment of place and community, to restore meaning, rootedness and human proportions of place (Ley, 1989). Such developments can be seen, for example, in neo-vernacular and neo-historicist forms of architecture, design and urban planning. They are also to be found in the postmodern recuperation of heritage and history, whether it be 'real, imagined or simply re-created as pastiche' (Harvey, 1987: 274). Whilst they appear to be quite contradictory, both these currents of postmodernism are, in fact, sustained

by shared concerns. They offer different responses to the same fundamental question of bearings and identity in the new global space.

So far, we have not considered the relevance of technology in the
formation of postmodern geographies. Whilst they should not be seen
as the determining and causal factor, it is undoubtedly the case that the
new information and communications technologies are playing a
powerful role in the emergence of new spatial structures, relations and
orientations. Corporate communications networks have produced a
global space of electronic information flows. The new media conglomerates are creating a global image space, 'a space of transmission [that]
cuts across – as a new geographic entity, which has its own sovereignty,
its own guarantors – the geographies of power, of social life, and of
knowledge, which define the space of nationality or culture' (Rath, 1985:
203). What the new technologies make possible is a new kind of rela
tionship between place and space: through their capacity to transgress
frontiers and subvert territories, they are implicated in a complex interplay of deterritorialisation and reterritorialisation (Dupuy, 1988). What
is particularly significant is the transformed relationship between
boundary and space that this entails. Things are no longer defined and
distinguished, in the ways that they once were, by their boundaries,
borders or frontiers (Ravlich, 1989). We can say that the very idea of
boundary – the frontier boundary of the nation state, for example, or
the physical boundaries of urban structures – has been rendered problematical. Paul Virilio describes how historically 'the boundary-surface
has been continually transformed, perceptibly or imperceptibly. Its most
recent transformation', he suggests, 'is perhaps that of the interface'.
Technological and physical topologies become, in some way, continuous.
The boundary has become permeable, an 'osmotic membrane', through
which information and communication flow (Virilio, 1987: 17, 21;
cf. Wark, 1988). These global systems – information networks, satellite
'footprints' – also lay an abstract space over concrete territorial configurations. Consequently, older communities and older, localised, senses of
community are undone. The question then is how network and community can be reconciled (Stiegler, 1987).

In particular, Europe has to position itself within new spatial hierarchies and a new international order. European integration is occurring in
response to the economic power of the United States and Japan, to the
emerging challenge of the so-called newly industrialising countries of
South East Asia and Latin America, and also to the dramatic change
taking place in Eastern Europe. A strategic response must be found to a
new hypermobile capital that has broken national bounds and undermined
national sovereignties. And sense must be made of the information
grids and image spaces that are increasingly creating new transnational
communication spheres, markets and communities.

What forms of political governance and regulation can be elaborated in these changing circumstances? There is a trenchant and conservative solution that looks to preserve the nation state and to maintain the integrity of national frontiers. Enoch Powell (1989) articulates the position of the British government: 'This is not a Europe "without frontiers". Nations have frontiers; and a Europe, Mrs Thatcher's Europe, of "independent sovereign nations" will be a Europe of frontiers'. Against this, there is a more imaginative and forward-looking strategy, beyond frontiers. In the idea of a European community there is an aspiration towards transnational regulation, through the formation of a multinational bloc. As yet, it is a precarious idea. The question is whether this vision can be directed towards emancipatory ends, or whether it will produce a European superstate, a kind of scaled-up nation state. The ambiguous potential is apparent in contrasting projections of, on the one hand, a 'social Europe', and on the other, the protectionism, statism and militarism of 'Fortress Europe'. What is 'community' to mean? As Eileen and Stephen Yeo (1988) emphasise, community is a contested concept. Historically it has had a range of meanings: community as mutuality; community as service; and more recently, community as state. This last sense, abstract and coercive, in which the ideal of community is made to coincide with state authority, threatens to prevail in the 1990s. Can we realise a European community that is more than this? Can the idea of community become more vital, more enabling?

THE COMMUNITY OF CULTURE

European culture is marked by its diversity: diversity of climate, countryside, architecture, language, beliefs, taste and artistic style. Such diversity must be protected, not diluted. It represents one of the chief sources of the wealth of our continent. But underlying this variety there is an affinity, a family likeness, a common European identity. Down the ages, the tension between the continent's cultural diversity and unity has helped to fuse ancient and modern, traditional and progressive. It is undoubtedly a source of the greatness of the best elements of our civilisation.

(Commission of the European Communities, 1983: 1)

Culture is at the very heart of the European project. It is seen as absolutely fundamental to the 'internal market' and to the ulterior objective of the European Community. Culture is the basis of European union, which has goals other than mere economic and social integration, however important this may be; European cultural identity 'is one of the prerequisites for that solidarity which is vital if the advent of the large market, and the considerable change it will bring in living conditions within the

Community, is to secure the popular support it needs' (Commission of the European Communities, 1987: 1). This concern with culture reflects an increasing awareness of the 'interrelationship between the economy, technology and culture' (ibid.: 3). The Commission invokes the richness and solemnity of 'a common cultural heritage characterised by dialogues and exchanges between peoples and men [sic] of culture based on democracy, justice and liberty', a heritage that is 'deeply rooted in the collective consciousness of its inhabitants' (ibid.: 1). What also runs as a leitmotiv through the European documentation is the theme of 'unity in diversity'. The seemingly paradoxical appeal is to 'the unity of European culture as revealed by the history of regional and national cultural diversity' (ibid.: 3).

The new communications technologies – particularly what is now being promoted as 'advanced consumer television' – are seen as fundamental to the evolution of this destiny. The Commission emphasises that the electronics, aerospace, telecommunications and audiovisual industries will constitute a major growth sector in the 1990s. In the case of the audiovisual industries, it will be necessary to develop a European technology and production base, in order to meet the challenge from external competitors. It is also stressed that a common market for broadcasting, particularly one that promotes the free flow of what is called 'commercial speech', should contribute to the achievement of an internal market for all goods and services. But, again, the overriding insistence is on the harmonious relationship between industrial and cultural renaissance. Television, it is argued, can be important in 'promoting the cultural identity of Europe'; it can help to develop a people's Europe through reinforcing the sense of belonging to a Community composed of countries which are different, yet partake of a deep solidarity (Commission of the European Communities, 1988b: 4). Television can actually be an instrument of integration. 'Television', the Commission maintains, 'will play an important part in developing and nurturing awareness of the rich variety of Europe's common cultural and historical heritage. The dissemination of information across national borders can do much to help the peoples of Europe to recognise the common destiny they share in many areas' (Commission of the European Communities, 1984: 28).

But how adequately does this come to terms with the changing geographies of this *fin de siècle*? Can the new communications media really be so unproblematically and straightforwardly instrumental in promoting a cohesive and coherent Europe for the twenty-first century? Indeed, is this project of European cultural integration, this ideal of 'unity in diversity', really as meaningful as the Commission seems to believe? What is this vision of Europe and its heritage?

The European Commission is seeking to revitalise and reactivate a sense of European identity associated with the heritage of Western civilisation.

The present push for economic, political and cultural unity 'is an attempt to refurbish the old image of princess Europe as wealthy, free and powerful' (Keane, 1989: 30). We can hardly be surprised by this resurgent appeal to a common culture and identity, to the 'collective consciousness' (whatever that might mean) of European citizens. But we must be troubled by its contemporary implications. It is difficult to see the relevance of this rearview sense of grandeur for any significant relocation of Europe in a changing world and for any genuine and meaningful reimagination of European identity.

A key issue in this context concerns our response to recent upheavals in Central and Eastern Europe. How far did the EC's idea of a 'Europe without frontiers' deal responsibly and effectively with Gorbachev's call for a 'common European home'? What will be the price of this failure, in the wake of the crisis in what was Yugoslavia? How will this idea of Europe confront the changing boundaries, real and imaginary, between East and West? As yet, there has been no real consideration of how these two Europes will relate. Milan Kundera points to the geographical and historical divisions: the West 'perceives in Central Europe nothing but a political regime . . . it sees in Central Europe only Eastern Europe' (1984: 118). At the same time, Central Europeans define their own identities in terms of Western civilisation and heritage: 'For them, the word "Europe" does not represent a phenomenon of geography, but a spiritual notion synonymous with the word "west"' (ibid.: 95). Ironically, indeed, their belief is that Western Europe 'no longer perceives its unity as a cultural unity'; in Western Europe itself 'Europe [is] no longer experienced as a value' (ibid.: 110, 118). How will the European Community come to terms with this other Europe, this 'lost' Europe? How might these different worlds, different Europes, enter into dialogue? Is it possible to expand the sense of collective and cultural identity to embrace both Europes? The past weighs heavily on such aspirations. It is difficult to accept, 'as Eurocratic optimists apparently do at present, that we can invent a new, humane culture *ex nihilo* and leave all the nasty bits out. Often, if not invariably, the skeletons in the cupboard persist in rattling' (Schlesinger, 1989: 15). This is not to say that the ideal is empty, but that its fulfilment will require political maturity and magnanimity.

Within the European Community, there are skeletons too: histories and memories that must be exorcised. If the idea of 'unity in diversity' is to be more than a bland slogan, then it will require the political will to confront the legacy of old systems of power, inequality and disadvantage. James Donald identifies a logic that has been at work in shaping the political and cultural map of Europe: 'culture can be seen as a field in which the forces of identity, standard speech, and the state exert a centripetal pull against the centrifugal forces of cultural difference, linguistic variation, and carnival' (1988: 33). Cultural diversity and homogeneity have been circumscribed by the forces of centralisation, standardisation and unity. Hitherto, it has been in the form of the nation state that this containing principle has been most highly developed. In the process, living but stateless cultures have been marginalised and have struggled to survive (de Moragas Spa, 1988). What is perceived as the rich tapestry of European cultural diversity is, in reality, a system of territorial and cultural hierarchies shaped through the power of the nation state.

The key question is whether European integration will take us beyond this logic of the nation state. Whether it will, indeed, as the European Commission supposes, stimulate a new and more egalitarian cultural geography. And what role might the new communications technologies play in this process? The partial answer to these questions is that to the extent that they transcend national territories, the new communications media may help to erode the authority of the nation state, and to open the way for new and varied forms of internationalism and regionalism. However, the corresponding danger is that the centripetal/centrifugal dynamics described by James Donald may, in fact, occur at a higher level, with a European mega-state as the centralising and containing force. In this case, ironically, we might then find ourselves defending national cultures as the very basis of cultural diversity, and, albeit reluctantly, supporting national sovereignty as a bulwark against global standardisation and homogenisation. The question is whether it is possible to transcend this nation-logic, to move beyond the 'nationalistic assumption . . . of a normative congruence of polity and culture', to reimagine 'a new form of human community in which polity and culture are decoupled' (Collins, 1988: 20). A genuine and radical cultural diversity would entail the more fundamental (and perhaps utopian) project of deconstructing this logic of containment, rather than simply and defensively reconstructing it at higher levels.

IMAGINARY AMERICA

What Milan Kundera says of the relationship between Central and Western Europe may also provide some help in understanding European attitudes towards America. At a time when its 'beloved Europe' appears to have abandoned culture as the realm of supreme values, *Mitteleuropa* asserts itself as the repository for Western civilisation: 'they are desperately trying to restore the past, the past of culture, the past of the modern era. It is only in that period, only in a world that maintains a cultural dimension, that Central Europe can still defend its identity, still be seen for what it is' (Kundera, 1984: 118). The drama of Central European identity, with its 'long meditations on the possible end of European humanity', evokes a fundamental insecurity:

Thus it was in this region of small nations who have 'not yet perished' that Europe's vulnerability, all of Europe's vulnerability, was more clearly visible before anywhere else. Actually, in our modern world where power has a tendency to become more and more concentrated in the hands of a few big countries, *all* European nations run the risk of becoming small nations and of sharing their fate. In this sense the destiny of Central Europe anticipates the destiny of Europe in general, and its culture assumes an enormous relevance.

(ibid.: 109)

The same vulnerability is apparent in the responses of the European nations to the great America of anti-culture. Here, too, there is a fight against 'the subtle, relentless pressure of time, which is leaving the era of culture in its wake' (ibid.: 118): America, the future, is counterposed to the values and traditions by which Europeans have understood themselves and identified themselves as European. Here, too, European identity must come to terms with the sense of threat and loss.

The real issues concern European identity in a changing world, and 'America' can be a vehicle for defensively containing, rather than resolving, these issues. Change and disruption are projected onto an imaginary America, and, in the process, traditional and conservative ideals of European and national identity are reinforced. This strategy is akin to what is described by psychoanalysts as projective identification. An aspect of European identity is split off and projected outwards. This can take the form of a 'benign defence which simply wishes to postpone confrontation with some experience that cannot yet be tolerated', or it can take a more trenchant form that 'aims really to *disavow* identification, and perhaps would be better called projective *dis*identification' (Grotstein, 1981: 131, our emphasis). The consequence is that the crisis of European culture is never directly confronted. And 'America', as the container of that 'experience that cannot be tolerated', assumes a fantasy dimension as that which always threatens to 'contaminate' or overwhelm European cultural integrity.

Of course, we are not suggesting that American culture is only powerful in fantasy. The US entertainment industry was, in 1986, second only to aerospace, in terms of its trade surplus of $4.9 billion (Hoskins and Mirus, 1988: 512). The United States is paramount in television production and trade. As Raymond Williams bluntly puts it, it is the case that the new communications media are 'reaching out to remake consciousness in [their] own images, and [are] scoring many successes' (1989: 311). This being the case, we must take very seriously the question of cultural power and domination in the contemporary world. But, we shall only be able to do this if we can first clarify and confront – through what Habermas (1984) calls 'therapeutic critique' – the systematic illusions and self-deceptions that distort our understanding of 'Americanisation'. A precondition is that we break out of that compulsion to repeat, which, from the time of Matthew Arnold to the present day, has characterised European discourse on its 'imaginary America'.

American culture is not irresistible. Thus, in the case of television production, there is evidence to suggest that 'US programmes do not overwhelm foreign audiences' and that, in the larger European countries at least, the 'most popular domestic programmes consistently outperform the leading US ones' (Waterman, 1988: 144). Michael Tracey suggests that the international communications system is more complex than is usually allowed for, and that there has been a gross underestimation of 'the strengths of national cultures, the power of language and tradition, the force that flows, still, within national boundaries' (1988: 22). Audiences arc also more discriminating than is generally acknowledged: 'US TV was never as popular, or even widespread as was assumed . . . national populations basically prefer national programming' (ibid.: 24). And, when they do watch American programming, audiences are less susceptible than is commonly supposed. The transmission model of the communication process has been powerfully criticised from a number of theoretical perspectives (Breton and Proulx, 1989: 186–90). Research that has situated audiences in everyday life contexts has tended to emphasise the active appropriation and negotiation of media messages. However still, scandalously, it seems that American culture may also be appealing and desirable to many within Europe and elsewhere. Its willing consumers have not seen American culture as monolithic and homogeneous. Rather,

> American popular culture – Hollywood films, advertising images, packaging, clothes and music – offers a rich iconography, a set of symbols, objects and artefacts which can be assembled and re-assembled by different groups in a literally limitless number of combinations. And the meaning of each selection is transformed as individual objects – jeans, rock records, Tony Curtis hair styles, bobby socks etc, are taken out of their original historical and cultural contexts and juxtaposed against other signs from other sources.
>
> (Hebdige, 1988b: 74)

It may be that the real problem at issue here concerns the alleged 'common cultural heritage', the 'collective consciousness' supposedly shared by the inhabitants of Europe. How substantial is this? 'In Paris, even in a completely cultivated milieu', rues the sentimental Kundera, 'during dinner parties, people discuss television programmes, not *revues*. For culture has already bowed out' (1984: 117). Kundera is right in suggesting that traditional European art and culture has lost the capacity to forge European cultural unity. But he is wrong to say that culture is dead. Culture is being transformed. The mass media are becoming increasingly significant, the line between 'high-brow' and 'low-brow' culture is becoming thin, and American cultural products are at the heart of this process. What is now being acknowledged, in some quarters, is that this has profound implications for traditional 'aesthetic' criteria. What is emerging is 'a notion of aesthetic value that wholly escapes the "modern" idea of art and literature, but also an audience that feels perfectly comfortable with the criteria of this new aesthetic' (Eco, 1985: 181). We need to come to terms with this postmodern – and, for some, post-cultural – aesthetic and its implications for European identities. What is called for is a creative and open, rather then defensively moralistic, stance towards American culture.

EUROPE AND ITS OTHERS

America is a source of discomfort. But there is something more disturbing for Euro-culture, something that eats at the soul of European identity. There is, writes Yasmin Alibhai, 'a respectable xenophobia mushrooming all over the continent, that is pushing some of the collective dreams for 1992 to cluster around a concept of Europe which is white, racist and much more powerful than any post-war individual state' (1989). National identities are being transformed into a 'white continentalism'. European unity is being defined against 'alien' culture and around a self-image of European superiority.

The same danger is indicated in Sivanandan's argument that 'we are moving from an ethnocentric racism to a Eurocentric racism, from the different racisms of the different member states to a common market racism'. 'Citizenship', he writes,

> may open Europe's borders to blacks and allow them free movement, but racism which cannot tell one black from another, a citizen from an immigrant, an immigrant from a refugee – and which classes all Third World peoples as immigrants and refugees and all immigrants and refugees as terrorists and drug-dealers – is going to make such movement fraught and fancy.
>
> (Sivanandan, 1988: 9)

The grave concern is that European union will be built on the back of an underclass of migrant and immigrant workers. The current reconstructuring process is commonly seen in terms of a high-tech revolution – robotics, telecommunications networks, electronic cottages, smart buildings – that is bringing about the end of work and the inauguration of a leisure society. The emphasis is on communications networks and the new economy of information flows. But there is a darker side:

82

Besides generating a large supply of high-income professional jobs, this new economic core also needs, directly and indirectly, a wide array of low-wage jobs. Immigration has been a supplier of low-wage and typically powerless workers, a not insignificant fact in [the] strategic centres for control and management of the world economy.

(Sassen-Koob, 1987: 60–1)

There is another economy of flows: the flows of human labour, of a 'cheap and captive labour force – rightless, rootless, peripatetic and tempo-rary, illegal even – without which post-industrial society cannot run' (Sivanandan, 1989: 29). For these migrants and exiles there is no promise of an end to work. Martin Walker (1988b) suggests that it is a dangerous efficiency we have built, that runs so sleekly even as it builds a perma-nent underclass of the condemned and the unwanted, the drones of Europe.

If we are seeing the emergence of postmodern geographies, then these developments are one manifestation. Mass immigration, displaced persons, refugees, exiles are a testament to the global–local nexus. This, too, is a question of empire, of empire within, of internal colonisation. 'There's a bit of apartheid happening right here among us – in our *democracy*', Gunter Wallraff angrily protests (1988: 2). What cultural or collective iden-tities can these extraterritorial beings lay claim to? Lacking root in an ongoing way of life, writes Bhikhu Parekh, 'unable to feel in their bones the deepest joys and agonies of their adopted home, cut off from the social well-springs of meaning and value, their lives lack depth and rich-ness, the commonest source of the experience of sacredness' (1989: 30). This is a poignant counterpoint to the appetite for roots, the sense of place and heritage, that seems now to preoccupy the core work-force of Western Europe. How might these nomad identities fit into an ideal of 'unity in diversity'? What community is there for them in Europe? How will they be accommodated within social Europe, the citizens' Europe, the Europe of culture?

These questions raise 'the deep, the profoundly perturbed and perturb-ing question of our relationship to others – other cultures, other states, other histories, other experiences, traditions, people and destinies' (Said, 1989: 216). They raise the question of how our historical relation to Others has been transformed into an ontological relation to the Other. Edward Said has described this in terms of the European discourse on Orientalism, 'a collective notion identifying "us" Europeans as against all "those" non-Europeans . . . the idea of European identity as a superior one in com-parison with all the non-European peoples and cultures'. Orientalism, Said writes, 'depends for its strategy on [a] flexible *positional* superiority, which puts the Westerner in a whole series of possible relationships with the Orient, without ever losing him the relative upper hand' (1978: 7).

Said relates this dimension of empire to the 'geographical disposition' of Europe, to philosophical and imaginative processes at work in the production, as well as the acquisition, subordination and settlement of space' (1989: 218). Out of a polarised geography of 'West' and 'East' is produced the tension between identity and alterity – 'one belongs either to one group or to another; one is either in or out' – which culminates in a 'frightening consolidation of patriotism, assertions of cultural superiority, mechanisms of control, whose power and ineluctability reinforce . . . the logic of identity' (1988: 56).

The European ideal is about an economic area where all barriers have been removed and the principles of solidarity applied. For some, it is also about coming to terms with social and political barriers. We are suggesting that there are also cultural and psychic barriers, and that these are the most profound obstacle to European unity. The most fundamental challenge is to confront the relation of superior to subaltern identity that is embodied in the construction of Otherness. The question is whether it is possible to create a kind of communication and community that can acknowledge difference (and not simply diversity); whether there is a capacity to use difference as a resource rather than fear it as a threat (Feraud-Royer, 1987). What would be needed is a quite fundamental reconsideration of the insularities and certainties of European identity and continuity.

A point, perhaps, with which to end this chapter is the experience of exile and immigration. If the objective is genuinely to open frontiers – cultural as well as geographical – then migrant experience could be an important resource. 'Exiles cross borders, break barriers of thought and experience', writes Edward Said. Exile is, indeed, a brutal and brutalising experience, but there are things to be learned from some of its conditions:

> Seeing 'the entire world as a foreign land' makes possible originality of vision. Most people are principally aware of one culture, one setting, one home; exiles are aware of at least two, and the plurality of vision gives rise to an awareness of simultaneous dimensions, an awareness that – to borrow a phrase from music – is *contrapuntal*.
> (Said, 1984: 170–2)

The point about this kind of experience is that it could serve to decentre a hegemonic and self-assured Euro-culture. Any meaningful European identity has to be created out of the recognition of difference, the acceptance of different ethnicities.

5

NO PLACE LIKE HEIMAT
Images of home(land)

Our story is the old clash between history and home. Or to put it another way, the immeasurable, impossible space that seems to divide the hearth from the quest.

(Jeanette Winterson, 'Orion')

Every country is home to one man.
And exile to another.

(T. S. Eliot, 'To the Indians who died in Africa')

Everybody needs a home, so at least you can have some place to leave, which is where most folks will say you must be coming from.

(June Jordan, 'Living Room')

INTRODUCTION

Our concern in this chapter is with the questions of identity and memory in the construction of definitions of Europe and European culture. It is in this context that we address the centrality of the idea of Heimat (home/land). We take as a particular instance the debates opened up in Germany by Edgar Reitz's 1984 film, *Heimat* (and further developed in his sequel *Die Zweite Heimat* (1990)), centred around the opposition between Heimat and Fremde ('homeland' and 'foreignness'). This provides the focus for a broader discussion of the relations between European and 'Other' cultures in the post-war period, and, more particularly, of the representation of the European past as constructed through the media. Our argument is that we see played out here, in these debates over who holds the franchise on the representation of the past, an illuminating 'echo' of debates as to who has the right to determine Germany's future. This is, of course, no local matter, but is crucial to the future of Europe as a whole. We take the 'German story' to be a symbolic condensation of many of the most problematical themes of the European past and a central issue in the contemporary *Realpolitik* of Europe. As

85

Magris bluntly puts it: 'Today, questioning oneself about Europe means asking oneself how one relates to Germany' (1990: 32).

If Germany, the past somehow reconciled (cf. Rond (1971) for a discussion of Jean-Marie Straub and Danièle Huillet's 1965 film *Not Reconciled*, itself based on Heinrich Böll's 1961 novel *Billiards at Half Past Nine*), is to be united in more than name, and Europe no longer divided by the 'Iron Curtain', then the question arises, inescapably, as to where Europe ends (what is the status of *Mitteleuropa* or Eastern Europe?), and against what 'Other' (besides America) Europe and European culture are to be defined, if no longer against Communism. Our argument is that, if America continues to supply one symbolic boundary, to the 'West', there is also, implicit in much recent debate, a reworking of a rather ancient definition of Europe – as what used to be referred to as 'Christendom' – to which Islam, rather than Communism, is now seen to supply the 'Eastern' boundary. Our concern is with identifying some of the threads from which this pattern is being woven – the better, hopefully, to unravel it.

BRINGING IT ALL BACK HOME

'Modern man', Peter Berger and his colleagues argue, 'has suffered from a deepening condition of "homelessness"': 'The correlate of the migratory character of his experience of society and of self has been what might be called a metaphysical loss of "home"' (1974: 77). To be modern, writes Marshall Berman,

> is to find ourselves in an environment that promises adventure, power, joy, growth, transformation of ourselves and the world – and, at the same time, that threatens to destroy everything we have, everything we know, everything we are. Modern environments and experiences cut across all boundaries of geography and ethnicity, of class and nationality, of religion and ideology; in this sense, modernity can be said to unite all mankind. But it is a paradoxical unity, a unity of disunity; it pours us all into a maelstrom of perpetual disintegration and renewal, of struggle and contradiction, of ambiguity and anguish.
>
> (1983: 15)

The project of modernity is, then, 'to make oneself somehow at home in the maelstrom' (ibid.: 345).

It is this idea of 'home' that interests us. Home in a world of expanding horizons and dissolving boundaries. Anthony Giddens draws attention to the implications of modernity for ontological security, for the confidence we have 'in the continuity of [our] self-identity and in the constancy of the surrounding social and material environments of action' (1990: 92). In pre-modern times, he argues, this sense of trust and security was rooted in kinship systems, in local community, in religious beliefs and in the continuity of tradition. The effect of the great dynamic forces of modernity – what Giddens calls the separation of time and space, disembedding mechanisms and institutional reflexivity – has been to 'disengage some basic forms of trust relation from the attributes of local contexts' (ibid.: 108). Places are no longer the clear supports of our identity.

If anything, this process of transformation has become accelerated, and time–space compression has come to be ever more intense. It is through the logic of globalisation that this dynamic of modernisation is most powerfully articulated. Through proliferating information and communications flows and through mass human migration, it has progressively eroded territorial frontiers and boundaries and provoked ever more immediate confrontations of culture and identity. Where once it was the case that cultures were demarcated and differentiated in time and space, now 'the concept of a fixed, unitary, and bounded culture must give way to a sense of the fluidity and permeability of cultural sets' (Wolf, 1982: 387). Through this intermixture and hybridisation of cultures, older certainties and foundations of identity are continuously and necessarily undermined. The continuity of identity is broken too. 'There are *lieux de mémoire*, sites of memory', writes Pierre Nora (1989: 7), 'because there are no longer *milieux de mémoire*, real environments of memory. . . . We speak so much of memory because there is so little of it left'. Indeed, we speak so much of memory, and also of place and community. As Michael Rustin (1987: 33–4) argues, there is an increasingly felt need for 'some expressive relationship to the past' and for attachment to particular territorial locations as 'nodes of association and continuity, bounding cultures and communities'. There is a desire to be 'at home' in the new and disorientating global space.

Home, homeland, Heimat. It is around the meaning of European culture and identity in the new global context that this image – this nostalgia, this aspiration – has become polemically activated. Consider Mikhail Gorbachev's appeal to a 'common European home':

> Europe is indeed a common home where geography and history have closely interwoven the destinies of dozens of countries and nations. Of course, each of them has its own problems, and each wants to live its own life, to follow its own traditions. Therefore, developing the metaphor, one may say: the home is common, that is true, but each family has its own apartment, and there are different entrances, too.
>
> (1987: 195)

This notion of a single Europe, from the Atlantic to the Urals, has an obvious appeal. But what does it really amount to? What kind of community does it offer? Perhaps Susan Sontag is right. Where once Europe symbolised empire and expansionism, the new idea of Europe is about retrenchment: 'the Europeanisation, not of the rest of the world, but . . . of Europe itself' (Sontag, 1989: 80). This is a defensive identity, a fortress identity, defined against the threat of other cultures and identities (American, Japanese, Islamic, African or whatever). This reassertion of European cultural identity amounts to a refusal to confront the reality of a fundamental population shift that is undermining 'the little white "Christian" Europe' of the nineteenth century. As Neal Ascherson argues, 'we are living in a new America which is reluctant to admit the fact; in a continent which the poor of the outside world are beginning to choose as a destination' (1990: 7). And as Hall notes,

> in the era of globalisation and migration, Europe's 'Other' has finally came home to roost. . . . The one-way ticket and the charter flight have brought Europe (which for so long dealt with its colonial outposts at arms' length) within reach of its 'Others'. . . . The barbarians are already within the gate.
>
> (1992a: 47)

Or, in Eco's more dramatic terms:

> We are facing a migration comparable to the early Indo-European migrations, East to West, or the invasion of the Roman Empire by the Barbarians. . . . The new migration will radically change the face of Europe. In one hundred years Europe could be a coloured continent.
>
> (1992: 96–7)

The European Heimat invokes the past grandeur of Europe as a bastion against future uncertainties. This is a Europe that divides those who are of the Community from those who are *extracommunitari* and, effectively, extraterrestrial.

There are those, however, who are less committed to this particular vision of a European home. They are, to appropriate Gorbachev's metaphor, more interested in the different apartments than in the common home. For them, a faceless Europeanism is inimical to the rich diversity of national cultures and identities that are, supposedly, the basis of a more authentic sense of belonging; they feel that it is only in the sense of nationhood that one can feel truly 'at home'. Throughout Europe, we can now see the rekindling of national and nationalist sentiments. It is more apparent in Central and Eastern Europe, where national aspirations of sixty and seventy years ago are currently being reactivated through the reassertion of ethnic, religious and cultural differences. But also in Western Europe, particularly in the context of German reunification (*Deutschland, einig Vaterland*), national allegiance is asserting itself as a powerful way of belonging. As Ian Davidson (1990) argues, 'western reactions to the prospect of German unification show that the civilised advances of European integration are very recent compared with the old reflexes of nationalism; and that despite 45 years of reconciliation, there are primitive national feelings which lie only millimetres below the skin'.

As an alternative to continental Europeanism and to nation statism, there is yet another kind of 'homely' belonging. This is the identity rooted in the Heimat of regions and small nations. According to Neal Ascherson (1989), the 'melting away' of the European nation states 'may allow other entities, smaller but more durable, to replace them'. He evokes the rich pluralism of regional traditions, languages, dialects and cultures as the true basis for authentic identities. The European community, Ascherson argues, 'will travel from the western Europe of nation-states via the Brussels superstate to the Europe of Heimats' (ibid.). This 'small is beautiful' ideal of a Europe of the regions clearly seems to offer a richer and more radical way to belong. There is a romantic utopianism in this celebration of small nationalism and regionalism, a utopianism of the underdog. 'The Irish, the Basques, the Corsicans, the Kurds, the Kosovans, the Azerbaijanis, the Puerto Ricans, the Latvians', writes John Berger (1990), 'have little in common culturally or historically, but all of them want to be free of distant, foreign centres which, through long bitter experience, they have come to know as soulless'. All of them 'insist upon their identity being recognised, insist upon their continuity – their links with their dead and the unborn'.

Yet Heimat is an ominous utopia. Whether 'home' is imagined as the community of Europe or of the nation state or of the region, it is steeped in the longing for wholeness, unity, integrity. It is about community centred around shared traditions and memories. As the German film-director Edgar Reitz puts it:

> The word is always linked to strong feelings, mostly remembrances and longing. Heimat always evokes in me the feeling of something lost or very far away, something which one cannot easily find or find again . . . . It seems to me that one has a more precise idea of Heimat the further one is away from it.
>
> (quoted in Birgel, 1986: 5)

Heimat is a mythical bond rooted in a lost past, a past that has already disintegrated: 'we yearn to grasp it, but it is baseless and elusive; we look back for something solid to lean on, only to find ourselves embracing ghosts' (Berman, 1983: 333). It is about conserving the 'fundamentals' of culture and identity. And, as such, it is about sustaining cultural boundaries and boundedness. To belong in this way is to protect exclusive, and therefore excluding, identities against those who are seen as aliens and foreigners. The 'Other' is always and continuously a threat to the security and integrity of those who share a common home. Xenophobia and fundamentalism are opposite sides of the same coin. For, indeed,

Heimat-seeking is a form of fundamentalism. The 'apostles of purity' are always moved by the fear 'that intermingling with a different culture will inevitably weaken and ruin their own' (Rushdie, 1990). In contemporary European culture, the longing for home is not an innocent utopia.

COMMUNICATIONS, MEMORY AND IDENTITY

These questions of identity, memory and nostalgia are inextricably inter-linked with patterns and flows of communication. The 'memory banks' of our times are in some part built out of the materials supplied by the film and television industries. It is to the role of these industries in the construction of memory and identity that we now turn.

In the preceding chapters, we have directly addressed the debates concerning the role of new communications technologies in the creation of 'electronic spaces' transcending established national boundaries, and in the reconfiguration of European culture. As argued earlier, within the prevailing framework, cultural identities are only conceived of as responsive and reactive to the controlling stimulus of communications technologies. What is needed is a better formulation of the problem, one that takes questions of cultural and national identity as both central and problematical categories.

One of the first questions concerns how we are to understand the 'national', and what the role of media institutions is in the construction of national identities. In the case of cinema, Andrew Higson notes that the concept of national cinema has almost invariably been mobilised 'as a strategy of cultural (and economic) resistance; a means of asserting national autonomy in the face of . . . Hollywood's international domination' (1989: 37). In that context, art cinema particularly has played a central role 'in the attempts made by a number of European countries both to counter American domination of their indigenous markets in film and also to foster a film industry and film culture of their own' (Neale, 1981: 11). The discourses of 'art', 'culture' and 'quality' have thus been mobilised against Hollywood and used to justify various nationally specific economic systems of support and protection for indigenous film-making.

The role of the state is crucial in this respect, in so far as government policies have often determined the parameters and possibilities of various national cinemas, in the context of recognition of 'the potential ideological power of cinema . . . as a national cultural form, an institution with a "nationalising" function' (Higson, 1989: 43). Stephen Heath has suggested that, just as nationhood is not given but 'always something to be gained', so 'cinema needs to be understood as one of the means by which it is "gained"' (quoted in ibid.: 44). This is, necessarily, a contentious business. Definitions of national cinema always involve the construction of an imaginary homogeneity of identity and culture, apparently shared by all national subjects; this involves mechanisms of inclusion and exclusion whereby one definition of 'the nation' is centralised and others are marginalised – what Higson refers to as a process of 'internal cultural colonialism'.

It is a question of recognising the role of the stories we tell ourselves about our past in constructing our identities in the present. One key issue concerns the power of the idea of the nation to involve people in a common sense of identity and its capacity to work as an inclusive symbol which provides integration and meaning as it constructs and conscripts public images and interpretations of the past 'to re-enchant a disenchanted everyday life' (Wright, 1985: 24). In this fashion 'the rags and tatters of everyday life take on the lustre of the idealised nation when they are touched by its symbolism. There is therefore no simple replacement of "community" by "nation" . . . but rather a constant . . . redemption of its unhappy remains' (ibid.: 24), as the idea of the national past is constantly reworked and represented within the historical experience of a particular nation state. Identity is a question of memory, and memories of 'home' in particular.

Film and television media play a powerful role in the construction of collective memories and identities. It is in this context that we address the centrality of the idea of Heimat, principally with reference to the debates opened up in the mid-1980s in the Federal Republic of Germany by Edgar Reitz's film/television series of that name. The Heimat film is, of course, a well-established genre in Germany. One obvious question concerns whether one can work within this traditionally reactionary genre and yet give the material new and different meanings. Reitz's attempts to do just this have to be seen in the context of the political revitalisation of the rural 'Heimat' tradition in West Germany in the 1970s – as an attempt by a coalition of ecological and anti-nuclear groupings to 'reclaim' these traditions for the left, by means of the rediscovery and revaluation of regional and folk traditions, dialect poetry and so on, in an anti-centralist (and anti-urban) political movement. This turn to ecology represents an important shift, and, in this context, Adolf Muschg noted how, in the face of the steady destruction of the environment, 'homeland' ceased to be a dirty word (quoted in Chalmers, 1984: 91). More cynically perhaps, Jean Baudrillard has observed that 'when the real is no longer what it used to be, nostalgia assumes its full meaning. There is a proliferation of myths of origin . . . and authenticity' (quoted in ibid.). Heimat is a place no one has yet attained, but for which everyone yearns. Reitz notes that 'Heimat, the place where you were born, is for every person the centre of the world'; the idea, or ideal, is not simply territorial, but rather invokes a 'memory of origin' and involves the notion of an 'impossible return' to roots or origins (quoted in Kaes, 1989: 163).

91

When the American-produced television series *Holocaust* was shown in West Germany in 1979 it was watched by more than twenty million Germans, who were confronted with this version of their own history in their own living rooms. When *Heimat* was shown in the autumn of 1984, it was much more than a television series: it provided the focus and stimulus for a wide-ranging debate on German identity and history, with the popular press proclaiming that 'Germany's theme this fall is Heimat' (quoted in ibid.: 184). As Thomas Elsaesser puts it:

> The move of some filmmakers (Reitz, Lanzmann) . . . to undertake projects whose scale can generate TV events can be seen as an attempt to use film and cinema as release mechanisms for a discursive activity that crosses the boundaries of entertainment, and even of the arts. When a documentary film makes it from the review pages to the front of newspapers or becomes the subject for late night talk shows it demonstrates television's potential for creating something like an instant public sphere.
>
> (1988: 133)

Both these series acquired the status of television events; it was absolutely necessary for the people to watch them if they were to be able to participate effectively in the public debates that were generated in daily conversation.

This raises the question of who has the power to structure discourse in the 'instant public sphere' (an issue that was again raised in early 1994 by the release of Spielberg's film, *Schindler's List*). Heinz Hone argued in *Der Spiegel*, that

> an American TV series, made in a trivial style, produced more for commercial than for moral reasons, more for entertainment than for enlightenment, accomplished what hundreds of books, plays, films . . . documents and the concentration camp trials themselves have failed to do in the three decades since the end of the war: to inform Germans about crimes against Jews committed in their name so that millions were emotionally touched and moved.
>
> (quoted in Buruma, 1989: 40)

Edgar Reitz, of course, explicitly conceived *Heimat* as the German 'answer' to this American series. For Reitz, *Holocaust* was a 'glaring example [of an] international aesthetics of commercialism [for which] the misery produced by the Nazis is nothing but a welcome background spectacle for a sentimental family story' (quoted in Kaes, 1989: 184). He was concerned that German film-makers should establish the 'rights' to their own history, reclaiming them from the Americans. For Reitz the real scandal was 'German history – Made in Hollywood': hence the subtitle to *Heimat*, 'Made in Germany'. With *Holocaust*, he believed,

the Americans had stolen our history . . . taken narrative possession of our past. . . . I watched the crocodile tears of our nation
and I saw how it was all taken seriously and how the question of
guilt in German history was being discussed by all the great German
intellectuals on the basis of this travesty.

(quoted in Hansen, 1985: 9)

It is worth noting that when *Heimat* was shown in the United States, many
critics responded negatively, deeming the series to be a dangerous whitewash of German history. Clearly, the history of a world war does
not belong to any single nation. In these debates over the politics of
representing the German past, what is at issue is who has the right to
determine Germany's future.

A number of useful parallels can be drawn between the debates
surrounding *Heimat* and the filmic representation of 'Vietnam' in the
United States. Here again we see the pertinence of the argument that the
representation of the past is very much a question of active processes in
the present – as the Vietnam War continues to be waged symbolically on
television, in bookshops and at a cinema near you. The historical Vietnam
War, a specific set of conflictual events, policies and conditions, has been
transformed into a symbolic 'Vietnam', just as with the German (and thus
the European) past in *Holocaust* and *Heimat*. In the case of both *Heimat*
and the Vietnam films, we have the questions not only of loss and
mourning, but also, and more problematically, the cultural blockage
created by questions of guilt, and how *that* is to be represented. In both
cases, we also have the question of whether it is possible to undertake a
'progressive' reappropriation of patriotic sentiment, along with the further
issue of the potential usurpation of the role of victim by the perpetrators
of the initial violence. And then, of course, we have the question of the
silences in these discourses: on the one hand, the marginalisation of
the Holocaust itself in *Heimat*'s sixteen hours; on the other, the almost
total absence of anything other than caricature representations of the
Vietnamese themselves in Hollywood's Vietnam films.

HOW GERMAN IS IT?

Everyone is passionately in love with outdoors, in love with what
they refer to as Natur, and the splendid weather is an added induce-
ment to put on their Lederhosen and spend several hours serenely
tramping through the woods.

(Walter Abish, 1983)

In his commentary on Adorno's essay, 'On the question: what is German?',
Thomas Levin notes that 'in order to say just what is the German language,
one must be able to establish the identity, limits and character of a natural

idiom' (1985: 111). Adorno maintains that the character or specificity of a natural idiom can best be ascertained by reference to those of its terms which cannot successfully be translated. 'Every language', he says, 'draws a circle around the people to which it belongs, a circle from which we can only escape in so far as one at the same time enters another one' (ibid.: 117). In his view, the very form of the question 'What is German?', presupposes 'an autonomous collective entity – "German" – whose characteristics are then determined after the fact'. In reality, however, it is quite 'uncertain whether there even is such a thing as the German person or specifically German quality or anything analogous in other nations' (ibid.: 121). These concerns inevitably take us back into questions of stereotyping and collective narcissism. In this process, the central dynamic is one in which 'the qualities with which one identifies oneself – the essence of one's own group – imperceptibly become the Good; the foreign group, the others, the Bad. The same thing then happens, in reverse, with the image the others have of the German' (ibid.). For our present purposes, the key issue concerns the way in which the images and identities of 'America' and 'Germany' have been, and continue to be, defined in relation to each other.

Wim Wenders notes that

America always means two things: a country, geographically, the USA, and an 'idea' of that country which goes with it. [The] 'American Dream', then, is a dream of a country in a different country that is located where the dream takes place. . . . 'I want to be in America', the Jets sing, in that famous song from *West Side Story*. They are in America already and yet still wanting to get there.

(1989: 117–18)

Similarly, Ian Buruma emphasises the necessity of distinguishing between 'Germany as a legal and political entity, a Reichstaat, and "Germany" as a romantic ideal, a "Heimat", devoid of politics, a land of pine forests, lonely mountain tops and dreamy *Wandervögel* anxiously searching for identity' (1989: 43).

Moving to the central term in our argument, Wenders draws attention to a crucial difference between the meanings of home in American and German culture:

They have that in America: 'Mobile Homes'. 'Mobile' is said with pride and means the opposite of 'bogged down' . . . [or] 'stuck'. 'Home' means 'at home', 'where you belong' . . . [whereas] what *makes* it a home in the German language is the fact that it's fixed somewhere.

(1989: 144)

94

In the context of the German debate, one of the crucial dimensions along which the term Heimat is defined is by contrast to all that is foreign or distant. The characteristics of the traditional Heimat film genre involve conflict between the stable word of the 'Heimat' and the threatening assault of the 'Fremde'. 'America', in particular, becomes the very antithesis of 'Heimat'.

Reitz's film follows exactly this pattern, in so far as it is structured around a central contrast between those (principally women) who stay in the village (*die Dableiber*) and those (men) who represent a culture of emigrants, who left home (*die Weggegangenen*). The moral universe of the film is structured around a set of contrasts: tradition/rootlessness; village/city; local/foreign; natural/modern; eternal/changing; feminine /masculine. Of these contrasts the final pair is perhaps the most significant. As Anton Kaes notes, in *Heimat*, the central female figure, Maria, embodies safety and permanence. The mother figure and the home itself are thus conflated, to the extent that Kaes claims that 'the film's secret message is: where she is, there is Heimat' (1989: 168).

Kaes also notes that a pervasive anti-Americanism recurs in *Heimat*, from the first mention of the United States as the 'land of the electric chair' (ibid.: 190). In Reitz's own production notes for the series, one of the central characters, Paul, is described as having 'become a real American . . . a man without a home, without roots, a sentimental globe-trotter' (Geisler, 1985: 63). To this extent, Reitz seems to fall into what Duncan Webster describes as a 'standard image of Americanisation . . . drawn from American horror films, the invasion of the alien, the replacement/transformation of the local, the community (viewers, consumers) becoming mindless zombies' (1989: 65). Reitz is projecting

> a mythical 'America', country of the perennially homeless . . . a land of loneliness, without history . . . without culture. . . . As the German Left is trying to renegotiate their traditional stance towards their 'Heimat', the exclusionary mechanisms find a new target in 'America'.
>
> (Geisler, 1985: 65)

The film's sympathetic treatment of the pre-war period, along with the focus on the destruction of the experience of Heimat in the post-war period, leads Reitz to imply that the loss of German identity is associated with its Americanisation.

Against this kind of perspective, Duncan Webster (1989: 65) points out that, when one of Wenders' characters in *Kings of the Road* says that 'the Americans have colonised our subconscious', it should be noted that the 'our' in question has a double resonance – 'we Germans' and 'we post-war consumers of popular culture' – and these resonances mark the site of intersection of generational, cultural and national identities.

What is at stake here is something more than any simple 'invasion' of other cultures by America. What Wenders poses is, rather, the specific appeal of American culture to a generation growing up in post-war Germany (Wenders was born in 1945) with a 'schizophrenic response to history, a double bind of remembering and forgetting fascism', in which 'one way of dealing with this was an involvement with other cultures' (ibid.: 67).

In similar vein, Gabrielle Kreutzner argues that, as a result of this history, intellectuals on the German left have taken on the heritage of an over-determined hostility towards popular phenomena of German culture. At the same time, she notes that it is common practice for the German left to supply its public events with music from the Third World (South America, Africa). Kreutzner suggests that this 'celebration of traditional music not only signifies a (romantic) desire for an "authentic" popular culture. It also suggests that the search for popular phenomena with which they can identify leads the German intellectual outside of her or his immediate cultural context' (1989: 245). It is only the popular phenomena of other lands that are felt to be free from ideological taint.

The appeal of American culture has to be seen, then, in the context of Germany's profound mistrust of sounds and images about itself. As Wenders puts it:

> In the early Fifties or even the Sixties, it was always American culture
> . . . . In other words, the need to forget twenty years created a hole,
> and people tried to cover this, in both senses, by assimilating
> American culture much more than French or Italian or British
> people did. The only radio I listened to was American Forces
> Network. But the fact that US imperialism was so effective over here
> was highly favoured by the Germans' own difficulties with their past.
> One way of forgetting it, and one way of regression, was to accept
> the American imperialism.
>
> (quoted in Webster, 1989: 67)

Rock and roll might have been 'foreign', but at least it had nothing to do with fascism.

A close parallel can be made between this contemporary analysis and Adorno's comments on the significance of 'foreign words' (*Fremdwörter*) in the German language. He recounts how, as a child, he delighted in the 'exterritorial and aggressive' character of these terms, which provided him with a refuge from the German chauvinism of the period. The *Fremdwörter*, he says, 'formed tiny cells of resistance against the nationalism in the First World War' (quoted in Levin, 1985: 115). The Nazis, not surprisingly, systematically eliminated these foreign words from the culture, in so far as they were able, in order to protect the 'purity' of the mother-tongue. In a similar way, Kaes (1989: 166) notes that the term

'Heimat' was a synonym for race (blood) and territory (soil) – a deadly combination that led to the exile or annihilation of anyone who did not 'belong'; under the National Socialists, 'Heimat' meant the murderous exclusion of anything 'un-German'.

Reitz has argued that 'the problem with us, in Germany, is that our stories are blocked by . . . history. In 1945 everything started happening from scratch, erasing all that had gone before. It's like a gaping hole in people's memories and feelings' (quoted in Ranvaud, 1985: 125). As he puts it:

It is our own history that is in our way. In 1945 the nation's 'zero hour' wiped out and created a gap in people's ability to remember . . . . an entire people has been 'unable to mourn' . . . unable to tell stories, because our memories are obstructed . . . we are still afraid that our personal stories could recall our Nazi past and remind us of our mass participation in the Reich.

(Reitz, quoted in *City Limits*, 15 February 1985: 11)

Thus, it is argued, 'Deutschland' became, in the post-war period, an entity which it was impossible to represent:

Nazism, the war . . . the defeat and its aftermath . . . produced a homelessness . . . in the feeling of a loss of 'right' to a homeland . . . even language no longer provided a 'home'. Even the image of Germany in the post-war period was part of this uprootedness. America [was] represented, for example, by the White House, England by Buckingham Palace . . . , France by the Arc de Triomphe. . . . Germany, however, [was always] represented by its division, above all by the Berlin Wall, marking the absence of certainty about home: separation, expulsion, exile.

(Chalmers, 1984: 93)

Prior to the success of *Heimat*, it could be argued that the West German audience for art cinema (in its enthusiasm for Bertolucci's *1900* or the Tavianis' *Padre Padrone*, for example) had compensated for the lack of an acceptable image of its own history and peasant culture by over-identifying in a plainly nostalgic way with the art cinema of its neighbours. The other side of this coin was that

Hollywood had a wonderful time after 1945, because they had limit-less possibilities for showing evil Nazis, whereas before they'd had to content themselves with a limited repertoire of (stereotypical) villains. But in reality, the personification of evil doesn't exist. The Nazi people were as ordinary as everyone else: in special moments . . . they acted as Nazi.

(Reitz, quoted in *City Limits*, 15 February 1985: 11)

In this process 'Nazi Germany' or 'Deutschland' readily becomes a cipher for an undefined, only superficially historicised, evil – a diabolical entity. The real horror of the war was evaded and, in a sense, defused. As Hans Magnus Enzensberger has commented, this is 'yet another transfiguration of the attribute "German" into a metaphysical entity – only this time it carries a negative charge . . . . Instead of Good, as before, it is now the absolute Evil, which is defined along biological or racial parameters' (quoted in Geisler, 1985: 32).

HOW EUROPEAN IS IT?

The problem with Germany is that it is too big and it's in the wrong place.

(Hans Magnus Enzensberger, 1992)

The debates around the concept of 'home' and 'homeland' occasioned by *Heimat* have now, of course, also to be seen in the transformed context of Gorbachev's call for the construction of a 'common European home' to transcend the Cold War division of Europe, which found its most dramatic expression in the division of Germany. As we have already suggested, the debates over who should hold the franchise rights on the story of the German past have many parallels in the debates as to who should have the right to determine Germany's future. Current debates concerning the reunification of the country have a necessary centrality to our argument, not least in so far as, in the context of *perestroika* and *glasnost*, the very concept of 'Europe' now becomes geographically less distinct.

Questions of religion and race are also lurking in the definition of Europe and European culture. As the Cold War order crumbles, we are seeing the reassertion of religion as both a buttress of cultural identity and a token of membership of the 'civilised' world. In this context, the debates generated by Turkey's application to join the European Community offer a number of interesting insights into the issues at stake.

At one level, the issue is simple. On the one hand Turkey, on account of its membership to NATO, its possession of a small but important triangle of land on the European side of the Bosphorus and the modern secular framework of institutions bequeathed by Kemal Atatürk, has a strong *prima facie* case for membership of the Community. On the other hand, there is a complex set of questions concerning trade barriers, the potential impact of cheap Turkish agricultural (and increasingly, electrical) products on existing member countries, and, of course, there is the continuing question of Turkey's record on human rights. However, we suggest that, at base, something far more fundamental is at stake: the question of whether in contemporary debates 'Europe' is being defined as co-extensive with what used to be called Christendom. Or, to put it the other way round, can an Islamic (albeit secularised) state be fully accepted as part of Europe? Consider that historically the Ottoman Empire provided an image of difference and threat (and, indeed, dread), against which Europe defined itself. Consider, too, that today's European Community was founded by Christian bureaucrats (indeed, Catholics) across Europe.

Certainly, in recent years there has been a marked increase in the anxiety and suspicion with which many Europeans view the Islamic world. Across Europe we can see an emerging pattern of racial hostility towards Muslims – dramatised in complex ways by the Rushdie affair in Britain, and by violence and hostility to Turkish immigrant workers in Germany and to North African immigrants in France and in Italy. One could argue that the oil crisis of the 1970s, images of PLO terrorists and Lebanese hostage-takers and the image of Islamic fundamentalism throughout the Middle East, have all been aggregated in the popular media to produce a greater sense of 'Islamic threat' to Europe than at any time since the seventeenth century. The French mass-circulation news magazine *Le Point* headlined a story about Islamic fundamentalism in Algeria 'The Holy War at our Gates', a story full of references to the Muslim 'danger' and its 'threat' to French national identity. Jean-Marie Le Pen, leader of the French National Front, claims Joan of Arc as his inspiration. The director of the Turkish Foreign Policy Institute in Ankara puts it quite simply: 'In Europe, many people see us as a new version of the Ottoman empire, attacking this time in the form of guest workers and terrorists' (quoted in *Newsweek*, 21 May 1990). It can be argued that Islam is now the primary form in which the Third World presents itself to Europe, and that the North–South divide, in the European context, has been largely inscribed onto a pre-existing Christian–Muslim division. Edward Said argues that 'the idea of the West . . . comes largely from opposition to the Islamic and Arab World', for the very good reason that 'Europe has always had Islam on its doorstep. . . . Islam is the only non-European culture that has never been completely vanquished. It is adjacent to and shares the monotheistic heritage with Judaism and Christianity. So, there is this constant friction' (1992: 111).

However, there is more to it than that, in so far as the relation between these two terms, or rather, the significance of this relation, has itself been shifted by the current transformation of East–West relations. As Edward Mortimer (1990) argues, the deep-seated anxieties about European identity (and the centrality of Christianity to that definition) were driven underground by the Cold War, during which Stalin's empire provided Europe with a *de facto* eastern frontier. During this period, whatever was not 'Communist' was 'Western' (that is, European). In this context, as a member of NATO, and a strategically crucial one at that, the European credentials of Turkey were accepted without much question. Certainly many Turks regard their membership of NATO as proof of their Western status. But with the collapse of the Soviet bloc, all this is now called into question. Central and Eastern Europe is reasserting its identity in large part as a Christian one. Europe is suddenly feeling the need to re-establish its psychic boundaries anew. And, as it redefines itself, the question of who is to be excluded – that is to say, in contra-distinction to whom or to what 'European' identity is to be defined – is being refocused. Turkey suddenly finds itself in a different context, one in which its European credentials have been dramatically devalued.

There is, it seems, no place like home – and apparently no place in that home for some who wish to dwell there. Our common European home remains to be built: but the stories we tell ourselves about our common (and uncommon) past are already shaping our understanding of how it should be constructed, how many floors it should have (a basement for the servants?), which way it should face and who should have the keys to the door.

'THE BORDER RUNS RIGHT THROUGH MY TONGUE'

Our discussion has, at various points, focused on Germany because of its particular strategic and symbolic importance in the contemporary transformation of Europe. Germany, once again the question mark of Europe. Germany has been divided against itself, and this divide has also marked the separation of the eastern and western halves of Europe. Now the dividing wall has been deconstructed: what was protectively solid has apparently evaporated into air. 'Germany is stretching its limbs', wrote Jens Reich shortly before the 9 November breaching of the Berlin Wall:

> The Federal Republic is shedding its geographical hair-shirt like a dried skin. The GDR is bursting its ideological corset, supposedly all that can give its existence legitimacy. Reunification or confederation, annexation or single cultural nation? – it is all equally alarming. The neighbours are on the qui vive and look for ways to keep the two components of the poison in their separate vessels. The pressure on the valves grows.
>
> (1990: 122)

Now the two components have come into direct contact. What compound mixture is being distilled in the process? If Germany had until recently been seen as a kind of 'post-national' society, questions of national culture and identity are once again on the political agenda. What does it mean to be German today, after forty years of division? What is 'German' now? The border ran right through German identity and now it has been dissolved and Germany re-encounters itself, across space and also across time. Ralf Dahrendorf (1990: 23) describes a kind of historical 'doppel-gänger' effect: West Germans must now see their past, their history, reflected back at them; and East Germans have the dislocating and disorientating experience of confronting their future. Who now are 'we the people'?

The tragedy will be if reunification provokes a defensive and exclusivist form of nationalism. The defeat will be if German identity is refounded in terms of a closed community, with boundaries drawn between those who belong and those who do not. 'Germany is one' and 'we are one people' were the slogans chanted outside the Berlin opera house in Karl Marx Square. One people. One homeland. For Edgar Morin, nationalist sentiments are akin to infantile attachments to the family. The nation, he argues, is both mother and father: 'It is maternal-feminine as the motherland (mère-patrie) that its sons should cherish and protect. It is paternal and virile as the just and commanding authority that calls to arms and to duty' (1990: 30). This complex allegiance, this 'matri-patriotism', expresses itself, Morin argues, in a strong sense of rootedness, of belonging to a home and a homeland ('un sentiment très fort de la patrie-foyer (Heimat, home), toit, maison'). One people, one family, one homeland: belonging together, with common origins. 'We the people' defined against the 'Others' who do not belong, and have different origins.

The question of a German home, as we have argued at length, has been a central motif in recent cultural debates in the Federal Republic. At the heart of the New German Cinema the problem of identity and the quest for origins has centred around the theme of the family, the damaged relation to the (absent) father and the fixation on the mother figure (Elsaesser, 1989). For many, this has been about trying to find a way home; it has been about becoming reconciled to German culture and identity. The romantic utopia of Heimat, with all its connotations of remembrance and longing has been about reconnecting with a national heritage and history. For others, however, the issue is far more complex. National integrity is a vain ideal; one people, a false utopia. The cinema of Wim Wenders, particularly, has been about the state of homelessness that seems to be a necessary expression of the condition of modernity. Wenders' work evokes 'a world of surfaces increasingly deprived of memory or self-reflection, where fantasy and reality have become so confused and the notion of self-identity so diluted that it no longer seems possible to tell one's story' (Kearney, 1988a: 324). In his films there is no easy recourse to the security of origins, rootedness and authenticity. As Thomas Elsaesser has argued, Wenders is concerned with journeys, with crossing borders, with exile, with the relation between inside and outside. What he seeks to explore, particularly through his relationship with 'America', are the realities of difference, Otherness and estrangement. For Wenders, there is no utopia of home and homeland:

The idea is that, not being at home [my heroes] are nevertheless at home with themselves. In other words, not being at home means being more at home than anywhere else. . . . Maybe the idea of being more oneself when one's away is a very personal idea. . . . Identity means not having to have a home. Awareness, for me, has something to do with not being at home. Awareness of anything.

(quoted in Elsaesser, 1985: 48)

Being away, not being at home, is what Wenders aspires to.

Not being at home is, of course, the permanent destiny of so many people and peoples ('involuntary cosmopolitans') in the modern world. It is the condition of those millions of so-called *Ausländer* or *Gastarbeiter* who live precarious and unsettled lives in the German homeland itself. As Ruth Mandel emphasises, 'Germany has a long history of confronting a salient other. The incorporation of "others" into the German *Volksgemeinschaft* has long been troublesome, as it has challenged the underpinnings of German notions of identity' (1989: 37): *Überfremdung* (overforeignisation) has been perceived as a threat to national integrity and culture. Now it is the 1.5 million Turks living in Germany who have become the salient and disturbing 'Other'. 'We the people' are now defined, in Germany, against the 'Islamic Other'. The question is whether Germany can come to terms with this 'Islam within', or whether the new nation will be imagined on the basis of an exclusive and excluding racism. It is also a question of whether Germany can understand that it is not one, can never be one, because it is multiple, because it contains many peoples, Germans of different ethnicities.

What must be recognised is that, if Germany is a home for some, then it is at the same time exile for others. What must be understood is the relation between Heimat and Fremde. If Heimat is about security and belonging, Fremde evokes feelings of isolation and alienation. Fremde is a 'synonym for separation, hardship, privation, homesickness, and the loss of a sense of belonging' (Suhr, 1989: 72). Germany – the real, rather than the imaginary, Germany – is at once Heimat and Fremde. Is it possible to come to terms with this relational truth, rather than taking refuge in the comforting absolute of Heimat? Is it possible to live with this complexity and ambivalence? In his poem 'Doppelmann', Zafer Şenocak writes of his Germany:

> I carry two worlds within me
> but neither one whole
> they're constantly bleeding
> the border runs
> right through my tongue.

(quoted in ibid.: 102)

It is this experience that is fundamental to questions of German – and also European – culture and identity today. And it is out of this tension – between homelessness and home – that we might begin to construct more meaningful, more complex, identities. As Zafer Şenocak puts it: 'The split can give rise to a double identity. This identity lives on the tension. One's feet learn to walk on both banks of the river at the same time' (ibid.: 103).

Our discussion has been about images of home and homeland, and it has arrived at the reality of homelessness. It has focused particularly on the idea of a German home to illuminate the powerful appeal of Heimat throughout a changing Europe. Whether it is in terms of a national home, a regional home or a common European home, the motivating force is a felt need for a rooted, bounded, whole and authentic identity. And yet Heimat is a mirage, a delusion. As Edgar Reitz recognises 'Heimat is such that if one would go closer and closer to it, one would discover that at the moment of arrival it is gone, it has dissolved into nothingness' (quoted in Birgel, 1986: 5). It is a dangerous delusion. Heimat is rooted in that intolerance of difference, that fear of the 'Other', which is at the heart of racism and xenophobia.

The crucial issue that now confronts European culture, we would argue, is whether it can be open to the condition and experience of homelessness. The questions posed by Wim Wenders are at the heart of the matter. Can we imagine an identity, an awareness, grounded in the experience of not having a home, or of not having to have a home? Can we see home as a necessarily provisional, always relative, truth? Writing of modern Irish culture and identity, Richard Kearney describes its multiple complexities and paradoxes:

> It is striking how many modern Irish authors have spoken of being in transit between two worlds, divided between opposing allegiances. They often write as *emigrés* of the imagination, conveying the feeling of being both part and not part of their culture, of being estranged from the very traditions to which they belong, of being in exile even while at home.
>
> (1988b: 14)

It is this experience of transit that is fundamental to the culture. 'The contemporary sense of "homelessness"', Kearney argues, 'which revivalism sought to remedy by the reinstatement of a lost homeland, becomes for modernism the irrevocable condition not only of Irish culture but of world culture' (ibid.).

There can be no recovery of an authentic cultural homeland. In a world that is increasingly characterised by exile, migration and diaspora, with all the consequences of unsettling and hybridisation, there can be no place for such absolutism of the pure and authentic. In this world, there is no longer any place like Heimat. More significant, for European cultures and identities now, is the experience of displacement and transition. 'Sometimes we feel that we straddle two cultures', writes Salman Rushdie (1982: 19) of his own experience, 'at other times we fall between two stools'. What is most important is to live and work with this disjuncture and ambivalence. Identity must live out of this tension. Our feet must learn to walk on both banks of the river at the same time.

6

TRADITION AND TRANSLATION

National culture in its global context

> Where once we could believe in the comforts and continuities of
> Tradition, today we must face the responsibilities of cultural
> Translation.
>
> (Homi Bhabha, 1989)

This chapter is about changing geographies – particularly the new forces
of globalisation that are now shaping our times – and what they mean for
the economic and cultural life of contemporary Britain. It is in this global
context, we believe, that we can begin to understand the emergence, over
the past decade or so, of both enterprise and heritage cultures. It is also
in this context that the problem of empire, for so long at the heart of
British national culture and identity, is now taking on a new significance.

TRADITION AND TRANSLATION

Recent debate on the state of British culture and society has tended to
concentrate on the power of Tradition. Accounts of the crisis of British
(or English) national traditions and cultures have described the cultural
survivalism and mutation that comes in the aftermath of an exploded
empire. As Raphael Samuel argues in his account of the pathology of
Tradition, the idea of nationality continues to have a powerful, if regressive, afterlife, and 'the sleeping images which spring to life in times of
crisis – the fear, for instance, of being "swamped" by foreign invasion –
testify to its continuing force' (1989: xxxii). It is a concern with the past
and future of British Tradition that has been central to Prince Charles'
declamations on both enterprise and heritage. A 'new Renaissance for
Britain' can be built, he suggests, upon a new culture of enterprise; a new
business ethos, characterised by responsibility and vision, can rebuild the
historical sense of community and once again make Britain a world actor.
What is also called for, according to the Prince's 'personal vision', is the
revival and re-enchantment of our rich national heritage. As Patrick
Wright argues, the Prince of Wales has been sensitive to 'the deepest

disruptions and disappointments in the nation's post-war experience' (1989: 27), and the Prince's invocation of so-called traditional and spiritual values is again intended to restore the sense of British community and confidence that has collapsed in these modern or perhaps postmodern times.

This prevailing concern with the comforts and continuities of historical Tradition and identity reflects an insular and narcissistic response to the breakdown of Britain. In a psychoanalytic account of early human development, Barry Richards describes a state of narcissistic omnipotence. It involves

> protective illusions which can stand in the place of the overwhelming anxieties to which we would be subject if the full helplessness of our condition were borne in upon us as infants. We can abandon these imperial illusions only to the extent that we can face the world without them, having been convinced that it is a sufficiently benign place for our weakness not to be catastrophic, and having gained some faith in our growing powers of independent functioning.
>
> (1989: 38–9)

Protective illusion, we shall suggest, has also been central to the obsessive construction of both enterprise and heritage cultures in these post-imperial days. The real challenge that we want to consider is about confronting imperial illusion (in both fantasy and literal senses). It is about recognising the overwhelming anxieties and catastrophic fears that have been born out of empire and the imperial encounter. If, in psychoanalytic terms, 'a stable disillusionment' is only achieved 'through many bruising encounters with the other-ness of external reality' (ibid.), then in the broader political and cultural sphere what is called for is our recognition of other worlds, the disillusioned acknowledgement of other cultures, other identities and ways of life.

This is what we take Homi Bhabha to mean by the responsibility of cultural Translation. It is about taking seriously 'the deep, the profoundly perturbed and perturbing question of our relationship to others – other cultures, other states, other histories, other experiences, traditions, peoples, and destinies' (Said, 1989: 216). This responsibility demands that we come to terms with the geographical disposition that has been so significant for what Edward Said calls the 'cultural structures of the West'. We could not have had empire itself, he argues, 'as well as many forms of historiography, anthropology, sociology, and modern legal structures, without important philosophical and imaginative processes at work in the production as well as the acquisition, subordination, and settlement of space' (ibid.: 218). Empire has long been at the heart of British culture and imagination, manifesting itself in more or less virulent forms, through insular nationalism and through racist paranoia. The relation of Britain to its

'Other' is one profoundly important context in which to consider the emergence of both enterprise and heritage cultures. The question is whether, in these supposedly post-imperial times, it is possible for Britain to accept the world as a sufficiently benign place for its weakness not to be catastrophic. The challenge is not easy, as the Rushdie affair has made clear, for 'in the attempt to mediate between different cultures, languages and societies, there is always the threat of mis-translation, confusion and fear' (Bhabha, 1989: 35). There is also, and even more tragically, the danger of a fearful refusal to translate: the threat of a retreat into cultural autism and of a rearguard reinforcement of imperial illusions.

THE MAKING OF GEOGRAPHY

Geography has always mattered. For many, it matters now more than ever. Edward Soja (1989: 1), for example, suggests that we are now seeing the formation of new postmodern geographies, and argues that today 'it may be space more than time that hides consequences from us, the "making of geography" more than the "making of history" that provides the most revealing tactical and theoretical world'. In the following sections we want to explore the spatial context in which enterprise and heritage cultures have been taking shape.

Geographical reconfigurations are clearly central to contemporary economic and cultural transformation. If, however, there is such a phenomenon as the postmodernisation of geography, then what is its organising principle? How are we to make sense of these complex spatial dynamics? What is needed is an understanding of the competing centrifugal and centripetal forces that characterise the new geographical arena. On this basis we can then begin to explore the implications for cultures and identities. More particularly, we can consider the significance of these developments for the geographical disposition that Edward Said sees as so much at the heart of western dominion. Are they likely to reinforce, to recompose or perhaps even to disconstruct, the geographical disposition of empire? Our central concern is whether the 'making of geography' can be about the 'remaking of geography'.

It is clear that geographical transformations are now being brought about through the international restructuring of capitalist economies. This has been associated with a changing role for the nation state (though in precisely what sense it is being transformed remains to be clarified). At the same time there has been a consolidation of supra-national blocs (such as the European Community) and a new salience for sub-national territories (regions and localities). The reorganisation of the international economic order has also changed the nature and role of cities, bringing about new and direct confrontations between city administrations and transnational corporations, and stimulating global competition between cities to attract ever more mobile investors. It has created new centres and peripheries, and also new territorial hierarchies. It has produced new relational contexts and configurations. Regions, for example, are now assuming a whole new significance in the context of a 'Europe of the regions'. And, beyond this, there is the overarching global context: 'regional differentiation becomes increasingly organised at the international rather than national level; sub-national regions increasingly give way to regions of the global economy' (Smith, 1988: 150).

This process of international restructuration is bringing change not only to the space economy, but to imaginary spaces as well. As territories are transformed, so too are the spaces of identity. National cultures and identities have become more troublesome (though they have a long and potent half-life). For many, European culture has offered a more challenging and cosmopolitan alternative, even if there are real difficulties, here too, in exorcising the legacy of colonialism, and even if recent events in Central and Eastern Europe raise questions about what Europe really means. Local and regional cultures have also come to be revalued (as is apparent in the growth of the heritage industry), and there is now a renewed emphasis on territorial locations as poles of identity, community and continuity.

The organising principle behind these complex transformations, both economic and cultural, as we shall argue in the following sections, is the escalating logic of *globalisation*. More precisely, as we shall then go on to make clear, the so-called postmodernisation of geography is about the emergence of a new *global–local nexus*. Historical capitalism has, of course, always strained to become a world system. The perpetual quest to maximise accumulation has always compelled geographical expansion in search of new markets, raw materials, sources of cheap labour and so on. The histories of trade and migration, of missionary and military conquest, of imperialism and neo-imperialism, mark the various strategies and stages that have, by the late twentieth century, made capitalism a truly global force. If this process has brought about the organisation of production and the control of markets on a world scale, it has also, of course, had profound political and cultural consequences. For all that it has projected itself as transhistorical and transnational, as the transcendent and universalising force of modernisation and modernity, global capitalism has in reality been about Westernisation – the export of Western commodities, values, priorities, ways of life. In a process of unequal cultural encounter, 'foreign' populations have been compelled to be the subjects and subalterns of Western empire, while, no less significantly, the West has come face to face with the 'alien' and 'exotic' culture of its 'Other'. Globalisation, as it dissolves the barriers of distance, makes the encounter of colonial centre and colonised periphery immediate and intense.

GLOBAL ACCUMULATION

Enterprise and heritage cultures must both be seen in the context of what has become a globally integrated economic system. What is new and distinctive about global accumulation, and what differentiates it from earlier forms of economic internationalisation? Globalisation is about the organisation of production and the exploitation of markets on a world scale. This, of course, has long historical roots. Since at least the time of the East India Company (founded in 1600), it has been at the heart of entrepreneurial dreams and aspirations. What we are seeing is no more than the greater realisation of long historical trends towards the global concentration of industrial and financial capital. Transnational corporations remain the key shapers and shakers of the international economy, and it is the ever more extensive and intensive integration of their activities that is the primary dynamic of the globalisation process: it remains the case, more than ever, that 'size is power'. What we are seeing is the continuation of a constant striving to overcome national boundaries, to capture and co-ordinate critical inputs, and to achieve world-scale advantages.

But if this process is clearly about the consolidation of corporate command and control, it is none the less the case that, to this end, we are now seeing significant transformations and innovations in corporate strategy and organisation. The limitations of nationally centred multinationals are now becoming clear, and the world's leading-edge companies are seeking to restructure themselves as 'flexible transnationals' on the basis of a philosophy and practice of globalisation. These companies must now operate and compete in the world arena in terms of quality, efficiency, product variety and the close understanding of markets. And they must operate in all markets simultaneously, rather than sequentially. Global corporations are increasingly involved in time-based competition: they must shorten the innovation cycle; cut seconds from process time in the factory; accelerate distribution and consumption times. Global competition pushes towards time–space compression. Globalisation is also about the emergence of the decentred or polycentric corporation. As business consultant Kenichi Ohmae points out, global operations require a genuine 'equidistance of perspective', treating all strategic markets in the same way, with the same attention, as the home market. He sees Honda, operating in Japan, Europe and North America, as a typical case: 'Its managers do not think or act as if the company were divided between Japanese and overseas operations. Indeed, the very word "overseas" has no place in Honda's vocabulary because the corporation sees itself as equidistant from all its key customers' (Ohmae, 1989: 153).

This whole process has been associated with a corporate philosophy centred around the 'global product'. A universalising idea of consumer sovereignty suggests that as people gain access to global information, so they develop global needs and demand global commodities, thereby becoming 'global citizens'. As noted earlier, in his influential book *The Marketing Imagination*, Levitt (1983) forcefully argues that the new reality is all about global markets and world-standard products. This is, of course, no more than a continuation of mass-production strategies which always sought economies of scale on the basis of expanding markets. However, whilst the old multinational corporation did this by operating in a number of countries and by adapting its products to different national preferences, today's global corporation operates as if the entire world (or major regions of it) were a single, largely identical entity; it does and sells the same things in the same way everywhere. Transcending vestigial national differences, according to Levitt, the global corporation strives to treat the world as fewer standardised markets rather than as many customised markets.

Of course, there is both hype and hyperbole in this. There has been a tendency to overemphasise the standardisation of products and the homogenisation of tastes. None the less, it would be a mistake to dismiss this globalising vision as simply another fad or fashion of the advertising industry. Levitt's position is, in fact, more complex and nuanced than is generally understood. What he recognises is that global corporations do, indeed, acknowledge differentiated markets and customise for specific market segments. The point, however, is that this is combined with the search for opportunities to sell to similar segments throughout the globe. These same insights have been taken up in Saatchi & Saatchi's strategies for pan-regional and world marketing. Their well-known maxim that there are more social differences between mid-town Manhattan and the Bronx than between Manhattan and the 7th *arrondissement* of Paris, suggests the increasing importance of targeting consumers on the basis of demography and habits rather than on the basis of geographical proximity; marketing strategies are 'consumer driven' instead of 'geography-driven' (Winram, 1984). What is at the heart of this economic logic of world brands remains the overriding need to achieve economies of scale, or, more accurately, to achieve economies of scale and scope – that is, to combine volume and variety production – at the global level.

Globalisation also demands considerable changes in corporate behaviour; the flexible transnational must compete in ways that are significantly different from the older multinational firm. In a world of permanent and continuous innovation, a world in which global span must be combined with rapid, even instantaneous, response, the global corporation must be lean and resourceful. In order to ensure its competitive position it must ensure a global presence: it must be 'everywhere at once'. This is bringing about significant changes in corporate strategy, with a huge burst of activity centred around mergers, acquisitions, joint ventures, alliances, inter-firm

110

agreements and collaborative activities of various kinds. The objective is to combine mobility and flexibility with the control and integration of activities on a world scale. The global corporation seeks to position itself within a 'tight–loose' network: tight enough to ensure predictability and stability in dealings with external collaborators; loose enough to ensure manoeuvrability and even reversibility, to permit the redirection of activities and the redrawing of organisational boundaries when that becomes necessary.

Truly global operations imply a quantum reduction in time–space compression. Global production and marketing depend upon a massively enhanced 'presence-availability', and this has been made possible by new computer communications systems. On the basis of an electronic communications network, the global corporation organises its activities around a new space of information flows. Through the use of these new technologies, corporate activities are organised, not in terms of an aggregate of discrete functions, but rather in terms of a systemic continuum. Through this cybernetic aspiration, the 'network firm' strives to articulate the spatial and temporal co-ordinates of its operations. In this process, the decentred and deterritorialising corporation transposes a new and abstract electronic space across earlier physical and social geographies. Globalisation is realised through the creation of a new spatial stratum, a network topography, an electronic geography (Robins and Hepworth, 1988). The strategic nodes of these electronic grids are the financial centres and skyscraper fortresses of 'global cities' like New York, Tokyo and London. These world cities are the command and control centres of the global economy.

GLOBAL CULTURE

The historical development of capitalist economies has always had profound implications for cultures, identities and ways of life. The globalisation of economic activity is now associated with a further wave of cultural transformation, with a process of cultural globalisation. At one level, this is about the manufacture of universal cultural products – a process which has, of course, been developing for a long time. In the new cultural industries, there is a belief – to use Saatchi terminology – in 'world cultural convergence'; a belief in the convergence of lifestyle, culture and behaviour among consumer segments across the world. This faith in the emergence of a 'shared culture' and a common 'world awareness' appears to be vindicated by the success of products like *Dallas* or *Batman* and by such attractions as Disneyland. According to the president of Euro Disneyland, Disney's characters are universal. 'You try and convince an Italian child', he challenges, 'that Topolino – the Italian name for Mickey Mouse – is American' (Shamoon, 1989).

111

As in the wider economy, global standardisation in the cultural industries reflects, of course, the drive to achieve ever greater economies of scale. More precisely, it is about achieving both scale and scope economies by targeting the shared habits and tastes of particular market segments at the global level, rather than by marketing, on the basis of geographical proximity, to different national audiences. The global cultural industries are increasingly driven to recover their escalating costs over the maximum market base, over pan-regional and world markets. They are driven by the very same globalising logic that is reshaping the economy as a whole.

The new merchants of universal culture aspire to a borderless world. BSkyB beams out its products to a 'world without frontiers'; satellite footprints spill over the former integrity of national territories. With the globalisation of culture, the link between culture and territory becomes significantly broken. A representative of Cable News Network (CNN) describes the phenomenon:

> There has been a cultural and social revolution as a consequence of the globalisation of the economy. A blue-collar worker in America is affected as much as a party boss in Moscow or an executive in Tokyo. This means that what we do for America has validity outside America. Our news is global news.

(quoted in Fraser, 1989)

What is being created is a new electronic cultural space, a 'placeless' geography of image and simulation. The formation of this global hyperspace is reflected in that strand of postmodernist thinking associated particularly with writers like Baudrillard and Virilio. Baudrillard, for example, invokes the vertigo, the disorientation, the delirium created by a world of flows and images and screens. This new global arena of culture is a world of instantaneous and depthless communication, a world in which space and time horizons have become compressed and collapsed.

The creators of this universal cultural space are the new global cultural corporations. In an environment of enormous opportunities and escalating costs, what is clearer than ever before is the relation between size and power. What we are seeing in the cultural industries is a recognition of the advantages of scale, and in this sphere too, it is giving rise to an explosion of mergers, acquisitions and strategic alliances. The most dynamic actors are rapidly restructuring to ensure strategic control of a range of cultural products across world markets. The most prominent example of conglomerate activity is, no doubt, Rupert Murdoch's News Corporation, which has rapidly moved from its base in newspapers into the audiovisual sector. Through the acquisition of Fox Broadcasting, 20th Century Fox and Sky Channel, Murdoch has striven to become involved at all levels of production and distribution. The most symbolic example of a global media conglomerate, however, is Sony. From its original involvement in consumer electronic hardware, Sony has diversified into cultural software through the acquisitions of CBS and Columbia Pictures. The Sony-Columbia-CBS combination creates a communications giant, a 'total entertainment business', whose long-term strategy is to use this control over both hardware and software industries to dominate markets for the next generation of audiovisual products (Aksoy and Robins, 1992). What is prefigurative about both News Corporation and Sony is not simply their scale and reach, but also the fact that they aspire to be stateless, 'headless', decentred corporations. These global cultural industries understand the importance of achieving a real equidistance, or equipresence, of perspective in relation to the whole world of their audiences and consumers.

If the origination of world-standardised cultural products is one key strategy, the process of globalisation is more complex and diverse. In reality, it is not possible to eradicate or transcend difference. Here, too, the principle of equidistance prevails: the resourceful global conglomerate exploits local difference and particularity. Cultural products are assembled from all over the world and turned into commodities for a new 'cosmopolitan' marketplace: world music and tourism; ethnic arts, fashion and cuisine; Third World writing and cinema. The local and 'exotic' are torn out of place and time to be repackaged for the world bazaar. So-called world culture may reflect a new valuation of difference and particularity, but it is also very much about making a profit from it. Theodore Levitt (1983: 30–1) explains this globalisation of ethnicity. The global growth of ethnic markets, he suggests, is an example of the global standardisation of segments: 'Everywhere there is Chinese food, pitta bread, country and western music, pizza and jazz. The global pervasiveness of ethnic forms represents the cosmopolitanisation of speciality. Again, globalisation does not mean the end of segments. It means, instead, their expansion to worldwide proportions'. Now it is the turn of African music, Thai cuisine, Aboriginal painting and so on, to be absorbed into the world market and to become cosmopolitan specialities.

Jean-Hubert Martin's exhibition at the Pompidou Centre in 1989, *Magiciens de la Terre*, was an interesting and significant barometer in the world of high art of this new climate of cultural globalisation. In his exhibition, Martin assembled original works by one hundred artists from all over the world: from the major artistic centres of Europe and America, but also from the 'margins' of Haiti, Nepal, Zaire and Madagascar. Here the discourse of high art converged with that of ethnography, the work of the Euro-American avant-garde was contiguous with that of Third World 'primitives'. Martin's aim in developing this 'truly international exhibition of worldwide contemporary art' was to question the 'false distinction' between Western cultures and other cultures, to 'show the real difference and the specificity of the different cultures', and to 'create a dialogue' between Western and other cultures. *Magiciens de la Terre* brought 'world art' into being. Artistic texts and artifacts were pulled out of their original contexts and then reinserted and reinterpreted in a new global context. The global museum was a decentred space: Martin cultivated an 'equidistance of perspective' in which each exhibit, in equal dialogue with all the rest, was valued for its difference and specificity.

Was *Magiciens de la Terre* about something more than simply absorbing new products into the international art market? 'What is it', in the words of Coco Fusco, 'that makes ethnicity attractive and marketable at a particular moment such as ours?' (1989: 13). Why does it resonate so much with the times? At one level, the project was genuinely exciting and challenging. This kind of cosmopolitanism is to be preferred to parochialism and insularity. There was indeed an immediate pleasure and exhilaration in seeing such a juxtaposition of diverse and vibrant cultures. But the exhibition touched deeper and darker chords. In its preoccupation with 'magic' and the 'spirituality' of Third World art, *Magiciens de la Terre* sought to expose a certain emptiness, a spiritual vacuum, in Western culture. There was, of course, something very suspect and problematical about this Western idealisation of 'primitiveness' and 'purity', this romance of the 'Other'. The exhibition in no way confronted or handled this inadequacy. None the less, even if there was no resolution, the exhibition did pose important questions about the nature of cultural identity, and about its relation to 'Otherness'. How do we now define ourselves as Western? And how does this Western identity relate to 'Other', non-Western, identities in the world?

If the global collection and circulation of artistic products has been responsible for new kinds of encounter and collision between cultures, there have also been more direct and immediate exchanges and confrontations. The long history of colonialism and imperialism has brought large populations of migrants and refugees from the Third to the First World. Whereas Europe once addressed African and Asian cultures across vast distances, now that 'Other' has installed itself within the very heart of the Western metropolis. Through a kind of reverse invasion, the periphery has infiltrated the colonial core. The protective filters of time and space have disappeared, and the encounter with the 'alien' and 'exotic' is now instantaneous and immediate. The Western city has become a crucible in which world cultures are brought into direct contact. As Neil Ascherson argues,

> the history of immigration into Europe over the past quarter century may seem like the history of increasing restrictions and smaller quotas. Seen in fast forward, though, it is the opposite: the beginning

114

of a historic migration from the South into Europe which has gained
its first decisive bridgehead.

(1990: 17)

It is a migration that is shaking up the 'little white "Christian" Europe' of
the past. Through this irruption of empire, the certain and centred
perspective of the old colonial order is confounded and confused.

Time and distance no longer mediate the encounter with 'Other'
cultures. This drama of globalisation is symbolised perfectly in the collision
between Western 'liberalism' and Islamic 'fundamentalism' centred
around the Rushdie affair. How we do cope with the shock of confrontation? This is perhaps the key political agenda in this era of space–time
compression. One danger is that we retreat into fortified identities.
Another is that, in the anxious search for secure and stable identities,
we politicise those activities – religion, literature, philosophy – that should
not be *directly* political. The responsibility of Translation means learning
to listen to Others and learning to speak to, rather than for or about,
Others. That is easily said, of course, but not so easy to accomplish.
Hierarchical orders of identity will not quickly disappear. Indeed, the
very celebration and recognition of 'difference' and 'Otherness' may itself
conceal more subtle and insidious relations of power. When Martin turned
world art into a spectacle in *Magiciens de la Terre*, might this not simply
have represented a new and enhanced form of Western colonial appropriation and assimilation?

GLOBAL–LOCAL NEXUS

Globalisation is about the compression of time and space horizons and
the creation of a world of instantaneity and depthlessness. Global space
is a space of flows, an electronic space, a decentred space, a space in which
frontiers and boundaries have become permeable. Within this global
arena, economies and cultures are thrown into intense and immediate
contact with each other – with each 'Other' (an 'Other' that is no longer
simply 'out there', but also within).

We have argued that this is the force shaping our times. Many commentators, however, suggest that something quite different is happening: that
the new geographies are, in fact, about the renaissance of locality and
region (compare the work of the GLC in London and other metropolitan authorities in Britain in the mid-1980s, and similar strategies adopted
to 'regenerate' the economies of many American cities). There has been
a great surge of interest recently in local economies and local economic
strategies. The case for the local or regional economy as the key unit
of production has been forcefully made by the 'flexible specialisation'
thesis. Basing its arguments on the economic success of the 'Third Italy'

115

(see chapter 2), this perspective stresses the central and prefigurative importance of localised production complexes. Crucial to their success, it is suggested, are strong local institutions and infrastructures: relations of trust based on face-to-face contact; a 'productive community' historically rooted in a particular place; a strong sense of local pride and attachment.

In the cultural sphere, too, localism has come to play an important role. The 'struggle for place' is at the heart of much of the contemporary concern with urban regeneration and the built environment. Prince Charles' crusade on behalf of community architecture and classical revivalism is the most prominent and influential example. There is a strong sense that modernist planning was associated with universalising and abstract tendencies, whilst postmodernism is about drawing upon the sense of place, about revalidating and revitalising the local and the particular. A neo-Romantic fascination with traditional and vernacular motifs is supposedly about the re-enchantment of the city. This cultural localism reflects, in turn, deeper feelings about the inscription of human lives and identities in space and time. There is a growing interest in the embeddedness of life histories within the boundaries of place, and with the continuities of identity and community through local memory and heritage. Witness the enormous popularity of the Catherine Cookson heritage trail in South Tyneside, of 'a whole day of nostalgia' at Beamish in County Durham or of Wigan Pier's evocation of 'the way we were'. If modernity created an abstract and universal sense of self, then postmodernity will be about a sense of identity rooted in the particularity of place: 'it contains the possibility of a revived and creative human geography built around a newly informed synthesis of people and place' (Ley, 1989: 60).

Whilst globalisation may be the prevailing force of our times, this does not mean that localism is without significance. If we have emphasised processes of delocalisation, associated especially with the development of new information and communications networks, this should not be seen as an absolute tendency. The particularity of place and culture can never be done away with, can never be absolutely transcended. Globalisation is, in fact, also associated with new dynamics of *re*-localisation. It is about the achievement of a new global–local nexus, about new and intricate relations between global space and local space. Globalisation is like putting together a jigsaw puzzle: it is a matter of inserting a multiplicity of localities into the overall picture of a new global system.

We should not idealise the local, however. We should not invest our hopes for the future in the redemptive qualities of local economies, local cultures, local identities. It is important to see the local as a relational, and relative, concept. If once it was significant in relation to the national sphere, now its meaning is being recast in the context of globalisation. For the global corporation, the global–local nexus is of key and strategic importance. According to Olivetti's Carlo de Benedetti, 'in the face of ever higher development costs, *globalisation* is the only possible answer'. 'Marketers', he continues, 'must sell the latest product everywhere at once – and that means producing *locally*' (quoted in Scobie, 1988). Similarly, the mighty Sony describes its operational strategy as 'global localisation'. NBC's vice-president, J. B. Holston III, is also resolutely 'for localism', and recognises that globalisation is 'not just about putting factories into countries, it's being part of that culture too' (quoted in Brown, 1989).

What is being acknowledged is that globalisation entails a corporate presence in, and understanding of, the 'local' arena. But the 'local' in this sense does not correspond to any specific territorial configuration. The global–local nexus is about the relation between globalising and particularising dynamics in the strategy of the global corporation, and the 'local' should be seen as a fluid and relational space, constituted only in and through its relation to the global. For the global corporation, the local might, in fact, correspond to a regional, national or even pan-regional sphere of activity.

This is to say that the 'local' should not be mistaken for the 'locality'. It is to emphasise that the global–local nexus does not create a privileged new role for the locality in the world economic arena. Of course local economies continue to matter. That is not the issue. We should, however, treat claims about new capacities for local autonomy and 'proactivity' with scepticism. If it is indeed the case that localities do now increasingly by-pass the national state to deal directly with global corporations, world bodies or foreign governments, they do not do so on equal terms. Whether it is to attract a new car factory or the Olympic Games, they go as supplicants. And, even as supplicants, they go in competition with one another: cities and localities are now fiercely struggling against each other to attract footloose and predatory investors to their particular patch. Of course, some localities are able successfully to 'switch' themselves in to the global networks, but others will remain 'unswitched' or even 'unplugged'. In a world characterised by the increasing mobility of capital and the rapid recycling of space, even those that manage to become connected in to the global system are always vulnerable to the abrupt withdrawal of investment and to disconnection from the global system.

What is more, the global–local nexus is not straightforwardly about a renaissance of local cultures. There are those who argue that the old and rigid hegemony of national cultures is now being eroded from below by burgeoning local and regional cultures. Modern times are characterised, it is suggested, by a process of cultural decentralisation and by the sudden resurgence of place-bound traditions, languages and ways of life. It is important not to devalue the perceived and felt vitality of local cultures and identities. But again, their significance can only be understood in the

117

context of a broader and encompassing process. Local cultures are over-shadowed by an emerging 'world culture' – and still, of course, by resilient national and nationalist cultures.

It may well be that, in some cases, the new global context is recreating sense of place and sense of community in very positive ways, giving rise to an energetic cosmopolitanism in certain localities. In others, however, local fragmentation may inspire a nostalgic, introverted and parochial sense of local attachment and identity. If globalisation recontextualises and reinterprets cultural localism, it does so in ways that are equivocal and ambiguous.

It is in the context of this global–local nexus that we can begin to understand the nature and significance of the enterprise and heritage cultures that have been developing in Britain over the past decade or so. We want now to explore two particular aspects of contemporary cultural transformation (each in its different way centred around the relationship between Tradition and Translation).

ON NOT NEEDING AND NEEDING ANDY CAPP

Why discuss enterprise and heritage together? Is there really any connection between the modernising ambitions of enterprise culture and the retrospective nostalgia of heritage culture? The argument put forward in this section is that there is in fact a close and necessary relation between them. The nature of this relationship becomes clear, we suggest, when we see that each has developed as a response to the forces of globalisation. Insight into this relational logic then helps us to understand the neurotic ambivalence that is, we believe, at the heart of contemporary cultural transformation.

Enterprise culture is about responding to the new global conditions of accumulation. British capital must adapt to the new forms of global competition and learn to function in world markets. It must pursue strategic alliances and joint ventures with leading firms in Europe, North America and Japan. In all key sectors – from pharmaceuticals to telecommunications, from automobiles to financial services – 'national champions' are being replaced by new flexible transnationals. In the cause of global efficiency, it is necessary to repudiate the old 'geography-driven' and home-centred ethos, and to conform to the new logic of placelessness and equidistance of perspective. The broadcasting industries are a good example. In the new climate, it is no longer viable to make programmes for British audiences alone. One way to understand the debate around 'public service versus the market' is in terms of the displacement of nationally centred broadcasting services by a new generation of audiovisual corporations operating in European and global markets. As the 1988 White Paper on broadcasting made clear, television is 'becoming an increasingly international medium' centred around 'international trade in ideas, cultures and experiences' (Home Office, 1988: 42). The consequence of these developments, across all sectors, is that the particularity of British identity is de-emphasised. In a world in which it is necessary to be 'local' everywhere – to be 'multidomestic' – certain older forms of national identity can actually be a liability. The logic of enterprise culture essentially pushes towards the 'modernisation' of national culture. Indeed it is frequently driven by an explicit and virulent disdain for particular aspects of British culture and traditions. This scorn is directed against what the self-styled 'department for Enterprise' calls 'the past anti-enterprise bias of British culture'. The spirit of enterprise is about eradicating what has been called the 'British disease': the 'pseudo-aristocratic' snobbery that has allegedly devalued entrepreneurial skills and technological prowess, and which has always undermined Britain's competitive position in world trade (see Robins and Webster, 1989, ch. 5).

If enterprise culture aims to refurbish and refine culture and identity, there are, however, countervailing forces at work. Globalisation is also underpinned by a quite contrary logic of development. As Scott Lash and John Urry argue, the enhanced mobility of transnational corporations across the world is, in fact, associated with an increased sensitivity to even quite small differences in the endowments of particular locations. 'The effect of heightened spatial indifference', they suggest, 'has profound effects upon particular places . . . contemporary developments may well be heightening the salience of localities' (Lash and Urry, 1987: 101–2). As global corporations scan the world for preferential locations, so are particular places forced into a competitive race to attract inward investors. Cities and localities must actively promote and advertise their attractions. What has been called the 'new urbanity' (Häussermann and Siebel, 1987) is very much about enhancing the profile and image of places in a new global context. It is necessary to emphasise the national or regional distinctiveness of a location. As Margit Mayer (1989: 12–13) points out, 'endogenous potentials' come to be cultivated: 'cities have come to emphasise, exploit and even produce (cultural and natural) local specificity and assets. . . . In this process, place-specific differences have become a tool in the competition over positional advantages'. In this process, local, regional or national cultures and heritage will be exploited to enhance the distinctive qualities of a city or locality. Tradition and heritage are factors that enhance the 'quality of life' of particular places and make them attractive locations for investment. An emphasis on tradition and heritage is also, of course, important in the development of tourism as a major industry. Here, too, there is a premium on difference and particularity. In a world where differences are being erased, the commodification of place is about creating distinct place-identities in the eyes of global tourists. Even in the most disadvantaged places, heritage, or the simulacrum of

119

heritage, can be mobilised to gain competitive advantage in the race between places. When Bradford's tourist officer, for example, talks about 'creating a product' – weekend holidays based around the themes of 'Industrial Heritage' and 'In the Steps of the Brontes' – he is underlining the importance of place-making in placeless times, the heightened importance of distinction in a world where differences are being effaced (see Page, 1986).

In the new global arena, it is necessary, then, simultaneously to minimise and maximise traditional cultural forms. The North East of England provides a good example of how these contradictory dynamics of enterprise and heritage are developing. In this part of the country, it is over the symbolic body of Andy Capp that the two logics contest. 'Andy Capp is dead – Newcastle is alive' (Whelan, 1989) – that is the message of enterprise. The region no longer has a place for Andy or for other cloth-capped local heroes like the late Tyneside comedian, Bobby Thompson. 'The real Northerner is no relation to Bobby or Andy', local celebrity Brendan Foster tells us. The 'Great North' promotional campaign put great emphasis on 'enterprise' and 'opportunity' and tried to play down the heritage of the region's old industrial, and later deindustrialised, past. At the end of the 1980s, Newcastle City Council employed the advertising agency, J. Walter Thompson, to change the city's image and to get rid of the old cloth-cap image once and for all. In order to position itself in the new global context, the region feels it must 're-image' and, ultimately, reimagine itself. The increasing Japanese presence in the region has become a key factor in this strategic identity switch. Japan is the very symbol of enterprise culture; Japan is the key to constructing the new model Geordie. The region's history is now being reassessed to emphasise the special relationship between Japan and the North East. We are told that the North East aided Japan's progress towards modernisation in the late nineteenth and early twentieth centuries, whilst today Japanese investment is contributing to the revitalisation of a region that followed a very different course in the post-war period (Conte-Helm, 1989). We must, it is stressed, adapt to changing times.

If the spirit of enterprise wants to kill off Andy Capp, there is, however, a counter-spirit that keeps him alive. The region's industrial past is its burden, but it is also its inheritance. It is clear that history can be made to pay. Beamish, The Land of the Prince Bishops, Roman Northumberland and Catherine Cookson Country are all heritage assets that can be exploited to attract tourists and investors alike. But if heritage is to be marketed, it becomes difficult to avoid the reality that the North East was once a region of heavy engineering, ship-building and coal mining. And around these industries there developed a rich working-class culture. For many in the region, the conservation of local culture and traditions is extremely important. The photographic work of Newcastle's Side Gallery, and also the productions of film workshops like Amber and Trade, have paid great attention to working-class heritage. The work of writers which include Jack Common, Sid Chaplin or Tom Hadaway has also contributed to the creation of a distinctive identity for the region (Pickering and Robins, 1984; 1989). Footballer Jackie Milburn is another powerful symbol of working-class heritage. So too is the 'little waster', Bobby Thompson, whom Brendan Foster sees as so much the embodiment of the Andy Capp myth. It is a strangely irrepressible image, and it is also in many ways an affirmative one. The gritty and anarchic humour of Andy and Bobby distinguishes the region, gives it a positive sense of difference.

Our objective is not to enter into a detailed account of enterprise and heritage cultures in the North East of England, but rather to emphasise how the region's new global orientation is pulling its cultural identity in quite contradictory directions: it involves at once the devaluation and the valorisation of tradition and heritage. There is an extreme ambivalence about the past. Working-class traditions are seen, just like 'pseudo-aristocratic values', as symptoms of the 'British disease', and as inimical to a 'post-industrial' enterprise ethos. But tradition and heritage are also things that entrepreneurs can exploit: they are 'products'. And they also have human meaning and significance that cannot easily be erased. At the heart of contemporary British culture is the problem of articulating national past and global future.

THE BURDEN OF IDENTITY

We want, finally, to return to the question of what postmodern geographies might imply for the question of empire. Postmodernism, as Todd Gitlin argues, should be understood as 'a general orientation, as a way of apprehending or experiencing the world and our place, or placelessness, in it' (1989: 101). Globalisation is profoundly transforming our apprehension of the world: it is provoking a new experience of orientation and disorientation, new senses of placed and placeless identity. The global–local nexus is associated with new relations between space and place, fixity and mobility, centre and periphery, 'real' and 'virtual' space, 'inside' and 'outside', frontier and territory. This, inevitably, has implications for both individual and collective identities and for the meaning and coherence of community. Peter Emberley describes a momentous shift from a world of stable and continuous reference points to one where 'the notions of space as enclosure and time as duration are unsettled and redesigned as a field of infinitely experimental configurations of space-time'. In this new 'hyperreality', he suggests, 'the old order of prescriptive and exclusive places and meaning-endowed durations is dissolving' and we are consequently faced with the challenge of elaborating 'a new self-interpretation' (Emberley, 1989: 755–6, 748).

It is in this context that both enterprise and heritage cultures assume their significance. Older certainties and hierarchies of British identity have been called into question in a world of dissolving boundaries and disrupted continuities. In a country that is now a container of African and Asian cultures, the sense of what it is to be British can never again have the old confidence and surety. Other sources of identity are no less fragile. What does it mean to be European in a continent coloured not only by the cultures of its former colonies, but also by American and now Japanese cultures? Is not the very category of identity itself problematical? Is it at all possible, in global times, to regain a coherent and integral sense of identity? Continuity and historicity of identity are challenged by the immediacy and intensity of global cultural confrontations. The comforts of Tradition are fundamentally challenged by the imperative to forge a new self-interpretation based upon the responsibilities of cultural Translation.

Neither enterprise nor heritage culture really confronts these responsibilities. Both represent protective strategies of response to global forces, centred around the conservation, rather than reinterpretation, of identities. The driving imperative is to salvage centred, bounded and coherent identities – placed identities for placeless times. This may take the form of the resuscitated patriotism and jingoism that we see in a resurgent Little Englandism. Alternatively, as we have already suggested, it may take a more progressive form in the cultivation of local and regional identities or in the project to construct a continental European identity. In each case, however, it is about the maintenance of protective illusion, about the struggle for wholeness and coherence through continuity. At the heart of this romantic aspiration is what Richard Sennett, in another context, calls the search for purity and purified identity. 'The effect of this defensive pattern', he argues, 'is to create in people a desire for a purification of the terms in which they see themselves in relation to others. The enterprise involved is an attempt to build an image or identity that coheres, is unified, and filters out threats in social experience' (Sennett, 1971: 15). Purified identities are constructed through the purification of space, through the maintenance of territorial boundaries and frontiers. We can talk of 'a geography of rejection which appears to correspond to the purity of antagonistic communities' (Sibley, 1988: 410). Purified identities are also at the heart of empire. Purification aims to secure both protection from, and positional superiority over, the external Other. Anxiety and power feed off each other. As William Connolly argues

> When you remain within the established field of identity and difference, you become a bearer of strategies to protect identity through devaluation of the other; but if you transcend the field of identities through which the other is constituted, you lose the identity

and standing needed to communicate with those you sought to inform. Identity and difference are bound together. It is impossible to reconstitute the relation to the second without confounding the experience of the first.

(1989: 329)

To question empire, then, is to call into question the very logic of identity itself. In this context, it is not difficult to understand the anxious and defensive efforts now being devoted to reinforce and buttress 'traditional' cultural identities.

Is it, then, possible to break this logic of identity? How do we begin to confront the challenge of postmodern geographies and the urgent question of cultural Translation? British enterprise and heritage cultures are inscribed in what Ian Buruma has called the 'antipolitical world of Heimat-seeking' (1989: 43). Against this ideal of Heimat, however, another powerful motif of the contemporary world should be counterposed. It is in the experience of diaspora that we may begin to understand the way beyond empire. In the experience of migration, difference is confronted: boundaries are crossed; cultures are mingled; identities become blurred. The diaspora experience, Stuart Hall argues, is about 'unsettling, recombination, hybridisation and "cut-and-mix"' and carries with it a transformed relation to Tradition, one in which 'there can be no simple "return" [to] or "recovery" of the ancestral past which is not re-experienced through the categories of the present' (1988: 30). The experience of diaspora, and also of exile, as Edward Said has powerfully argued, allows us to understand relations between cultures in new ways. The crossing of boundaries brings about a complexity of vision and also a sense of the permeability and contingency of cultures. It allows us 'to see others not as ontologically given but as historically constituted' and can, thereby, 'erode the exclusivist biases we so often ascribe to cultures, our own not least' (Said, 1989: 225).

The experience of diaspora and exile is extreme, but, in the context of increasing cultural globalisation, it is prefigurative, whilst the quest for Heimat is now regressive and restrictive. The notion of distinct, separate and 'authentic' cultures is increasingly problematical. A culture, as Eric Wolf argues, is 'better seen as a series of processes that construct, reconstruct, and dismantle cultural materials'; 'the concept of a fixed, unitary and bounded culture must give way to a sense of the fluidity and permeability of cultural sets' (1982: 387). Out of this context are emerging new forms of global culture. There is, to take but one example, a new cosmopolitanism in the field of literature. Writers like Isabel Allende, Salman Rushdie or Mario Vargas Llosa are recording 'the global juxtapositions that have begun to force their way even into private experience', 'capturing a new world reality that has a definite social basis in

123

immigration and international communications' (Brennan, 1989: 4, 9). For Rushdie these literary exiles, migrants or expatriates are 'at one and the same time insiders and outsiders', offering 'stereoscopic vision' in place of 'whole sight' (1982: 19).

The point is not at all to idealise this new cosmopolitanism (the Rushdie affair is eloquent testimony to its limits and to the real and profound difficulties of cultural Translation). It is, rather, to emphasise the profound insularity of enterprise and heritage cultures and to question the relevance of their different strategies to re-enchant the nation. As Dick Hebdige emphasises, everybody is now 'more or less cosmopolitan'; '"mundane" cosmopolitanism is part of "ordinary" experience' (1990: 20). If it is possible, then it is no longer meaningful, to hold on to older senses of identity and continuity. In these rapidly changing times, Hanif Kureishi writes, the British have to change: 'It is the British, the white British, who have to learn that being British isn't what it was. Now it is a more complex thing, involving new elements' (1989: 29).

The argument of this chapter has been that the emergence of enterprise and heritage cultures has not been a matter of the purely endogenous evolution of British culture, but rather a response to the forces of globalisation. If, however, over the past decade or so, both of these cultural developments have been provoked and shaped by those forces, neither has been open to them. The question is whether we will continue to insulate ourselves with protective and narcissistic illusions, or whether, in the new global arena, we can really find 'a new way of being British'.

7

UNDER WESTERN EYES
Media, empire and Otherness

The helicopter landed with the body in a metal casket, which revolutionary guards carried on their shoulders a short distance to the grave. But then the crowd surged again, weeping men in bloody headbands, and they scaled the barriers and overran the gravesite.

The voice said, Wailing chanting mourners. It said, Throwing themselves into the hole.

Karen could not imagine who else was watching this. It could not be real if others watched. If other people watched, if millions watched, if these millions matched the number on the Iranian plain, doesn't it mean we share something with the mourners, know an anguish, feel something pass between us, hear the sigh of some historic grief? . . . If others saw these pictures, why is nothing changed, where are the local crowds, why do we still have names and addresses and car keys?

(Don DeLillo, *Mao II*)

Already by action we maintain a living relationship with a real object; we grasp it, we conceive it. The image neutralises this real relationship, this primary conceiving through action.

(Emmanuel Levinas, 1983)

MEDIA IMPERIALISM

One of the distinguishing characteristics of the present period is the role played by improved systems of physical transportation and by various forms of symbolic communication in linking the different parts of the world together. It has been observed that the role of geographical distance in human affairs is much diminished (Meyrowitz, 1985), and that 'time–space compression' is constitutive of our supposedly postmodern condition (Jameson, 1985; Harvey, 1989). These might be seen as no more than extrapolations of Marshall McLuhan's well-worn adage about the contribution of communications media to the construction of a 'global village'. However, as many of McLuhan's critics have emphasised, this is no mere technological phenomenon, not least in so far as the media technologies in question have a very particular (Western or Euro-American) point of origin and are controlled by identifiable interests (Walt Disney, News Corporation, Berlusconi, Time Warner, Bertelsmann or whatever), engendering a largely one-way 'conversation', in which the West speaks and the Rest listen.

All of this clearly points to the need to pay close attention to the role of the media in this process of cultural encounter. How are we to understand this influence of the media? Within media studies, there is a long-standing tradition which has addressed the issue in terms of 'media imperialism'. In the work of, for example, Armand Mattelart *et al.* (1984), Herbert Schiller (1969) and Jeremy Tunstall (1977), there has been considerable analysis of the cultural consequences of the West's long-exercised control over the world's media systems. The flaw in this body of work, however, has been in its reliance on a simplistic 'hypodermic' model of media effects – a model, long discredited within the mainstream of media studies, in which it is assumed that media products have direct and necessary cultural 'effects' on those who consume them. This is not to fall prey to any kind of foolish presumption that the media do not exercise profound forms of cultural influence, but it is to insist that the ways in which they have influence over their audiences are rather more complex than any hypodermic model can allow (Morley, 1992), and it is to insist that, in analysing the implication of the media for transcultural encounters, we must adequately deal with that complexity.

We referred earlier (see chapter 3) to the debates which went on throughout the 1980s over the almost global popularity of the American television series *Dallas*. As we noted, by the mid-1980s *Dallas* had become the privileged hate symbol for all those who saw the worldwide popularity of the programme as an indication of the growing threat to the variety of world cultures that was posed by American dominance over the world's media industries.

The problem with this argument, or assertion, is that all the subsequent audience research on the consumption of *Dallas*, in different cultural contexts, far from demonstrating any automatic 'media effects', has tended, rather, to demonstrate that viewers from different cultural backgrounds 'read' the programme in quite different ways, depending on their own cultural contexts. Thus, Ien Ang (1985) demonstrates how many Dutch women interpreted the programme ironically, through the grid of their own feminist agenda. Eric Michaels (1988) showed how Australian Aboriginals reinterpreted *Dallas* through their particular conceptions of kinship so as to produce quite different readings from those intended by the programme's makers. And, most exhaustively, Tamara Liebes and

126

Elihu Katz (1991) have demonstrated the ways in which viewers from American, Russian, North African and Japanese backgrounds came to see quite different things in the programme and took quite different 'messages' from their encounter with *Dallas*. However, against this, Gripsrud (forthcoming) makes the important point that, while these ethnographic findings concerning varieties of reception in different contexts are of considerable interest (as counter-evidence to any simple-minded theory of 'hypodermic' media effects), we would be foolish to conclude that the continuing world dominance of the Hollywood film and television production base is therefore of no consequence.

Certainly, one should not overestimate the freedom of the media consumer to make whatever he or she likes of the material transmitted. Even if they could, their choice of materials to reinterpret would still be limited to the 'menu' constructed by powerful media organisations. Moreover, such programmes are usually made in such a way as to 'prefer' one reading over another (Hall, 1981) and to invite the viewer to 'take' the message in some particular way, even if such a 'reading' can never be guaranteed. Clearly, we should not respond to the deficiencies in the hypodermic model of media effects by romanticising the consumption process and cheerfully celebrating the 'active' viewer as a kind of semiotic guerrilla, continuously waging war on the structures of textual power (Curran, 1990). We must balance an acceptance that audiences are in certain respects active in their choice, consumption and interpretation of media texts, with a recognition of how that activity is framed and limited, in its different modalities and varieties, by the dynamics of cultural power.

Equally, we should not fall into any technologically determinist argument. Even if media technologies have, historically, been developed and controlled by the powerful countries of the West, they are, none the less, always capable of being appropriated and used in other ways than those for which they were intended. Eliut Flores (1988), for example, describes how expatriate Puerto Rican families in New York use video conferencing facilities (designed for business applications) during evenings and weekends, when rates are low, to substitute for an air trip 'home'. Similarly, Stephen Greenblatt describes certain uses of modern video technology in Bali in which the technology is in effect incorporated into traditional rituals, to the extent that it is unclear who is assimilating whom in the process through which the villagers incorporate a sophisticated version of international capitalism's representational machinery into their own patterns of activity. We should resist a priori ideological determinism, he argues, and recognise that cultures have 'fantastically powerful assimilative mechanisms . . . that work like enzymes to change the ideological composition of foreign bodies'. In this example, video technology is by no means 'unequivocally and irreversibly the bearer of the capitalist ideology that was the determining condition of [its] . . . creation'

127

(Greenblatt, 1992: 4). In a similar vein, Daniel Miller (1992), one of the few anthropologists who has offered any direct analysis of processes of media consumption, in an analysis of the viewing of the American series *The Young and the Restless* in Trinidad, helpfully offers the concept of 'indigenisation' (on the model of digestion, incorporation and assimilation) as a way of understanding how 'local' cultures are continually refashioned out of elements initially produced elsewhere. Criticising the traditional model in which authentic local cultures are seen as being invaded by 'foreign' and 'corrupting' influences, Miller suggests we should accept an alternative approach in which 'authenticity' is defined a posteriori, as a matter of local consequences rather than of local (or 'foreign') origins.

So far, we have been concerned principally with debates about the consequences of Western media for other cultures. In addressing this issue, we have kept to the terms of a fairly conventional model of communications, which many authors (for example, Baudrillard, 1988b; Harvey, 1989) would argue is, in fact, inadequate to our present situation. In their view, the condition of so-called 'postmodernity' is in fact characterised by a new ordering of experience and the creation of a new sense of place, a complex process in which the media play a particularly vital role.

CULTURE, GEOGRAPHY AND MEDIA

The central issue here concerns the effects of modern media in constructing new geographies. Already apparent in some of the examples we have given is the fact that the media have consequences for the way we imagine space and place. Doreen Massey (1991a) has argued that places themselves should no longer be seen as internally homogeneous, bounded areas, but as 'spaces of interaction' in which local identities are constructed out of resources (both material and symbolic) which may well not be at all local in their origin, but are none the less 'authentic' for all that.

In an anthropological context, James Clifford (1992) takes up the same issue, noting that 'villages', inhabited by 'natives' and conceived as bounded sites of residence which stand as metonyms for a whole culture, have long been the focus of anthropological fieldwork. Against this traditional preoccupation of anthropology, however, he emphasises that cultures are not 'in' places in any simple sense. The focus on 'rooted', 'authentic' or 'native' culture and experience fails to address 'the wider world of intercultural import-export in which the ethnographic encounter is always already enmeshed'. Clifford supports Arjun Appadurai's contention that 'natives, people confined to and by the places to which they belong, groups unsullied by contact with a larger world, have probably never existed' (Appadurai, 1988: 39). We should work, Clifford argues, not only with a model of eccentric natives, conceived in their multiple external connections, but with a notion of places as sites of travel encounters as much as sites of residence. Clifford suggests that we should be attentive to 'a culture's farthest range of travel, while *also* looking at its centres; to the ways in which groups negotiate themselves in external as much as internal relations; to the fact that culture is also a site of travel for others and that one group's core is another's periphery'. This is to argue for a multi-locale ethnography of both 'travelling-in-dwelling' and 'dwelling-in-travelling', when it comes to those 'permanently installed in the wanderground between here and there', those facing the question not so much of where they are from, as of where they are between (Clifford, 1992: 107–9). Clifford's arguments are well supported by those of Gupta and Ferguson (1992), who argue that 'people have undoubtedly always been more mobile and identities less fixed than the static and typologising approaches of classical anthropology would suggest', not least because that conventional anthropological approach allowed the 'power of topography to conceal successfully the topography of power' (ibid.: 8–9).

Eric Wolf makes the fundamental criticism that, on the whole, the 'concept of the autonomous, self-regulating and self-justifying society and culture has trapped anthropology inside the bounds of its own definitions' (1982: 18). His point is that the methodological tail of anthropology's commitment to 'fieldwork' has too much wagged the discipline's theoretical dog, in terms of the basic model of what constitutes a 'society' or a 'culture'. As 'fieldwork' has become a hallmark of anthropological method, heuristic considerations have often been improperly converted into theoretical postulates about society and culture. As Wolf argues, 'limitations of time and energy in the field dictate limitations in the number and locations of possible observations and interviews, demanding concentration of effort on an observable place and on a corps of specifiable informants' (ibid.: 13–14) – which is then treated relatively unproblematically as a metonym of the larger 'society' or 'culture' being studied. As far as he is concerned, the problem with the study of the 'living cultures' of specified populations in 'locally delimited habitats' is that the model wrongly presumes an a priori closure in its conception of its unit of study. In the context of centuries of imperialism and cross-cultural contact, we would do better to think of human societies as open systems 'inextricably involved with other aggregates, near and far, in weblike, netlike connections' (Alexander Lesser, quoted in ibid.: 19).

The conventional model of cultural exchange, then, presumes the existence of a pure, internally homogeneous, authentic, indigenous culture which becomes subverted or corrupted by foreign influences. The reality, however, is that every culture has, in fact, ingested foreign elements from exogenous sources, with the various elements gradually becoming 'naturalised' within it. As Said argues, 'the notion that there are geographical spaces with indigenous, radically "different" inhabitants who can be defined on the basis of some religion, culture or racial essence, proper to that geographical space is a highly debatable idea' (quoted in Clifford, 1988: 274). As argued earlier (cf. Appadurai, 1990; Bhabha, 1987; Hall, 1987), cultural hybridity is, increasingly, the normal state of affairs in the world, and in this context, any attempt to defend the integrity of indigenous or authentic cultures easily slips into the conservative defence of a nostalgic vision of the past.

Let us consider more carefully how the media are implicated in this transformation of both real and imaginative geographies. At its simplest, the point was well expressed some sixty years ago by the art historian Rudolf Arnheim, who speculated that the principal social consequences of television followed from the fact that it is 'related to the motor car and the aeroplane – as a means of transport for the mind'; as such, it 'renders the object on display independent of its port of origin, making it unnecessary for spectators to flock together in front of an original' (quoted in Rath, 1985: 199). If, in days of old, explorers and anthropologists set off on long journeys into the unknown to bring us back written accounts of the strange customs of exotic Others in distant places, today we are all ethnographers to the extent that all kinds of Others are exposed to our gaze (nightly on the regular television news and hourly on CNN) in the form of electronic representation on the television screens in our own living rooms. These days we have only to sit on the couch and press a button to behold the Other or the Exotic.

As early as 1946, Max Read recognised how media technologies can shape our perceptions of social reality:

> The radio not only reports history, it seems to make it. The world seems to originate from the radio. People still see things and events, but they become real only after the radio has reported the event and the newspaper has run a picture of it. The radio apperceives, registers and judges for people. Our souls are immediately connected to the radio and no longer to our own sensory organs. People no longer have an inner history, an inner continuity, the radio today is our history, it validates our existence.
>
> (quoted in Kaes, 1989: 197)

In a classic article, Donald Horton and Richard Wohl argued that through the new mass media, remote people are met 'as if they were in the circle of one's peers' in a 'seeming face-to-face relationship', a 'simulacrum of conversational give and take which may be called para-social interaction' (1956: 215). In a more recent extension of this perspective, the German psychoanalyst Claus-Dieter Rath (1985: 203) has argued that, increasingly, we all live within a 'television geography', where what counts is the space of electronic transmission, which often cuts across national borders, as we view television representations of 'planetary affairs which we face privately in our cosy living rooms' (Rath, 1989: 88). On occasion, these televisual forms of para-social contact can be celebratory – sometimes literally, as when a recent papal ruling concluded that, for the sick and the ill who are unable to go to church, the celebration of mass 'live', through television, was valid (though it was not if recorded and time-shifted on video because of the consequent loss of 'immediacy'). At other times, the contact may be felt to be intrusive, as was the case with the American television series *Julia*, one of the first to show black people in leading roles on prime-time American television, where the producers received a number of irate letters from white viewers, complaining that, having succeeded in physically keeping blacks out of their neighbourhoods, they did not want to come home and find them 'invading' their living rooms through the television screen (Bodroghkozy, 1992).

On occasion, even trauma can be transmitted through this para-social kind of interaction. In 1990, in response to claims made by relatives of those who died in the televised tragedy at Hillsborough football ground, the Liverpool High Court ruled that people who suffer psychological illness after watching live television coverage of tragedies involving close relatives are eligible to claim damages in the same way as those witnessing the events *in situ* (*The Guardian*, 1 August 1990). Indeed, the judge pointed out that a television watcher might be even more traumatised, by virtue of the camera's ability to bring into sharp focus events that might not be as clear to an observer of the real event. The point is that television,

> allows us to share the literal time of persons who are elsewhere. It grants us . . . *instantaneous* ubiquity. The telespectator of a lunar landing becomes a vicarious astronaut, exploring the moonscape at the same time . . . as the astronauts themselves. The viewer of a live transmission, in fact, can in some respects see better than those immediately on the scene.
>
> (Stam, 1983: 24)

In this respect television 'transforms us into "armchair imperialists"; through its all encompassing viewpoint, we become "audio-visual masters of the world"' (ibid.: 25).

This is a situation rife with its own ironies. *The Guardian*'s Southern Africa correspondent, David Beresford, offers a telling account of the transformed meaning of 'being there' geographically, in relation to news events in the contemporary media environment, on the occasion of his own attempt to report Nelson Mandela's speech on his release from prison in April 1990. For Beresford, being physically 'on the spot', but merely one of hundreds of reporters, jostling for position, unfortunately entailed

131

being unable either to see or hear Mr Mandela. Beresford recounts this as an experience of both 'being there and not being there', where being the 'man on the spot' had the perverse effect of making him unable to witness the images and hear the words being clearly relayed, via the well-positioned television cameras, to the global audience at home.

In a similar vein, Joshua Meyrowitz has offered a fascinating analysis of the impact of electronic media on social behaviour, in transforming the 'situational geography of human life'. Meyrowitz's concern is for the way in which electronic media have undermined the traditional relationship between physical setting and social situation to the extent that we are 'no longer "in" places in quite the same way' we once were, or thought we were (1989: 333). The media, he argues, make us 'audiences to performances that happen in other places and give us access to audiences who are not physically present' (1985: 7). Meyrowitz's central contention is that these new media redefine notions of social 'position' and 'place', divorcing experience from physical location. Thus, 'Live Aid was an event that took place nowhere but on television' (1989: 329), the ultimate example of the freeing of communications experience from social and physical constraints. The electronic media have transformed the relative significance of live and mediated encounters, bringing 'information and experience to everyplace from everyplace' as state funerals, wars or space flights become 'dramas that can be played on the stage of almost anyone's living room' (1985: 118).

In this way, the media create new 'communities' across their spaces of transmission, bringing together otherwise disparate groups around the common experience of television, and bringing about a cultural mixing of here and there. Television thereby becomes the basis of common experiences and interactions: 'to watch television is to look into the common experience and to see what others are watching' (ibid.: 145–7). Thus, the millions who watched the assassination of Kennedy

> were in a 'place' that is no place at all . . . the millions of Americans who watch television every evening . . . are in a 'location' that is not defined by walls, streets or neighbourhoods but by evanescent 'experience' . . . more and more, people are living in a national [or international] information-system rather than in a local town or city.
> (ibid.: 146)

It is in this sense that the electronic media are transforming our sense of locality and relocating us in terms of the 'generalised elsewhere' of distant places and 'non-local' people. As Lidia Curti puts it:

> In every country the media pose the problem of the shifting boundaries between the national and the foreign, otherness and sameness, repetition and difference. Italia TV shows sharply how different

132

countries mingle and blend on the national screen, in a flow of fictions . . . it highlights how *Dallas* is naturalised in . . . Naples, how California-ness can become part of the imaginary of a Southern Italian housewife, how the proximity of a poor Roman 'bargata' to a petty bourgeois household in Rio, to a mansion in Denver, Colorado is made acceptable and plausible, by its appearing on the same flat screen in the same household in close succession.

(1988: 16–17)

Through the electronic media we have seen the construction of a new experience of virtual space and place and of virtual community. It is with virtual reality that we now have to come to terms. As Christopher Coker has suggested, 'the impact of television lies not at the level of opinion and concepts, but [at the level of] "sense ratios" and patterns of perception. A profound structural change in the world has been brought about in human relations in terms of scale, models and habits' (1992: 197).

LIVING IN A MEDIATED WORLD

The media now make us all rather like anthropologists, in our own living rooms, surveying the world of all those 'Others' who are represented to us on the screen. Edward Said (1978) has argued against any comforting notion that technically improved communications media will necessarily improve inter-cultural relations, claiming that the media have, if anything, increased regressive tendencies. Indeed, he goes on, one aspect of the electronic postmodern world is that there has been a reinforcement of the stereotypes by which the Orient is viewed: 'So far as the Orient is concerned, standardisation and cultural stereotyping have intensified the hold of the nineteenth-century academic and imaginative demonology of the "mysterious Orient"' (ibid.: 26).

Seeing by way of the media may even be an obstacle to understanding. Paul Hartmann and Charles Husband (1972) long ago offered good evidence that, largely as a result of media images of black people, racism in Britain is strongest in areas where white people have less day-to-day contact with them and are thus more dependent on media images for their knowledge of blacks (indeed, largely as a result of media obsessions with 'numbers' in debates about race, the average white person overestimates the number of black people in Britain by a factor of ten).

We are all largely dependent on the media for our images of non-local people, places and events, and the further the 'event' from our own direct experience, the more we depend on media images for the totality of our knowledge. It is at this point that the question of media representations of Otherness relates directly to the growing debate within anthropology concerning the ethics of anthropological depictions of the Other. In the

133

light of the contributions of Clifford and Marcus (1986), Marcus and Fischer (1986) and Said (1978), many anthropologists have begun to address the Foucauldian version of the question of representation – as always involving a relation of power, as well as a relation of knowledge, between representer and represented (whether or not the Other concerned is wearing 'exotic' tribal dress). Put crudely, the question is, of course, 'who are we to represent them?' (Rabinow, 1986). As James Clifford (1986: 13) insists, we must always be sure to ask: 'Who speaks? When and where? With or to whom? Under what institutional and histori-cal constraints?' At its strongest, the case is put by authors such as the late Bob Scholte, who suggested that anthropology as a whole may simply be 'a way Europeans have invented of talking about their darker brethren or sisters' (1987: 35–6). 'Ethnography' itself is a word that carries a heavy ideological burden, in so far as, if its denotative meaning can be defined innocently as 'the description of peoples', connotatively the implication is always that the 'peoples' to be described are Others – non-whites, non-Europeans, non-Christians: 'Them' (Fabian, 1990: 758). Trinh Minh-Ha explores the metaphor of anthropology's attempt to 'grasp the marrow of native life' as itself a cannibalistic rite, arguing that today 'the only possible ethnology is the one which studies the anthropophagous [metaphorically cannibalistic] behaviour of the white man' (1989: 73).

The point of the analogy is that just as, historically, it is Western anthro-pology that has arrogated to itself the right to represent the 'native', so today, given the largely one-way nature of the flow of international communications, it is the Western media which arrogate to themselves the right to represent all non-Western Others, and thus to provide 'us' with the definitions by which 'we' distinguish ourselves from 'them'. To extend, and complicate, our central metaphor, the television screen on which the Other is represented to (and for) us functions at a number of different levels. If, in one sense, screening means that 'they' are made present to 'us' in representation, it is also the case that the image of 'them' is screened in the different sense of being filtered, with only certain selected images getting through. At the same time, in a psychic sense, the screen is not only the medium through which images are projected for us, but also the screen onto which we project our own fears, fantasies and desires concerning the Others against whom our identities are defined and constructed. If this is a routine process, at particular moments of crisis, its operations can be highlighted, as basic dilemmas are thrown into dramatic relief, under the glare of the world media spotlight.

The crucial question, then, is 'who are we who are screening them?' The reflexive question is the vital one:

> The viewer experiences events, not at first hand, but through percep-tion. What he perceives will inevitably trigger an individual response

to the nature of identity. There is a vital connection between what the world imposes and the mind demands, receives and shapes. Everything seen on the screen says something about ourselves. It challenges us to respond, to relate what we see to what we are. It compels us to validate our own identity.

(Coker, 1992: 197)

What we have to come to terms with are our watching technologies and the watching behaviour they make possible. What should concern us is how, through the screen, we devour images of the Other. The screen is implicated in the construction of the fundamental antimonies of 'self-us-good' versus 'Other-them-bad'. Kobena Mercer (1990: 69) has referred to the 'sheer difficulty of living with difference', and Paul Hoggett (1992: 352) to the fundamental psychic dilemma in which 'unity without difference' is the only form of unity tolerable to the troubled psyche. We are not suggesting that any of this is new. Tzvetan Todorov's masterly analysis of the representation of the Other by the Spanish, in the process of conquest and colonisation of the 'New World', addresses the same fundamental dilemma. On the one hand, the Spaniards can conceive of the Indians as human, and therefore as 'identical' to themselves and having equal rights, in which case they are then ripe for the 'assimilation' of Spanish values; alternatively, they can recognise difference, but that is then immediately translated into the terms of superiority and inferiority, into the belief that the Indians are sub-human, and therefore into a justification for their enslavement. As Todorov puts it, 'what is denied is the existence of a human subject truly other, someone capable of being not merely an imperfect state of oneself'; what is at stake is 'the failure to recognise the Indians, and the refusal to admit them as a subject having the same rights as oneself, but different. Columbus discovered America but not the Americans' (Todorov, 1984: 42, 49).

UNDER WESTERN EYES

Nowadays, our 'discoveries' of Otherness are made not so often by means of long and perilous sea crossings as by use of the remote-control, as we flick between the varieties of exotica on offer on different television channels. In televisual encounters, however, we find many of the same fundamental processes in play, the same compulsion to split Good from Evil in some absolute way, the same inability to tolerate difference without relegating the different to the sub-human or inhuman category of the 'monster'. This we saw very clearly when the Gulf War was brought under Western eyes. In the media presentation of the war, Saddam Hussein was portrayed as representing all the forces of irrational barbarism that must be contained and controlled by the forces of reason and sanity. It was up to Europe and its civilisational offspring, America, to slay the dragon, to vanquish the alien: the UN crusaders had to take on the 'beast of Baghdad' and his 'empire of terror'. Reason, supposedly universal reason, had to be made to prevail. The problem, of course, is that it is all too easy to project all the evil outwards, and then to believe that all is well in our own community. The demonisation of the enemy and the accusations against the Evil Other for their criminality and bestiality were related to the desire to purify our own culture and civilisation. To see the Evil Other as the embodiment of irrationality was to be certain of our own rational cause and motives. The symbolic damnation of Saddam–Hitler revealed, then, a great deal about the fears, anxieties and guilt at the heart of Western modernity and rationality.

It is important to attend to the media dimension of such events. This is, not least, because it was as an experience mediated by CNN that most people outside Iraq were put into some kind of relation to, and given some form of knowledge of, the actual events that took place. Our principal interest here lies in the role of various media in constructing a sense of the reality (or otherwise) of events in one place for people in other places. On a visit to the United States during the Gulf War, Judith Williamson observed:

> It is the unreality of anywhere outside the US, in the eyes of its citizens, which must frighten any foreigner. Like an infant who has yet to learn there are other centres of self, this culture sees others merely as fodder for its dreams and nightmares. . . . It isn't that Americans don't *care* (God knows, they care) but that, for most of them, other lands and other people cannot be imagined as real.
>
> (1991: 21)

Having earlier criticised 'hypodermic' theories of media effects at the social or cultural levels, we have no intention of reinstating such a theory at the psychic level (see Morley, 1992, ch. 2, for a critique of such tendencies in cultural theory). However, we would argue that in order to explore adequately the unconscious dynamics in play in the reception of media materials, we do need recourse to concepts derived from a psychoanalytic perspective (cf. Robins, 1993, for an elaboration of this perspective).

The intensive encounter with other cultures, brought about by imperialist expansion, has always been one of the driving forces defining the modern West. The historian Albert Hourani argues that something new in history was 'created by the vast expansion of the European mind and imagination so as to appropriate all existing things' (1980: 13). In its quest to appropriate the world, the West learned to define its own uniqueness against the Other, against 'non-Europe'. If the political reality has always been one of conflict and disunity, the construction of an imaginary Orient helped to give unity and coherence to the idea of the West.

This Orient was, moreover, a mirror in which Europe (and subsequently America) could see its own supremacy reflected. In learning to account for its difference from non-Europe, it also had to account for this supremacy, for the unquestionable success it had had in imposing its hegemony on 'inferior' cultures.

Fundamental to both its difference and its inherent superiority, it seemed, was the principle of reason. It was on the basis of reason, embodied in modern science and technology, that Europe had triumphed throughout the world and had made itself the universal point of reference. This reason it came to see as the basis of a universal culture; the justification for its claim to define universal values, to define its values as universal. Modernity was defined against pre-modernity, reason against irrationality and superstition; and this divide was, as we know, then mapped onto a symbolic geography that counterposes the West and its Orient. *Its* Orient, because if 'the West' did not exist, then the Orient could not exist either. It is 'the West' that has given both existence and identity to 'the Orient'. And the existence and identity it has bestowed is one of constitutive inferiority and deficit. Oriental culture is defined as a subaltern culture, conceived through the very process of its subjugation and subordination to the universal culture. And it is a culture defined by what it lacks (modernity, rationality, universality); its 'Otherness' is defined in terms of the backwardness, the irrationality and the particularity of its values. This confrontation, as Edward Said (1978) has so powerfully demonstrated, has assumed its most intense and confrontational form in the encounter with Islam.

Hourani describes how the encounter with the West has led to a sense of secondariness in modern Arab and Islamic identity: 'It is no longer to have a standard of values of one's own, not to be able to create but only to imitate; and so not even to imitate correctly, since that also needs a certain originality' (1946: 70–1). In the face of self-proclaimed Western universalism, Islamic and Arabic culture was shaken to its foundations. Within the terms of this self-proclaiming universal culture, moreover, there could be no escape from this degradation. Islam was inferior in its very essence. Under Western eyes (though contrary to historical evidence) it was constituted as a conservative culture, a culture of dogmatism and fanaticism. History and progress were possible only in the West. Islam, by contrast, was a static culture, an eternally medieval and feudal culture: it was the culture of impossible modernisation. And it could not be otherwise because the very difference and supremacy of the West were constructed around this image of Arab and Islamic Otherness. 'Our' civilisation was defined against 'their' barbarism; 'our' beauty against 'their' bestiality. If that irrational culture had access to our rationality and science, what would be the implications for the Western sense of difference and uniqueness? If that backward culture would modernise itself, where should we then find the mirror to reflect our superiority?

This unthinkable predicament of modernity in the Orient was what confronted the West at the time of the Gulf War. In that war, Saddam Hussein was assaulting the norms that have defined Western uniqueness and superiority; he was violating the boundaries that have differentiated rationality and irrationality, Western modernity and the pre-modern Orient. He armed himself with the munitions of modernity, not only with conventional arms but also with an arsenal of nuclear, biological and chemical weapons. But, according to the Western myth, he was by nature – by his Arab and Oriental nature – irrational. When equipped with the scientific instruments of warfare, Saddam's inherent irrationality could only become explosive; with modern technologies he was a monstrous and psychotic force. The armies of Reason then had to suppress this crazed, monstrous Unreason.

The media presented Saddam as the embodiment of evil, of all that 'we' are not, in terms which stand diametrically opposed to our civilisation and culture. He was 'imagined' as absolutely and monstrously 'Other'. To see him in this way made it possible – made it logical and rational – to set fire to the night skies of Iraq. But Saddam used our weapons, the weapons that we sold him, and he used them, like us, in a rational and calculating way. Saddam embodied the aspirations and logic of modernity; he was modernity as it now exists in that part of the world. Saddam was a mirror – a distorting mirror perhaps, but a mirror none the less – reflecting an image of us. The West did not like what it saw in that mirror. But let us be clear about just what it is that it was seeing: it was the monstrous side of its own modernity; it was the irresistible spread of its own project, a project that has been marked by both rationality and violence. Saddam was not an alien monster, a monster against modernity, but rather a monster born of modernity, a monster within modernity.

Many commentators have described the creation of a Frankenstein's monster in Iraq. Like Mary Shelley's creature, Saddam was a monster created through the global spread of modernity. In him, too, our fear of modernity's monstrous aspect was projected onto an elemental hatred of the 'Other'. Saddam had to be seen as a member of a race apart. If Iraq was to be seen as in the process of modernisation, then it had to be an alien kind of modernity that could never be acceptable to the civilised world. Like Frankenstein's monster, Saddam Hussein had to be banned from civilisation. Only through his exclusion could reason be reclaimed in the name of universal progress and humanity.

And so the 'smart' technologies of Western reason were mobilised to smash the 'Other'. And courtesy of the latest media technology, we could sit in front of our television screens, safe at home, and watch, as in a video game, as the bombs homed in on their targets. The media then allowed us a kind of para-social, thrilled involvement in the obliteration of the monstrous Other.

WESTERN SCREEN, WESTERN PSYCHE

Writing from a psychoanalytic perspective, Paul Hoggett describes how all human beings carry a primordial fear, a persistent dread, a sense of imminent catastrophe, within themselves:

> So what is this fear, what is this catastrophe that stalks us like a crazy dog? We cannot say because we cannot name it. But it is there, right in our guts, and as soon as we find the means to do so we seek to represent it, despite the fact that it cannot be represented. We construct an endless series of misrepresentations all of which share one essential quality, the quality of otherness, of being not-me.
>
> (1992: 345–6)

Whatever the political realities, the Gulf War offered itself as an occasion, a rich opportunity, to rid ourselves, for a while at least, of this 'crazy dog' through the projection of our fears outwards. This time the 'not-me' we used to embody the sense of catastrophic danger was Saddam Hussein vilified as child-molester, rapist, murderer and monster. His scuddish evil, George Bush assured the Western world, confirmed us as the guardians of enlightened and civilised values. In so far as Saddam symbolised the forces of irrationality, it became possible for us to imagine ourselves as all reason. To protect our new-found peace of mind, it seemed both reasonable and inevitable that we should attack the 'new Hitler'. Now that the 'crazy dog' of our fears had a name we would 'cut it off' and 'kill it'.

What is, of course, significant about a world historical event like the Gulf War is how individual fantasies are drawn into a collective strategy of psychic defence. The collective expulsion of fear becomes the basis for reaffirming group solidarity. Membership of a social group, of a society, is never an easy or an uncomplicated matter: belonging to it is associated with feelings of discomfort, from indifference to resentment and anxiety. At particular historical moments, however, such tensions are eased, as the collectivity reasserts itself through what, following Didier Anzieu (1984), we might call the working of the 'group illusion'. The group discovers its common identity at the same time as its individual members are able to avow that they are all identical in their fears, and then that they are consensual in the defensive violence and hatred they direct against the threat that is 'not-us'. It is a moment in which the individual can fuse with the group: for a time, at least, the defence of individual identity can be displaced onto the collectivity. And for as long as danger and threat can be projected from its midst, the group experiences a sense of exultation through its new-found wholeness and integrity. It was this exultation that infused the *esprit de corps* of the coalition nations in the Gulf War. What it reflected was the pleasure of experiencing harmonious community and in joining in righteous struggle (the just crusade). It was, however, like so many times before, predicated on a consensual misrepresentation: on the illusory belief that the dangers and threats were all simply 'out there' and that the crazy dog really was Saddam.

In an essay on the Gulf War – one that can be read as both symptom and diagnosis – Lloyd deMause (1990), an American psycho-historian, suggests that, prior to the conflict, American national culture had been characterised by feelings of guilt, depression and sinfulness – partly linked to the 'Vietnam Syndrome'. He describes this condition as a 'shared emotional disorder'. In this context, the Gulf War could be seen as a cleansing and purifying experience, through which, in George Bush's words, America could finally 'kick the Vietnam Syndrome'. What the war offered was the possibility of renewal and revitalisation: America could rediscover its moral purpose and emotional wholeness. Of course, there is a simplification in this account of the Gulf War as a kind of morality play. But there is also a persuasive truth in it. For a moment, a brief moment, this epic spectacle sustained a sense of national integrity and moral regeneration. The Gulf War was to purify America by exorcising an 'evil' – which was projected as being outside ('in a desolate Middle Eastern desert').

Television was fundamental to this process. We have drawn attention to the group processes at work, rather than invoking the more conventional agenda of the media as public sphere, because we are, for the moment, more concerned with the emotional and libidinal, rather than the rational, dimensions of collective behaviour. In most discussions of Gulf War television, there was a tendency to privilege the informational role of television, and to overlook the significance of the screen and the screening process for the psyche-at-war. As the conflict developed, however, the television screen played a crucial role, first in projecting our fears outwards and creating the image of external threat, and then in mobilising defensive violence against that threat. It was perhaps in the form of the television audience (the audience-as-group) that the 'group illusion', functioning as a defensive mechanism against persecutory anxieties, manifested itself most powerfully. The screen mediated between the dangers we imagined out there and the fear, anger and aggression we were feeling inside (Robins, 1993).

The nature and functioning of the screen are crucial. The screen can allow us to witness the world's events while, at the same time, protecting us – keeping us separate and insulated – from the reality of the events we are seeing. It can expose audiences to the violence and catastrophe of war while they still remain safe in their living rooms. But how do we learn to live with this violence? To ask this question is to consider the mechanisms through which we manage to screen ourselves from evil. Our exposure to the violence of the Gulf War was through the mediation of the screen, as a 'media event'. The screen is a powerful metaphor for our times: it symbolises how we now exist in the world, our contradictory condition of engagement and disengagement. Increasingly we confront moral issues through the screen, and the screen confronts us with increasing numbers of moral dilemmas. At the same time, however, it screens us from those dilemmas. It is through the screen that we disavow or deny our human implication in moral realities.

'To suffer is one thing', writes Susan Sontag, 'another thing is living with the photographed images of suffering, which does not necessarily strengthen conscience and the ability to be compassionate' (1979: 20). Yet, through the distancing force of images, frozen registrations of remote calamities, we have learned to manage our relationship to suffering. The photographic image at once exposes us to, and insulates us from, actual suffering. It does not, and cannot, of itself implicate us in the real and reciprocal relations necessary to sustain moral and compassionate existence. Cinema, too, has kept the viewer at a distance from the consequences of violent action. Screen violence is routinely presented 'as a ritual, distant experience, like listening to news of a tragedy in a place you've never heard of' (Leith, 1993). With video screens and electronic images, this moral chasm has been made wider. As we have become exposed to, and assaulted by, images of violence on a scale never before known, we have also become more insulated from the realities. It may no longer be a question of whether this strengthens conscience and compassion, but of whether it is actually undermining and eroding it. If we are to come to terms with this moral condition, we must consider the nature of our engagement with screen culture.

To the ordinary audience member, the screen affords access to experiences of the unfamiliar and the extreme, the fantastic, aberrant and frightening. In this respect, the screen has the potential to extend and amplify human awareness and sensibility. And, of course, this can be liberating. But it can also be very problematical. The screen also encourages a morbid voyeurism. So the screen affords access to experiences beyond the ordinary. But experience and awareness for what, we might ask. What does it mean to be 'fascinated' by a missile-eye perspective on death? What does it mean to become quickly 'bored' by pictures of slaughter and suffering? What does it mean to turn to horror movies to satisfy a 'need to be terrified'? The spectator-self can rove almost at random from one visual sensation to the next; a cruising voyeur. The screen exposes the ordinary viewer to harsh realities, but it also tends to screen out the harshness of those realities. It has a certain moral weightlessness. It grants sensation without demanding responsibility. It can involve us in a spectacle without engaging us in the complexity of its reality. This clearly satisfies basic needs and desires. Through its capacity to project frightening and threatening experiences, we can say that the screen provides a space in which to master anxiety, and allows us to rehearse our fantasies of omnipotence to overcome this anxiety.

SCREENING BOSNIA

More recently, as a horrific sequel to the Gulf massacre, we have seen another war filling our screen time. This time in Europe itself, we have seen the horrors of concentration camps, massacre, rape and terror. As Branka Magas puts it, 'the year 1992, scheduled to be a milestone on the road to European unity, has seen Sarajevo and other Bosnian cities slowly bombarded to pieces and their inhabitants starved before the television eyes of the world' (1992: 102). This is a war that is closer to the quick of our own lives here in the west end of Europe. 'The crisis of Bosnia', as Akbar Ahmed says, 'is the crisis of Europe itself' and 'in failing to salvage Bosnia, it is clear that Europe is failing to salvage itself' (1992a: 14). This war is closer, dangerously closer, to home.

Writing from Croatia, Slavenka Drakulić movingly describes her own experience of the war: how, from being a distant reality, an external event, it entered into her soul and changed her life. 'All last year', she writes,

> war was a distant rumour, something one managed to obscure or ignore – something happening to other people, to people in Knin or Slavonia on the outskirts of the republic, but never to us in the centre, in Zagreb. We were busy with our private lives, with love, careers, a new car. War was threatening us, but not directly, as if we were somehow protected by that flickering TV screen – we might just as well have been in Paris or Budapest.
>
> (1993a: 18)

For some time, it was possible to keep the war at a distance, to see it only as 'familiar media images':

> While it still seemed so far away, it had a mythical quality. Everyone knew about its existence, but not many people had seen it and the stories we heard sounded so horrible and exaggerated that it was difficult to believe them. Everyone read reports, listened to the news and looked at the television images but its mythical dimension remained preserved by the distance – the majority of us had no direct experience.
>
> (Drakulić, 1993b: xiv)

But it was not possible to go on screening out the reality of the conflict: 'For a long time we have been able to fend off the ghost of war; now it comes back to haunt us, spreading all over the screen of our lives, leaving no space for privacy, for future, for anything but itself' (Drakulić, 1993a: 18). Living in the war zone has meant coming to live with war and coming to be profoundly changed by it.

Outside the war zone, we are still protected by the flickering screen; the mythical dimension of the war is still preserved through the distancing effect of the screen images. Beyond that zone, there is a sense of comfort in the knowledge that the war is not only happening to other people but that it is happening to another kind of people. In Western Europe, the war is seen as an atavistic affair, being acted out by primitive and tribal populations. Arjun Appadurai describes how, in anthropological theory, places become associated with what he calls 'gatekeeping concepts', that is to say 'concepts that seem to limit anthropological theorising about the place in question, and that define the quintessential and dominant questions of interest in the region . . . . The point is that there is a tendency for places to become showcases for specific issues over time' (1986: 357–8). This is not, of course, restricted to theoretical anthropology. And, in the case of the Balkans, what limits our understanding is the ideologically conceived association of this unfortunate region with the passions of ethnic hatred and primordial violence. Our cherished reason may then recoil, as we witness what to us are irrational and incomprehensible acts of savagery. This is a mad place, we say, and these are mad people, unlike us.

The fear is that the madness might be contagious. 'New tribalism threatens to infect us all', proclaims a recent article in *The Guardian* (Hutton, 1993). 'In the place of evil empires', as Paula Franklin Lytle (1992: 304) observes, 'are resurgent nationalisms, and the terms used to describe them are images of infection and disease'. The point about this kind of imagery is that it interprets events in the former Yugoslavia as pathological and as the consequence of some kind of catastrophic natural force. The Balkans are seen 'as a body infected by nationalism, rather than as a war possibly amenable to any form of mediation or intervention' (ibid.: 316). The viral metaphor excuses Western inaction or ineffectiveness. More than this, it comes to legitimate a policy of disengagement and withdrawal: 'In the absence of an effective vaccine the alternative response to viral contagion is quarantine' (ibid.: 306). We must be screened from the infecting body.

The television screen may well be the key mechanism through which this distancing has been achieved. Press coverage has also drawn attention to the 'shocking images' of ethnic cleansing: 'Now the grim results are finally showing up on television screens and the front pages of newspapers. Pictures sear the conscience of the world'. And yet, it goes on, 'the response of the outside world so far – a lot of hand-wringing and a few relief supplies for one besieged city, Sarajevo – looks pathetically inadequate' (*Newsweek*, 17 August 1993: 8). The television images do not necessarily involve us in the plight of those distant Others: what they may rather do is to bring us voyeuristically, and perhaps even cognitively, closer, whilst maintaining an emotional distance and detachment. The screen is then a separation, a shield, a protection.

In considering what he calls 'the postmodern call of the other reaching towards us from the mediatised image', Richard Kearney poses the crucial question: 'Are not those of us who witness such images (as well as those who record and transmit them through the communications network) obliged to respond not just to surface reflections on a screen but to the call of human beings they communicate?' (1988a: 387–8). Most of us know what we would want to answer individually. We are also aware of what our collective response has ended up being. How are we to explain the uses of the screen that seem to preclude moral response and engagement?

At one level, of course, we can see it in terms of a mutation in television journalism which is associated with an increasing 'analytical paralysis' in its account of the world (Ferro, 1993). According to Paolo Carpignano and his colleagues, we have seen the demise of journalistic authority and the creation of a state of affairs in which 'information has created a world rich in events but devoid of shared experience' (1990: 36).

But it is more than just the transformation in media technologies and journalistic techniques that is at issue. There is something more fundamental at work in the process of screen mediation, something that is more than a technological matter. The journalistic organisation of the 'world as a show' responds to individual and collective psychological demands. In this respect, it can be said that 'the media are used by the unconscious mind as an auxiliary system [the screen], which stabilises and takes care of the personal and direct relationships which are too painful and lie between dream and reality' (Dufour and Dufour-Gompers, 1985: 320). In looking at the television screen, the watcher can say to himself or herself:

> I see that these anxieties, hatreds, killings and destructions are not me
> . . . . I can see that these hungers for power and these continual con-
> frontations are not me . . . . I see that these inhibited, distorted sex-
> ual appetites are not me . . . in a word, all this craziness is not me.
>
> (ibid.: 321)

The television screen can be seen as functioning, then, in terms of psychic defence and screening. What we must take into account is how the imaginary institution of television can become a collective mechanism of defence.

What needs to be understood, as much as what is actually happening in the Balkans, is what is going on in the TV audience, watching the war from a safe distance. We are invited, by the nature of the TV coverage

144

to take up the position of the 'armchair anthropologist', gazing at the 'Other' on the screen, in the living room. We must recognise that, in so far as this war is 'viewed' as something (mythical) happening to 'Other' people, this can make its viewers insensitive to their own psychic investments in the material viewed. We must be attentive, then, not only to the ethics of everyday depictions, but also to the psychic investments we make in such depictions. We have organised our collective fantasies around the idea of 'the Balkans as the Other of the West', but in so doing we have failed to see how, 'far from being the Other of Europe, ex-Yugoslavia was rather Europe itself in its Otherness, the screen on to which Europe projected its own repressed reverse' (Žižek, 1992). What should concern us is how the screen helps us to organise reality in the cause of our own psychic fantasies and defences.

In all of this, the relation to the 'mediated' and the 'real' is a complex one. It could certainly be argued that the airlift of wounded children from Sarajevo in August 1993 was a real event almost entirely shaped by the media. The strategy seemed mainly designed to boost the standing of the Western powers in their own voters' eyes, by virtue of the 'good publicity' generated through the consequent photo-opportunities for politicians to pose with 'rescued' children. However, when it became clear that strictly medical priorities would mean that the first plane-load of evacuees would contain, not only sick children, but also some severely wounded adults, the British popular media were outraged, running headlines complaining of Muslim duplicity in 'tricking' the Western charities and doctors. The presence of wounded Muslim adults among the evacuees was certainly taken to represent a kind of 'pollution' of the Western crusade on behalf of innocent children. It seems that wounded Muslim children were predominantly seen as part of the universal 'race' of children, and thus deserving of help, whereas wounded adults were predominantly seen as Muslims, and thus represented 'matter out of place' on a Western crusade. The cynicism of the British Government in the whole episode, its attempt to exploit this tragic situation for political publicity, was perhaps best summed up in the words of a UN representative, Sylvana Foa (*The Guardian*, 14 August 1993): 'Does this mean Britain only wants to help children? Maybe it only wants children under six, or blond children, or blue-eyed children?' Our own analysis would lead us to believe that her question, even if rhetorical, is none the less pertinent for that.

'What can happen next, is this the end of the horror?' asks Slavenka Drakulić (1993b: xiii) in a letter to her publisher in London. 'No, I am afraid that we will have to live with this war for years. But you too will have to live with it, and it will change you, not immediately, but over time.' For the moment, we are still watching the flickering screen. For the moment, we still have names and addresses, and car-keys. But, in

Sarajevo, it was reported (*The Guardian*, 26 August 1993) that the price of an almost new Volkswagen Golf had fallen to around $150, as few people could get hold of the petrol needed to run a car: in which context, what price car-keys?

8

TECHNO-ORIENTALISM
Japan panic

Every western politician has either actual or cinematic experience of
the brutalities Japan inflicted on its prisoners-of-war. No one, whether
in Asia or beyond, has fond memories of Japanese expansionism.
Which is why, as Japan's economic power expands anew, the Japanese
would do better to face up to the darker aspects of their past.

(Leader article in *The Economist*, 24 August 1991)

Today, the modern era is in its terminal phase. An awareness of its
imminent demise has made Americans, the most powerful
Caucasians since World War II, increasingly emotional, almost
hysterical, about Japan.

(Shintaro Ishihara, 1991)

Our concern in this chapter is with what has been called 'the problem of
Japan', that is to say Japan as a problem for the West. Our interest here
is in tracing a set of discursive correspondences that have been, and are
still being, developed in the West between 'Japan', the 'Orient' and the
'Other'. More specifically, we want to explore why, at this historical
moment, this particular Other should occupy such a threatening position
in the Western imagination. The former French prime minister, Edith
Cresson, publicly declared her belief that 'the Japanese have a strategy
of world conquest'. The Japanese, she said, are 'little yellow men' who
'stay up all night thinking about ways to screw the Americans and
Europeans. They are our common enemy'. Most tellingly, Mme Cresson
likened the Japanese to 'ants'. Her fear was that those 'ants' were
colonising the world and taking possession of the future. What are these
fears and anxieties that Japan arouses in the Western psyche?

THE JAPAN THAT IS SAYING NO

For nearly five centuries now, Japan has been among the West's Others.
It has been seen as the exotic culture (zen, kabuki, tea-ceremonies,
geishas) of aesthetic *Japonisme*. And it has been seen as an alien culture,

147

a dehumanised martial culture (kamikaze, ninjutsu, samurai), to be feared. Its difference has been contained in the idea of some mysterious ambiguity. Japan is both 'the chrysanthemum and the sword':

> The Japanese are, to the highest degree, both aggressive and unaggressive, both militaristic and aesthetic, both insolent and polite, rigid and adaptable, submissive and resentful of being pushed around, loyal and treacherous, brave and timid, conservative and hospitable to new ways.
>
> (Benedict, 1974: 2)

It is this complexity and ambiguity in the image of Japan that has given it a particular resonance in Western fantasies. But, if it has been complex, it has always been possible symbolically to control this image of Japan. As Mark Holborn writes:

> The dialogue between Japan and the West is frequently described in terms of Japan's absorption of the West. The pattern of imitation, absorption and finally reinterpretation of Western ideas is explicit.
> . . . In contrast, the West's absorption of Japan is inconclusive and rarely described. *Japonisme* was the first stage in the imitation of a Japanese aesthetic. It was primarily decorative and involved the borrowing of Japanese motifs and design elements. Oriental views provided the West with spectacle.
>
> (1991: 18)

Japan absorbed the culture of the West because this was its 'destiny'. This was the logic and the nature of history, development, progress. The West's absorption of Japan is 'rarely described', or is only described in a displaced and sublimated way, through the discourse of exotica and aesthetica. The dialogue between Japan and the West was not one between equals, and the integrity of the West was never challenged by Japanese culture.

But no more. That integrity is now being assaulted by a Japan that is no longer content only to provide the West with spectacle. This became most dramatically apparent with the appearance of *The Japan That Can Say No*, by the Liberal Democratic politician and former Minister of Transport, Shintaro Ishihara (1991). Ishihara directly accuses the United States of adopting a racist attitude towards Japan, even suggesting that American planes used atom bombs against the Japanese, and not the Germans, 'because we are Japanese' (ibid.: 28). He also suggests that the bases of Western economic and cultural supremacy are being undermined. If it is the case that 'Caucasians deserve much credit in the creation of modern civilisation' (ibid.: 107), it is also true that their creative energies are being exhausted. Japan has a growing lead in new technologies, to the extent that the US nuclear weapons industry is dependent on Japanese suppliers. Technology is the key to the future:

Technology gives rise to civilisation, upon which, in time, culture thrives. Nations decline when they self-indulgently let life-styles become more important than workmanship and neglect their industrial and technological base. That is the lesson of history.

(ibid.: 57)

According to Ishihara, Japanese technological superiority now puts it 'on the verge of a new genesis' (ibid.: 29). Europe and the United States, in contrast, are on the verge of decline. The modern era that was shaped by the West is now in its terminal phase:

Americans should realise the modern era is over. Their cherished beliefs in materialism, science, and progress have borne bitter fruit. The defeat in Vietnam, despite raining Napalm and Agent Orange on the countryside for ten years, showed the futility of military power. America harnessed science and technology and spent a fortune to get to the moon, only to find a barren rock pile. All that money and effort and what does the nation have to show for it?

(ibid.: 123)

Japan is held up as the future, and it is a future that has transcended Western modernity. 'How preposterous', Ishihara suggests, 'to assert that somehow modern Japan sprang full-blown from Western seeds!' (ibid.: 107). He appeals to 'our national gift for improving and refining everything from Buddhist art to semiconductors', and celebrates Japan's 'Eastern ways and values' (ibid.: 58, 123). 'We are', writes Ishihara, 'in and of the Orient' (ibid.: 124). According to Ishihara, Japan is of the future; it is riding on the crest of a great historic wave and will shape the next age, a more human age beyond Western modernity.

STEALING AMERICA'S SOUL

Japan is calling Western modernity into question, and is claiming the franchise on the future. And this has provoked a defensive response from the West. As Akio Morita, ex-chairman of Sony, points out, 'they have the feeling that strangers, or something foreign, has entered their midst. This gives them strong feelings of fear and anxiety' (*The Sunday Times*, 29 October 1989). Anti-Japanese feeling grows strong as Japan seems to invade the symbolic strongholds of the West. Nippon Television Network paid around $3 million for the restoration of the Sistine Chapel ceiling, making it 'an unlikely symbol of the new balance of East–West power' (Januszczak, 1990a: 194). Manhattan's Rockefeller Center has been acquired by Japanese real-estate interests. And, most symbolically of all, Hollywood has now been 'invaded' by Japanese corporate capital. Having acquired CBS Records for $2 billion in 1988, Sony went on to purchase

149

Columbia Pictures in 1989 for $3.4 billion. Then, in 1990, followed Matsushita's 'copycat' purchase of MCA-Universal for a massive $6 billion. If there were other Japanese infiltrations – $600 million of Japanese investment in Walt Disney Corporation; JVC's investment of $100 million in Largo Entertainment; Pioneer Electronics' acquisition of a ten per cent share in Carolco Pictures – the Sony and Matsushita manoeuvres were 'most potent and symbolic' (Aksoy and Robins, 1992).

Both Sony and Matsushita were involved in a strategy to achieve global dominance in the new image industries through control over both hardware and software markets. Both companies use the term 'synergy' to describe their objective of controlling different media products (books, records, films, television programmes) across different distribution channels. As one commentator puts it:

> Now Sony can control the whole chain. Its broadcast equipment division manufactures the studio cameras and the film on which movies are produced; in Columbia it owns a studio that makes them and crucially, determines the formats on which they are distributed. That means it can have movies made on high definition televisions, and videoed with Sony VCRs. It can re-shoot Columbia's 2700-film library on 8 mm film, for playing on its video Walkmans.
>
> (Cope, 1990: 56)

What Sony and Matsushita have both recognised is that a successful industry depends on having appropriate software to support hardware. They have also recognised that the industry is becoming a global one, and that economies of scale and increasing corporate integration are necessary to control world markets. Sony describes its strategy now as one of 'global localisation', meaning that while it operates across the globe it aims to gain 'insider' status within regional and local markets. They are set to conquer the world.

Europe and the United States have been put on the defensive. Herbert Schiller points to the irony of the situation:

> The buyout of MCA/Universal – one of the Hollywood 'majors' – by the Japanese superelectronics corporation Matsushita has already had one beneficial effect. It has caused the American news media, along with the government foreign-policy makers, to recognise a problem whose existence they have steadfastly denied for the past twenty-five years – cultural domination by an external power.
>
> (1990: 828)

Suddenly there is an anxiety about exposure to, and penetration by, Japanese culture. The fear is that Japanese investors are 'buying into America's soul'. There is a fear that, in contrast to Western openness, Japan is characterised by a culture of self-censorship: 'It is not that any overt censorship takes place, but rather that the norms of a society well attuned to subtle signals make unnecessary rigid rules about what is acceptable discourse' (Sanger, 1990). Would Sony or Matsushita be prepared to make a movie about a taboo subject such as the war-time role of the late Emperor Hirohito? There is also a fear that Japan might turn 'cocacolonisation' into 'sake imperialism'.

What is apparent, too, is the sense that Japanese culture is incompatible with the Hollywood ethos. Whereas America is characterised by 'ethnic democracy' and pluralism, Japan is seen as a culture of 'ethnic purity' and homogeneity. Japan is seen as a consensus and conformist society, the obverse of the individualistic and creative ethos that made Hollywood a world culture. Most vocal of all is Jeffrey Katzenberg, chairman of Disney Studios. 'Film-making at its essence', he asserts, 'is about the conveyancing of emotion'. And what is clear about the Japanese is that they are lacking in emotion. The Japanese

> culturally err on the side of withholding emotion. In saying this, I am not simply offering an American perspective. The Japanese are the first to tell you this about themselves.
>
> This sense of discipline and self-control has no doubt been a major factor in achieving the Japanese economic miracle that has turned a small island nation into one of the world's pre-eminent industrial powers.
>
> But it is also why I firmly believe that the recent marriages between Japanese hardware makers and American moviemakers may not be ones made in entertainment heaven.
>
> There will be a chasm in the fundamental understanding of the movie business that will likely prove exceedingly frustrating for Japanese and Americans alike.
>
> (quoted in *Variety*, 4 February 1991: 26)

If the Japanese are investing in Western popular culture it is, according to a vice-president of Disney, because 'they respect us for our ability to create magic – I think they admire something about the American spirit of ingenuity – almost a wildness or recklessness, a sense of fun – that the more conservative cultures aren't capable of' (quoted in Huey, 1990: 54). Respect – respect from an inferior culture – is one thing. The 'invasion of Hollywood' and the loss of a 'national heritage' are quite another.

At one level, the response is obvious, and it is made forcefully by Ishihara: 'The sentimental attachment to a Hollywood institution like Columbia Pictures and a New York landmark like Radio City Music Hall is understandable. But the American public . . . should realise that it takes two to make a deal: Americans put these properties on the market' (1991: 89). What is made clear is that Japan is not in the business of making movies, but in the business of making money. Within the United

States, too, there has been criticism of cultural and economic protectionism. 'Bruce Springsteen doesn't lose his value because he's working
for Sony Chairman Akio Morita instead of CBS Chairman Larry Tisch',
says economist Robert Reich (quoted in Tran, 1990). According to Reich,
this kind of defensive cultural chauvinism and techno-nationalism is no
longer appropriate to an era in which frontiers and borders are being
eroded. In the context of rapid globalisation, the question 'who is us?' is
increasingly problematical and perhaps even irrelevant (Reich, 1987;
1990).

At one level, perhaps, this is true. But, at another level, America still
believes it has a 'soul', a national soul, and to see Japan as the enemy
now is one way to bring the identity of that soul back into focus. Despite
the apparent logic of Ishihara's and Reich's arguments, what seems clear
is that the West both needs and wants its Japan problem. The idea of 'the
coming war with Japan' seems to meet a desire of some kind.

JAPAN RISING?

At the psychic level, the question 'who is us?' arouses profound disquiet.
That the Japanese are unlikely to hijack Bruce Springsteen or Michael
Jackson is beside the point. What is so disturbing is the manner in which
Japanese interests appear to work behind the scenes, remotely manipu-
lating Western concerns, operating through the chameleon-like strategy of
global localisation. Japanese economic strategies appear to be unfair and
adversarial. Rather than buying American or European products, they
prefer to buy raw materials or even whole businesses. And they operate
with an unnerving dedication to this cause. James Fallows (1989a) sees
this in terms of 'Japan's lack of emotional connection to the rest of the
world', in terms of a kind of asceticism and dedication that is almost
inhuman (cf. van Wolferen, 1988; 1989). In *You Only Live Twice*, James
Bond's police contact, Tiger Tanaka (who had hoped to be a kamikaze
pilot during the war), describes the martial art of *ninjutsu*:

> My agents are trained in one of the arts most dreaded in Japan –
> *ninjutsu*, which is, literally, the art of stealth or invisibility. All the
> men you will see have already graduated in at least ten of the eigh-
> teen martial arts of *bushido*, or 'way of the warrior', and they are
> now learning to be *ninja*, or 'stealers-in', which has for centuries
> been part of the basic training of spies and assassins and saboteurs.
> (quoted in Johnson, 1988: 108)

The villain, Shredder, in *Teenage Mutant Ninja Turtles*, hidden away in
the darkness of the sewer system, operates by the same ninja principles,
to erode and undermine American civilisation. What these popular
cultural expressions reflect is an anxiety about the 'stealth' of Japanese

corporations. The Japanese stealers-in are perceived as having a robot-like dedication to achieving world hegemony and to undermining the principles of Western modernity.

These anxieties must be seen in the context of an increasing sense of insecurity about European and American modernity. Modernity has always been that 'mysterious and magical word that puts a barrier between the European [and American] ego and the rest of the world' (Corm, 1989: 14). If it was the West that created modernity, it was also modernity that created the imaginary space and identity described as 'Western'. As Agnes Heller and Ferenc Feher (1988) argue, however, the very dynamism of modernity also worked to undermine its Western foundations. The modernisation project was cumulative, future-orientated, based upon the logic of technological progression and progress. Its various elements were also designed to be exported and to transcend their European origins and exclusiveness. Modernisation and modernity, with their claims to universalism, could be transposed to other host cultures. In Japan this project found a fertile environment. The technological and futurological imagination has now come to be centred here; the abstract and universalising force of modernisation has passed from Europe to America to Japan. 'In the future', Jean Baudrillard writes,

> power will belong to those peoples with no origins and no authenticity, who know how to exploit that situation to the full: Look at Japan, which to a certain extent has pulled off this trick better than the US itself, managing, in what seems to us an unintelligible paradox, to transform the power of territoriality and feudalism into that of deterritoriality and weightlessness.
>
> (1988a: 76)

Japan has now become modern to the degree of seeming postmodern, and it is its future that seems to be the current measure for all cultures. And, thereby, the basis of Western identity is called into question.

From 1848 to 1914 Great Britain was the leading creditor nation in the world. Then the United States assumed that role for the next seventy years. In 1985, it became the turn of Japan. It is the largest creditor and the largest net investor in the world, and its surplus on current and capital accounts is the highest ever recorded. Half the world's goods and services and half its population now come from the fifty countries that rim the Pacific – and the world's economic centre of gravity has begun to shift, from the Atlantic to the Pacific – from the Greenwich Meridian to the International Date Line (Wilkinson, 1983; Shibusawa, Ahmad and Bridges, 1991).

The roles have been reversed in other spheres, too. In the nineteenth century, Europeans and Americans regarded Japan as an exotic playground, while the Japanese regarded Europe and the United States as disciplined, group-orientated societies possessing the secrets of efficient industrial production. Today, it is the Japanese who flock to the United States and to Europe for exotic tourism, and it is the Americans and Europeans who regard Japan as an austere and disciplined society, with frighteningly efficient industries. In a reversal of the traditional aestheticised image of Japan, its people are now increasingly seen as workaholics, as 'economic animals' under the governance of a 'Japan Inc.' pursuing GNP growth at the expense of everything else, spreading pollution and spawning intimidating futuristic megalopolises.

If the 'Pacific era' is finally coming into being, then it has been long and anxiously anticipated. In 1903, its imminence was announced by President Roosevelt: 'The Mediterranean era died with the discovery of America; the Atlantic era is now at the height of its development and must soon exhaust the resources at its command; the Pacific era, destined to be the greatest of all, is just at its dawn' (quoted in Knightley, 1991). This geo-economic and geo-political ascendancy of Japan has always seemed an awesome prospect. The (potential) rise of Japan has always threatened to put 'us' in danger. From the late nineteenth century onwards, fears of the 'Yellow Threat' have constantly resurfaced in the popular imagination. At its most fantastic, there is an image in which 'Japanese and Chinese hordes spread out over all Europe, crushing under their feet the ruins of our capital cities and destroying our civilisations, grown anaemic due to the enjoyment of luxuries and corrupted by vanity of spirit' (René Pinon, quoted in Wilkinson, 1983: 59).

The early years of the twentieth century saw the growing popularity of *Fu Manchu-* and *Yellow Peril*-type literature in Europe and the United States. The basic fear has long been of a Japan that is seen as being engaged in an inexorable struggle with the West, whether by military means, or, more recently, through trade wars (cheap, 'shoddy' goods from Japan have been a persistent source of anger and anxiety). The image of 'Japan Inc.' can readily be seen as an echo of the West's age-old fear of 'Oriental Despotism' – a phrase first used by the ancient Greeks to describe the Persians, but one which still provides the inherited script according to which the West now imagines (post)modern Japan.

SEMITES AND ORIENTALS

Edward Said's premise in *Orientalism* was that

> as both geographical and cultural entities – to say nothing of historical entities – such locales, regions, geographical sectors as the 'Orient' and the 'Occident' are man-made . . . . Therefore, as much as the West itself, the Orient is an idea that has a history and a tradition

of thought, imagery and vocabulary that have given it reality and presence in and for the West.

(1978: 4–5)

Naoki Sakai develops the point further:

the Orient does not connote any internal commonality among the names subsumed under it, it ranges from regions in the Middle East to those in the Far East. One can hardly find anything religious, linguistic or cultural that is common among these varied areas. The Orient is neither a cultural, religious or linguistic unity. The principle of its identity lies outside itself: what endows it with some vague sense of unity is that the Orient is that which is excluded and objectified by the West, in the service of its historical progress. From the outset the Orient is a shadow of the West. If the West did not exist, the Orient would not exist either.

(Sakai, 1988: 499)

The 'Orient' exists because the West needs it; because it brings the project of the West into focus.

Until the Renaissance, Europe belonged to a 'regional tributary system' that included Europeans and Arabs, Christians and Muslims. Before then, the countries of Western Europe only occupied the north-western edge of a geographical complex whose centre was at the eastern end of the Mediterranean basin. Subsequently, however, a 'North–South split, running through the Mediterranean – which only replaced the East–West division at a late date – [was] falsely projected backward' and was 'presented as permanent, self-evident and inscribed in geography (and therefore – by implicit false deduction – in history)' (Amin,: 1989: 93; cf. Corm, 1989). In this transition, northern Europe became redefined as the centre of the system, and all other regions were relegated to the status of its peripheries. In all of this, history is rewritten: Christianity is annexed arbitrarily to Europe, and becomes one of the central terms by which Europe understands itself (despite the fact that Christianity is Middle Eastern in origin). A further crucial step involved the arbitrary annexation of Hellenic culture to Europe. As Samir Amin emphasises, the history of 'Western thought' is conventionally traced back to ancient Greece, and it is generally considered to come of age with the Renaissance reappropriation of Greek culture and philosophy (Amin, 1989: 90, 94). The problem with this 'fabrication of ancient Greece' is that the ancient Greeks themselves were quite clear about their Oriental roots, claiming significant Phoenician and Egyptian cultural ancestries quite at odds with the 'Aryan' definition of Greek culture constructed by nineteenth century 'Hellomania' (see Bernal, 1987). In this connection Kearney reminds us that the very name 'Europe' is itself 'derived from a tradition lying some-

155

where between Africa and the Middle East' (1992: 10) in so far as, in the legend, Europa was carried by her father across the Mediterranean to Greece, without ever abandoning her non-European origins.

It has become a commonplace to observe that, from the time of the Crusades, and then, more dramatically even, from the moment of the Ottoman army's arrival at the gates of Vienna in 1683, it has been the 'threat from the East' which has produced attempts at European unification, both as a defensive response and as a rationalisation for aggressive policies of expansion and the consolidation of white, Christian, 'civilised' Europe against its Other. Indeed, historians of late antiquity have been known to assert that, without Mohammed, there could have been no Charlemagne, in so far as attempts at the unification of what we have come to know as 'Europe' have always developed in response to perceived external threats. However, the 'East' is not always or necessarily 'outside'. It can also designate the 'Other within'. German writers referred to Jews as 'Asiatics' or 'Orientals' right up to the present century, and both Samir Amin and Edward Said stress the way in which the category 'Europe' – through the category 'Aryan' – has, at least since the time of Renan, been defined by way of contrast with the category 'Semitic' (a category which includes both Jew and Arab). We are, as Robert Young argues, forced to consider the relation of anti-Islamic and anti-Arab feeling to its 'dark shadow', anti-Semitism: 'in this context the Jews came to represent the Orient within, uncannily appearing inside when they should have remained hidden, outside Europe: thus the logic of their expulsion, or extermination, becomes inextricably linked with Orientalism itself' (1990: 139). Within the terms of European racism, both Arab and Jew are subsumed together in the figure of the Orient, against which the Western world struggles to differentiate itself.

As if all that were not enough, there are yet further complications. To speak of 'the Jews' is not only to specify a particular racial or ethnic group. It is also to invoke a figure of suspicion within Western culture. In fact, it identifies a symbolic space that can be occupied by different groups at different times. A number of commentators have recently shown that it is the Japanese who are now coming to occupy that space in the imagination of the West. In a short discussion of the new European nationalism, Ian Buruma (1991a) quotes from a disturbing piece of recent racist propaganda: 'With the wholesale appropriation of western ways, Jewry struts about in borrowed plumage, as does foremost Japan in the world at large'. Slavoj Žižek draws attention to the dangers:

> Our perception of 'real' Jews is always mediated by a symbolic-ideological structure which tries to cope with social antagonism: the real 'secret' of the Jew is our own antagonism. In today's America, for example, a role resembling that of the Jew is being played more and

more by the Japanese. Witness the obsession of the American media with the idea that the Japanese don't know how to enjoy themselves. The reasons for Japan's increasing economic superiority over the USA is located in the somewhat mysterious fact that the Japanese don't consume enough, that they accumulate too much wealth.

(1990: 156)

Similarly, Judith Williamson (1990) has pointed to the parallel between anti-Semitism and anti-Japanese racism:

Anti-semitism fed off notions of 'rich Jewish bankers'; anti-Arab mythologies blossomed in the seventies with the buying up of British landmarks by oil sheikhs. And now we have Japan take-over fear, alongside a popular fascination with inscrutable customs, currant-eyed criminals and bad guys on Suzukis.

Ben-Dasan (1972) writes of how 'the position of being a middleman or go-between invites persecution'. The Japanese, he argues, 'known to the great masses of the non-white peoples of the world for the excellence of their products and services, are in a position similar to that of the Alexandrian Jews. They are honorary white men as the Jews were once, in a sense, honorary Greeks in Alexander's city' (ibid.: 164–5). The Japanese, he goes on to say, 'may one day find themselves facing a general hostility that will differ little from that which has inspired persecution of the Jews in many lands' (ibid.: 166). From a Jewish perspective, Shillony (1991) offers an analysis of the analogies between the experience of the Japanese and the Jews, in their interactions with the Christian West.

In relation to American anxieties about the Japanese takeover of Hollywood, the analogy is quite apt. As Gabler (1988) notes, historically, it was Jews who played the key roles in 'establishing' Hollywood: Adolph Zukor (the founder of Paramount Pictures), William Fox (founder of the Fox Film Corporation), Louis B. Mayer (founder of Metro-Goldwyn-Mayer) and Benjamin Warner (founder of Warner Bros) were all from Eastern European Jewish families. As Gabler puts it: 'the American film industry . . . the quintessence of what we mean by "America", was founded, and for more than thirty years operated, by Eastern European Jews, who themselves seemed to be anything but the quintessence of America' (ibid.: 1). In Gabler's analysis, the point is that it was the anti-Semitism which proscribed their entry to more established industries, which effectively directed these entrepreneurs to new areas, like the burgeoning film industry, where such proscriptions held less force. Gabler's argument is that, having established their own companies,

Within the studios and on the screen . . . [they] could simply create a new country – an empire of their own, so to speak. . . . They could fabricate their empire in the image of America, as they would

157

fabricate themselves in the image of prosperous Americans. . . . This was *their* America and its invention may be their most enduring legacy. . . . Ultimately, American values came to be *defined* largely by the movies the Jews made. Ultimately, by creating their idealised America on the screen . . . [they] reinvented the country in the image of their fiction.

(ibid.: 6–7)

From our point of view the crucial question is not so much whether the category 'Jewish' and the category 'Japanese' share some common substance, or display any essential similarity; it is, rather, that they increasingly occupy a comparably unfavourable position in the demonology of the West.

In 1989, the Japanese overtook the Russians in opinion polls as the nation which Americans fear most. The 'official' explanation of this is in economic terms. As McKenzie Wark (1991) says, this scenario reflects the loss of American mastery: a scenario in which 'manifest destiny' turns out to lead 'from Fordism to Sonyism', and, thereby, to the premature end of the American century. It is, however, not simply a matter of economic hegemony. More significant is the racism and paranoia evoked when the Japanese are seen to be buying up things – Hollywood studios, record companies, the Rockefeller Center and so on – that are somehow felt to be properly or quintessentially 'American'. It is a question of strangers 'stealing in' on the American Dream. And the Japanese are, as Waldemar Januszczak (1990b) says, now the 'ultimate 20th century strangers' (cf. Mme Cresson, quoted on p. 147). As he observes:

if the Canadians (rather than the Japanese) had bought Columbia Pictures or Mickey Mouse or the Rockefeller there would have been no point in an outcry. Canadians, after all, are just like Americans, only less so. The Japanese, according to the occidental popular imagination are aliens from the East who are probably trying to take over the West.

(ibid.)

This, as Januszczak goes on to argue, is

a position in the Caucasian imagination that has hitherto been occupied by freemasons and foreign agents and Rosicrucians and little green men from outer space cunningly disguised as humans; and, of course, Jews. Like the Jews, the whole Japanese nation seems to add up to one huge secret society, bent on making money out of Christians.

(ibid.)

Contemporary expressions of anti-Japanese feeling incorporate a long tradition of racist fascination and fear, one whose language and imagery is being reforged in contemporary political and cultural rhetoric. As Judith Williamson (1990) notes by way of example, at the centre of Ridley Scott's highly successful film *Black Rain*, there is the antagonistic interplay of American cultural imperialism and Japanese 'economic' expansion. Michael Douglas complains: 'You Japanese sit on what you've got so tight I can't even pull it out of your arse'. His Japanese co-star, Ken Takakura, dismissively retorts: 'Music and movies are all your culture is good for. . . . We make the machines'. There is, of course, a specificity to American–Japanese relations. When *The Japan That Can Say No* was officially published in English in 1991, one of the most contentious (and most often cited) passages was that in which Ishihara claims that there was a 'virulent racism' in the American decision to drop nuclear bombs on Hiroshima and Nagasaki. It is hardly incidental, in this context, that the motive for *Black Rain*'s chief villain swamping America with counterfeit dollars is revenge for the 'black rain' which fell on Hiroshima.

MODERNITY AND ETHNICITY

We must recognise how abruptly and dramatically the histories and geographies of the dominated were fissured by their encounter with the West. National and regional geographies were disrupted by this contact, and histories and stories of the past had to be retold in a new light:

> It is as if the pre-contact time had been wrenched off and replaced by an unfamiliar temporal system that would efficiently dissolve the residual old. Peoples were also displaced from their sundry geographic centralities to the peripheral positions assigned by the Western metropolis: thus appellations like the Middle East and the Far East . . . . A new history and [a] new geography combined to produce the magical peripheries of the primitive.
>
> (Miyoshi and Harootunian, 1988: 388)

Naoki Sakai (1988) stresses the involuntary nature of modernity for the non-West: modernity for the 'Orient' was primarily about subjugation to the West's political, economic and military control. The modern Orient was born only when it was invaded, defeated and exploited by the West; only when the Orient became an object for the West did it enter 'modern times'. For the non-West, 'modernity means, above all, the state of being deprived of its own subjectivity'; it is possible, then, 'to define the Orient as that which can never be a subject' (ibid.: 498–9). What is clear is that the 'West' is not simply and straightforwardly a geographical category: 'it is, evidently, a name always associating itself with those regions, communities and peoples that appear politically or economically superior to other regions, communities and peoples' (ibid.: 476–7). Onto the geography of 'East' and 'West' is directly mapped the distinction between the 'pre-modern' and the 'modern'. The category 'West' has always signified the positional superiority of Europe, and then also of the United States, in relation to the 'East' or 'Orient'.

It is on this basis that we can begin to understand the contemporary hysteria and panic about Japan. Japan has come to exist within the Western political and cultural unconscious as a figure of danger, and it has done so because it has destabilised the neat correlation between West/East and modern/pre-modern. If the West is modern, Japan should be pre-modern, or at least non-modern. That is the case if it is to fit the terms of the established scheme by which 'we' order our sense of space and time and allocate their place in it to 'them'. The fact that Japan no longer fits throws the established historico-geographical schema into confusion, creating a panic of disorientation (if not yet, to be sure, of dis-Orientalism).

Western social science has understood 'modernisation' as a unilinear process of economic and social transformation, stretching from the cultural and intellectual world of seventeenth-century Europe to the post-1945 United States. It finds the emergence of Japan as an economic superpower hard to reconcile with this model (based as it is on a Euro-American definition of modernity). The scandalous and unthinkable possibility is raised that the West may now have to 'learn from Japan' – that is, to 'Orientalise' itself in order to become economically competitive with the emerging economies of a 'Confucian zone' in the twenty-first century. The unpalatable reality is that Japan, that most Oriental of Oriental cultures, as it increasingly outperforms the economies of the West, may now have become the most (post)modern of all societies.

What Japan has done is to call into question the supposed centrality of the West as a cultural and geographical locus for the project of modernity. It has also confounded the assumption that modernity can only be articulated through the forms the West has constructed. Indeed, what it has made clear are the racist foundations of Western modernity. If it is possible for modernity to find a home in the Orient, then any essential, and essentialising, distinction between East and West is problematised. Japan can no longer be stereotyped as the 'Orient'; it is not possible to marginalise or dismiss Japanese modernity as some kind of anomaly. Its distinctiveness insists that we take it seriously. And, at the same time, it insists that we seriously consider the implications of this for the West's own sense of privilege and security.

ORIENTALISM AND OCCIDENTALISM

In his book, *White Mythologies*, Robert Young emphasises 'the relation of the Enlightenment, its grand projects and universal truth-claims, to the history of European colonialism' (1990: 9). 'The appropriation of the other as a form of knowledge within a totalising system', he argues, 'can thus be set alongside the history (if not the project) of European imperialism, and the constitution of the other as "other" alongside racism and sexism' (ibid.: 4). Drawing on Derrida, he makes the point that, through the development of Western culture, 'the white man [has taken] his own mythology, Indo-European mythology, his own *logos*, that is, the *mythos* of his idiom, for the universal form of that he must still wish to call Reason' (ibid.: 7). In the deconstruction of this Europeanisation of culture and knowledge, the work of Edward Said has clearly been of particular importance. *Orientalism* offers a cogent analysis of the process through which the 'Orient' has been produced as an object, not only of knowledge, but also of power, inscribed in both the discourses and the institutions of imperialism and colonialism.

Said's work on the 'Middle East' is clearly of relevance in looking at the West's construction of a 'Far East', but as Richard Minear rightly stresses, 'the historical relation between "the West" and Japan was very different from that which obtained between "the West" and Said's Orient' (1980: 508). Thus, whilst it did succumb to Western force in the nineteenth century, and also in the middle of the twentieth, 'Japan did not become a colony'. 'Nor', Minear adds, 'did the abiding cultural ties which bound the West to the Orient exist between Japan and the West. Japan held no special interest'. This meant that the particular relation between Orientalist knowledge and imperial and military power, which has been so important in the case of the Middle East, did not hold in the case of Japan: Japanese studies 'never experienced the naked "authority over the Orient" which Said sees as an integral part of Orientalism'. 'Nor', Minear continues, 'did Japan wait for the West to discover its own past, its history, its identity'. Japan was always a sophisticated and literate culture, and, indeed, some of the most widely read books on Japan in Western languages were written by Japanese. What is clear is that 'the West had very little to teach Japan about itself' (ibid.: 514–15). This apparent hermetic integrity of Japanese culture has been crucial to the way it has functioned within the Orientalist *imaginaire*.

Its irreducible difference has been the source of both fascination and anxiety. Far Orientalism – from Lafcadio Hearn's *Japan: An Attempt at Interpretation* through to Roland Barthes' *The Empire of Signs* – has been seduced by the elaborate and arcane rituals of Japanese culture; this Orientalism has been one in which Japan functions as a locus of self-estrangement and cultural transcendence. In his account of *The Japanese Tradition in British and American Literature*, Earl Miner suggests that 'Japan, a civilisation as highly refined as the West, is familiar and congenial in its modern conveniences, in addition to having the additional grace for a world-weary Westerner of new and idealised forms of behaviour and art' (Miner, 1958: 270; cf. Melot, 1987/8). In contact with this refined exoticism, the world-weary Westerner has indulged in

161

unashamed aestheticism, eroticisation and idealisation. Japan has been the 'proper meeting-ground of East and West', where Western rationalism might seek fulfilment through its 'marriage' with Eastern mysticism (Miner, 1958: 271).

Yet this uniqueness of Japanese culture, which makes it exceptionally seductive, may also provoke fear and anxiety. There is a fear of what lies behind the enigmatic façade of Japanese aestheticism and spiritualism. There is a fear that Japan's irreducible difference will remain aloof from, and impenetrable to, Western reason and universalism. A fear, too, that Western culture might itself be overwhelmed by the Oriental Other. This is now a fundamental issue in discussions of the 'Japan problem'. A leader article in the *Financial Times* (19 September 1991) symptomatically suggested that 'Britain, though not Britain alone, fears some emasculation'. Bruce Cumings reveals the existence of an unpublished report, commissioned from Rochester Institute of Technology by the CIA, which tries to address the question of how different the Japanese are from 'us':

> The report deems the Japanese 'creatures of an ageless, amoral, manipulative and controlling culture . . . suited only to this race, in this place.' Which 'creature' do they most resemble, you might ask. Well, the Japanese get along 'as does the lamprey eel living on the strength of others.' The lamprey eel will not stop sucking the lifeblood of the rest of us, this 'treatise' implies, until it has devoured the entire world.
>
> (Cumings, 1991: 365)

This represents a kind of response to Ishihara's *The Japan That Can Say No*. What we have here, as Cumings puts it, is 'the America that can say yo!' It may be ludicrous, even comical, but it is racist. It may be extreme, but it reflects a prevailing attitude towards the Japanese 'Other'.

'The most consistently interesting questions caused by Japan', according to James Fallows (1991a: 7), 'involve its differentness'. If difference can be seductive, it is always disturbing, dangerous, and ultimately intolerable. The 'Other' must be assimilated or excluded: within 'our' universe there is no place for difference as such. 'What is at issue', writes Cornelius Castoriadis (1992: 4), 'is the apparent incapacity to constitute oneself as oneself without excluding the other – *and* the apparent inability to exclude the other without devaluing and, ultimately, hating them'. It is almost always the case in the encounter between cultures, Castoriadis argues, that the Other is constituted as inferior:

> The simplest mode in which subjects value their institutions evidently comes in the form of the affirmation – which need not be explicit – that these institutions are the only 'true' ones – and that therefore

the goods, beliefs, customs, etc., of the others are false. In this sense the inferiority of the others is only the flipside of the affirmation of the *truth-proper* of the institution of the society-Ego.

(ibid.: 6)

The sole foundation for the institution of ('our') society 'being belief in it and, more specifically, its claim to render the world and life coherent, it finds itself in mortal danger as soon as proof is given that other ways of rendering life and the world coherent and sensible exist' (ibid.). Difference is not easy to live with. But what if another culture were to seem, and to claim itself, 'equivalent' or even superior to 'ours'? What if it will not be excluded or converted? What if, as is the case with the Japanese, it seems to flaunt its differentness?

The 'Japan problem' is, in one sense, the problem of Japan's irreducible difference. Japan's differentness is a very particular problem for the West. The Japanese Other plays the West at its own game. Western Orientalism appears to have found its match in what seems to be an 'Orientalism in reverse'. In his discussion of Said's *Orientalism*, Sadik Jalal al-'Azm addresses the question of Islamic revivalism and fundamentalism. Its discourses on the inherent superiority of Islamic culture, he argues, 'simply reproduce the whole discredited apparatus of classical Orientalist doctrine concerning the difference between East and West, Islam and Europe. This reiteration occurs at both the ontological and epistemological levels, only reversed to favour Islam and the East in its implicit and explicit value judgements' (1981: 22). The 'dichotomising' tactic of Orientalism is by no means the hallmark of Western thought alone, and 'Orientalism in reverse' is, in the end, 'no less reactionary, mystifying, ahistorical and anti-human than Orientalism proper': a tendency well demonstrated in recent Islamic fundamentalist critiques of 'Occidentiosis' (defined as the 'infection' of Islamic cultures by 'corrupt' Western values).

In this case, however, the argument is posed abstractly and is divorced from the question of power – here the institutional power of the West, which has ensured the authority of its Orientalism. As Lata Mani and Ruth Frankenberg argue,

it is within the context of a specific set of unequal economic, social and political relationships between West and East that Western descriptions are produced. It is these relationships that lend them strength and endurance. Until this world-historical context changes, it does not make sense to speak of a 'reverse Orientalism'.

(1985: 187)

Where power is missing, it is not really meaningful to talk of 'Orientalism in reverse'. But what about Japan?

In the case of Japan, it is of some interest to interrogate the recent flourishing of what might actually be understood as a form of 'Orientalism in reverse'. We are referring to the rise of *nihonjinron* discourses of 'Japaneseness', 'Japanese uniqueness', 'Japanese superiority' and 'Japan as Number One'. *Nihonjinron* discourses are works of cultural nationalism concerned with the ostensible uniqueness of Japan. They display a number of assumptions, centred principally around the idea that the Japanese constitute a culturally and socially homogeneous racial entity, the essence of which is both unchanged throughout history and quite different from all other races. *Nihonjinron* discourses are by no means new: these 'discussions of the Japanese' (a literal translation of *nihonjinron*) have been going on for at least the last hundred years (Dale, 1987). As Richard Minear observes,

> with or without power in its favour, Japan has a long tradition of racist and ethnocentric behaviour; what nation does not? Perhaps European and American ideas about the 'non-Western' world are exceptional only in that during the past several centuries Europe and America have had the military power to put them into action.
>
> (1980: 516)

What is at stake now, however, is the changed function these discourses have in the new context of a shifting balance of power between Japan, Europe and the United States. As Japan comes to assume a hegemonic position in the spheres of technology, manufacturing and finance, and as the question of Japanese military capacity increasingly comes onto the political agenda, there are growing fears about whether Japan might now have power in its favour and might now be inclined to put its ideas into action. In the context of these changing power relations, *nihonjinron* discourses are taking on a new significance, as are European and American reactions to them.

Historically, the West has provided the universal point of reference in relation to which Others have been defined as particular. Thus, Japan has existed 'as a particularity, whose sense of identity is always dependent upon the Other. Needless to say, this Other is a universal one, in contrast to which Japanese particularism is rendered even more conspicuous' (Sakai, 1988: 484). If the discourse of *nihonjinron* has stressed innumerable cases of Japan's difference from the West, thereby defining Japan's identity in terms of deviations from the West, 'this is nothing but the positing of Japan's identity in Western terms, which in return establishes the centrality of the West as the universal point of reference' (ibid.: 487). None the less, the desire has been to change this situation so that the Japanese would occupy the position of the centre and of the subject which determines other particularities in its own universal terms. In more recent developments of *nihonjinron* discourse what we are seeing seems to be a series of 'tryouts in rewriting world history and geography with the first world and Japan as the joint master-narrators' (Miyoshi and Harootunian, 1988: 390). Western anxieties about Japan are an expression of resentment at this emergence of a threat to what has been seen as the West's natural and proper claim on universalism.

Japanese culture has developed a kind of reverse Orientalism, what Roland Robertson (1991: 192) describes as 'Occidentalism', based on claims as to the selfish individualism, materialism, decadence and arrogance of Westerners (particularly Americans), and also on an explicit pride in Japanese racial purity, which has been contrasted with the allegedly debilitating consequences of American racial and ethnic heterogeneity. This kind of Japanese self-projection and self-assertion can assume highly provocative and confrontational forms. When, in the context of the Gulf War, one Japanese commentator described the Americans as 'our white mercenaries' (Buruma, 1991b: 26), it was difficult for the Western forces to take. When Ishihara throws out a warning to 'the Caucasians' that their creative energies are becoming exhausted and their civilisation is in its terminal phase, this can be decidedly unnerving and destabilising. To be warned that the future belongs to those who are 'in and of the Orient' exposes a raw nerve.

There have been two kinds of Western response to these 'Occidentalist' challenges. The first has been defensive, reflecting a certain disorientation and loss of self-confidence. Perhaps Japan has become Number One? The 1980s saw a quite significant shift in American perspectives on Japan, especially following the publication of Ezra Vogel's widely read *Japan as Number One* (1979), and the emergence of the question of what America could 'learn from Japan'. This has also translated itself into attempts to reassert national self-image and self-esteem by recovering the essence of American difference. Indeed, what one sees is 'something like an American equivalent of *nihonjinron*, with much debate about the ways in which American national culture could be enhanced and protected from global relativisation. In certain respects the idea of American exceptionalism is the equivalent of the idea of Japanese uniqueness' (Robertson, 1991: 189). Thus, James Fallows (1989b) has argued that America could be made great again by capitalising upon the 'American talent' for disorder and openness and by rejection of the 'Confucianism' which he says has taken hold of American society in the form of credentialism, reliance upon educational testing and so on. This is not to suggest that the idea of American exceptionalism is new. Manifestly, it is not. What is new is the centrality of Japan as the point of reference in relation to which (or against which) 'Americanness' is being defined.

But if there have been such responses of adjustment, there has also been a more aggressive retaliation against what is seen as Japanese provocation. An outburst of 'Japan-bashing' flared up around 1987, and it did so as an immediate consequence of the thawing relations between the West and the Soviet bloc. It is the transformation to the so-called New World Order that is now changing American and European attitudes to Japan. Now there is a growing hostility to what is seen as its ruthless and dedicated economic expansionism, anger at this insensitivity to global concerns (the environment, famine) and resentment about its lack of political solidarity (the Gulf War). Ishihara (1991: 77–8) reports a conversation in which a US congressman said: 'US–Soviet ties have dramatically improved and it's quite possible that the partnership between Washington and Tokyo might be dissolved'. 'Do you mean that Americans and Russians have rediscovered their mutual identity as Caucasians?', Ishihara responded. The congressman nodded in agreement.

Two recent Japan-bashers, Michael Silva and Bertil Sjögren, suggest that we have to cast our minds back to the wartime period if we want to gain insights into 'the Japanese mind set' (1990: 156). In trying to understand Japanese economic strategy, these authors explicitly use Pearl Harbor as a reference point, one that 'more than vaguely parallels today's economic confrontations'. And, in a much-cited article, James Fallows points to 'Japan's ever-present fears that the rest of the world is about to gang up on it and exclude it' (1989a: 40). The last time Japan felt like this, Fallows goes on, was the moment of Pearl Harbor, when the country's military leadership 'was convinced that the West had decided to choke Japan to death, with boycotts, so Japan might as well strike' (ibid.). Japanese 'narcissism', a 'weakness of universal principles' and a 'lack of emotional connection to the rest of the world', all add up to make Japan seem a powerful figure of danger. Japan is different: a natural enemy. The Western mood is resentful and belligerent. The talk is of 'the coming war with Japan' (Friedman and LeBard, 1991).

Orientalism and Occidentalism head to head: cultures in contestation. Who is to be the 'unmarked' (the natural) point of universal reference? Who is to occupy the 'centre', in relation to which the 'Other' must define its particularly and marginality? 'West' against 'East'. We could say that it should not, need not, be like this. In the words of Ihab-Hassan, Occident and Orient 'have "contaminated" one another, and this is, mainly, to the good' (1990: 74). These interactions, we might say, 'hint at the possibilities of human understanding, an understanding neither universal nor stubbornly local' (ibid.: 83). And yet what we have is mutual paranoia: 'This idea that the others are quite simply others, which in words is so simple and so true, is a historical creation that goes against the "spontaneous" tendencies of the institution of society' (Castoriadis, 1992: 6). There are powerful psychic investments in the desire to exclude the Other.

166

TECHNO-ORIENTALISM AND THE FUTURE OF MODERNITY

In one sense, then, the West's 'Japan problem' is about the confrontation between cultural narcissisms. But to leave it at that would be too easy. There is something that is even reassuring about the possibility that Japan's phenomenal economic and technological success is attributable to 'the Japanese mind'. To invoke Oriental conformity, stealth and ruthless dedication is to suggest that Japan does not play by the rules. The comparative lack of success of the European and North American economies must then be a consequence of abiding by universal principles and moral codes. Through such reasoning, it is possible, even in the face of competitive failure, to reaffirm the essential (that is, civilisational) supremacy of Western culture.

Differentness is functional: it cannot be willingly or easily relinquished. Through the manic assertion of difference, the identity of Western culture and identity can be sustained. And if the encounter with difference is painful, what it averts – what it represses, denies or disavows – is something that is more painful still. What it defers is the encounter with Western self-identity and self-interest, as well as the recognition of what is common in both the Japanese and Western experiences of modernity.

The functioning and the significance of technology in Western identity is crucial to understanding what this means. What would the West be without its vaunted technological supremacy? Technology has been central to the potency of its modernity. And now, it fears, the loss of its technological hegemony may be associated with its cultural 'emasculation'. Technology is held to be the key to the future, and Japan now has a growing lead in key areas of technological development. Symbolically, American military capacity is increasingly dependent on Japanese high-tech components. This Japanese rise to power has been a perfectly conscious strategy. From the nineteenth century, 'Japan's leaders knew the country would be colonised, like Malaya or China, if it did not haul itself into the modern age'; and, following defeat in the Second World War, 'Japan's tattered postwar leadership understood that technology and industry were the only means of recovering independence of any kind' (Fallows, 1991b: 34). Akio Morita has described how he deliberately set out to make Sony's image synonymous with 'technical quality'. This was necessary in order to avoid the negative connotations of products being perceived as 'Japanese', given the level of anti-Japanese feeling in the immediate post-war period. In a BBC interview in the mid-1980s, Morita recalled the task that faced him:

> When I first visited Europe in 1953, I discovered that Japan had a very bad image in Europe because of the war . . . and I thought 'unless we make a real high technical quality product we cannot sell

anything here'. So we have been trying to change our image, to concentrate on quality in technical standards.

Through its strategies of technological innovation, Japan has more than recovered its independence, and has now hauled itself perhaps even beyond the modern age.

Lummis (1984) has argued that this is the society where technology and rationalisation have fused perfectly. Technological prowess has become associated with Japanese enterprise (Sony, Nissan, Matsushita, Panasonic, Toshiba, Toyota . . .). In Don DeLillo's *White Noise*, Jack Gladney's daughter utters two clearly audible and haunting words in her sleep, 'Toyota Celica':

> How could these near-nonsense words, murmured in a child's rest-less sleep, make me sense a meaning, a presence? She was only repeating some TV voice. Toyota Corolla, Toyota Celica, Toyota Cressida. Supranational names, computer-generated, more or less universally pronounceable. Part of every child's brain noise, the substatic regions too deep to probe.
>
> (DeLillo, 1985: 155)

High-technology has become associated with Japaneseness. Out of this a new techno-mythology is being spun. Japan can be projected as 'the greatest "machine-loving" nation of the world', a culture in which 'machines are priceless friends' (Kato, 1991). Japan has become synony-mous with the technologies of the future – with screens, networks, cyber-netics, robotics, artificial intelligence, simulation. What are these Japanese technologies doing to us? The techno-mythology is centred around the idea of some kind of postmodern mutation of human experience. 'The Japanese are not altering the way we see the real world, they are doing something far more radical', writes Charlie Leadbeater (1991): 'They are taking us further and further into a different world of electronic images and sounds. . . . In future, the line between the real and the electronic will probably blur even further to the extent that it may not be fully recog-nisable'. The Japanese are creating a new domain of artificial reality. Karaoke, *pachinko*, computer games, virtual reality. Japanese technologies are 'blurring the line between the real and the simulated . . . producing the sensation that reality is only part of a world of simulation' (Isozaki, 1991).

If the future is technological, and if technology has become 'Japanised', then the syllogism would suggest that the future is now Japanese too. The postmodern era will be the Pacific era. Japan is the future, and it is a future that seems to be transcending and displacing Western modernity. In so far as a nation's sense of identity has become confused with its tech-nological capability, these developments have, of course, had profoundly disturbing and destabilising consequences in Europe and the United States. The West has had to try to come to terms with everything that this technological 'emasculation' entails. As the dynamism of technological innovation has appeared to move eastwards, so have these postmodern technologies become structured into the discourse of Orientalism. Through these new technologies, the contradictory stereotypes of Japaneseness have assumed new forms; the new technologies have become associated with the sense of Japanese identity and ethnicity.

One response is to see *pachinko* and computer games simply as the postmodern equivalents of zen and kabuki. Like 'traditional' forms of Japanese culture, they too embody the exotic, enigmatic and mysterious essence of Japanese particularism. This is apparent in the postmodern romanticisation of Japan as a space somewhere between the real and the imaginary. Tokyo is the centre for a new phenomenon of 'postmodern tourism': 'the paradigm of the modern decentred metropolis. It's not so much that [it] disorientates you – rather that you never get orientated in the first place' (Thackara, 1989: 35). In cyberpunk fiction this aestheticism and exoticism become quite apparent. William Gibson's *Neuromancer*, as Yoshimoto Mitsuhiro (1989: 18) observes, combines 'futuristic high-tech images of contemporary Japan and anachronistic images of feudal Japan still widely circulating in the popular American imagination'. The same can be said of Ridley Scott's *Blade Runner*. Stephen Beard describes this as 'the re-invention of Japan as a land of high-tech enchantment':

> manga, techno-porn, high-density urbanism, mobile fashion, hyper-violent movies, video-phones, fax cameras, hand-held televisions, video-games, disposable buildings, even a new breed of 'radically bored' teen information junkies, *otaku*, who shun body contact and spend all their waking hours gathering data on the most trivial bit of media.
>
> (1991: 25)

Through the projection of exotic (and erotic) fantasies onto this high-tech delirium, anxieties about the 'importance' of Western culture can be, momentarily, screened out. High-tech Orientalism makes possible 'cultural amnesia, ecstatic alienation, serial self-erasure' (ibid.).

But there is another, more resentful and more aggresively racist, side to this techno-orientalism. The association of technology and Japaneseness now serves to reinforce the image of a culture that is cold, impersonal and machine-like, an authoritarian culture lacking emotional connection to the rest of the world. The *otaku* generation – kids 'lost to everyday life' by their immersion in computer reality – provides a good symbol of this. These children of the media 'despise physical contact and love media, technical communication, and the realm of reproduction and simulation in general' (Grassmuck, 1991: 201); they are characterised by a kind of 'vacuousness' and by 'self-dissociation in hyper-reality' (ibid.: 207):

> In the age of cyber-medialism with its emphasis on simulation, the hi-tech media become the condition for survival . . . . The media cyborgs in their electronic womb are also called *aliens* . . . it's an empty, content-less joy of technology that drives them.
>
> (ibid.: 213)

These kids are imagined as people mutating into machines; they represent a kind of cybernetic mode of being for the future. This creates the image of the Japanese as inhuman. Within the political and cultural unconscious of the West, Japan has come to exist as the figure of empty and dehumanised technological power. It represents the alienated and dystopian image of capitalist progress. This provokes both resentment and envy. The Japanese are unfeeling aliens; they are cyborgs and replicants. But there is also the sense that these mutants are now better adapted to survive in the future. The *otaku* are the postmodern people. To use Baudrillard's phrase, the future seems to have shifted towards artificial satellites.

There is something profoundly disturbing in this techno-orientalism. Following Castoriadis, we have suggested that Western xenophobia and racism are motivated by the apparent incapacity of a culture to constitute itself without excluding, devaluing and then hating the Other. That the Others must be instituted as inferior, Castoriadis (1992) describes as the 'natural inclination' of human societies. This is the logic of a kind of self-love that constructs itself in terms of a cultural and national narcissism. But there is something more, something deeper, something we might even describe as 'unnatural' in this logic of techno-orientalism. As Castoriadis goes on to suggest, hatred of the Other can also be seen as the 'other side of an unconscious self-hatred'; a hatred that is 'usually for obvious reasons intolerable under its overt form, that nourishes the most driven forms of the hatred of the other' (ibid.: 9). To explore this possibility speculatively, and perhaps only metaphorically, we might suggest that the resentment expressed against Japanese technology (rationality, development, progress) reflects an unconscious and primal hatred of this aspect of Western maturity. There is perhaps a (delirious) refusal, rejection, detestation of that modernity into which our own culture has been transformed; of that (totalitarian) element of modernity that threatens some deep-seated aspect (or cultural monad) in Western society.

Perhaps Japan is just a mirror of our own modernity and of its discontents. Maybe Japan simply reflects back to us the 'deformities' in our own culture. As it asserts its claims on modernity, and as it refuses the investment of Western Orientalist fantasies, there might just be the possibility really to 'learn from Japan'. We shall increasingly be compelled to take seriously this Japan that can say no. Perhaps we should be less concerned with what we think it reveals about 'them', and more attentive to what it could help us to learn about ourselves and our own culture. Japanese no-saying is important because of the radical challenge it currently presents to our understanding of modernity and of the cultural and ethnic conditions of its existence until now. Japan is significant because of its complexity: because it is non-Western, yet refuses any longer to be our Orient; because it insists on being modern, yet calls our kind of modernity into question. Because of this Japan offers possibilities. It potentially offers us a way beyond that simple binary logic that differentiates modern and traditional, and then superimposes this on the distinction between Occident and Orient. In so far as Japan complicates and confuses this impoverished kind of categorisation it challenges us to rethink our white modernity.

This kind of intellectual and imaginative challenge cannot, and will not, obviate conflicts between Europe and America and Japan, but it could make it possible to handle real differences of interest in more complex ways. What Japan tells us is that we have to move beyond a worldview that confronts Western modernity with its (pre-modern) Other. Contrary to Ishihara's argument, the modern era has not entered its terminal phase with the displacement of 'Caucasian' modernity. Modernity is now, more than ever, the condition of all cultures in this world. The issue is on what terms they are inserted into that modernity, and on what terms they will co-exist. Japan's achievement is that it is now no different from Europe or the United States in terms of its modernity. What is significant about Japan is its ethnicity, and the fact that it is the first non-white country to have inserted itself into modernity on its own terms. In so doing it has exposed the racist foundations of modernity as it has hitherto been constructed.

JAPAN PANIC

The West resents what it sees as the inscrutable, the remote and the ambiguous nature of Japanese culture. What disturbs it most of all is that this alien culture has now become 'Number One', the model of economic and technological progress. In the United States and in Europe there is a powerful sense of Japanese *otherness* and a growing fear of the might and power of that 'Other'.

It is in this context that we can situate the Japan Festival, held in Britain in 1991, described as 'a nationwide celebration of Japanese culture and society'. As Mark Holborn wrote in the catalogue for the Barbican's *Beyond Japan* exhibition, 'the dialogue between Japan and the West is frequently described in terms of Japan's absorption of the West . . . . In contrast, the West's absorption of Japan is inconclusive and rarely described'. With this festival we might, perhaps, have been forced to confront and absorb that other culture. The question was whether we would be able to use this opportunity to get ourselves 'beyond Japan', beyond a fantasy of the mysterious and sinister Orient, which says a great deal about the xenophobic and neurotic condition of contemporary Western culture and which works to obstruct any more adequate understanding of, and negotiation with, the Japanese Other.

Western stereotypes of the Japanese hold them to be sub-human, as if they have no feelings, no emotions, no humanity. One way in which this Japanese character is held to manifest itself is in terms of bestial and brutal behaviour. In the late 1980s, the British newspaper *The Star* described a 'Banquet of Blood' in which 'raw whale meat was on the menu at a sickening feast for Jap VIPs'. 'During the banquet in Tokyo', it went on, 'they gorged themselves on chunks of the animal's tongue and uncooked slices of its skin'. The Japanese are held to be cold, callous and threatening because of some 'lack' of emotional connection to the rest of the world. In *The Enigma of Japanese Power*, Karel van Wolferen (1989) describes the active suppression of the personal inclinations of the Japanese through a programme of character-moulding that helps to ensure predictable and disciplined behaviour. Japan has come to figure in our cultural unconscious as the symbol of barbarism.

What seems contradictory is that even while the Japanese are perceived as alien and barbaric, there is also a recognition that they may be more modern and advanced in certain ways than the West itself. Japan is seen as the society where technology and rationalisation have fused perfectly. It is now virtually synonymous with the technologies of the future – screens, networks, robotics, artificial intelligence, simulation. Any contradiction here is only apparent, however. Japanese 'achievements' do not make them seem any less alien. As the dynamism of technological innovation has moved eastwards, so have these new technologies become subsumed into the discourse of racism. As these technologies have become associated with Japanese identity and ethnicity, they have reinforced the image of a culture that is cold, impersonal and machine-like. The barbarians have now become robots.

It seems that the West can never see Japan directly. It is as if the Japanese were always destined to be seen through the fears and the fantasies of Europeans and Americans. Japan is the Orient, containing all the West most lacks and everything it most fears. Against Japanese difference, the West fortifies and defends what it sees as its superior culture and identity. And so the West's imaginary Japan works to consolidate old mystifications and stereotypes: 'they' are barbaric and 'we' are civilised; 'they' are robots while 'we' remain human; and so on.

What is at stake is the identity of Western modernity, no less. It was the West that created modernity and modernity has always been associated with that imaginary space and identity called 'Western'. On this basis, we can say that modernity was endowed with an ethnicity (albeit an ethnicity that was invisible to the West itself). Modernity was conceived through a barrier between Europe and America, on the one hand, and the rest of the world, on the other. This barrier was always vulnerable, however. The logic of technological progression and progress which underpinned the modernisation project was always dynamic, always expansionary, always threatening to transcend and betray its Western origins and exclusiveness.

Now it seems to have found a new and ideal host culture in Japan. It is as if the future had passed from Europe to America to Japan, from 'us' to 'them'. This has created a disturbing sense of insecurity around Western modernity. If the Japanese can become modern, then what is still distinctive about the West? Where and what is the West now? Who is us? This is what the Japan panic is about. If it is possible for modernity to find a home in the Orient, then any essential, and essentialising, distinction between East and West is problematised. Japan can no longer be handled simply as an imitator or mimic of Western modernity. It is not possible to dismiss Japanese modernity as some kind of anomaly. Its distinctiveness insists that we take it seriously.

As we move into the mid-1990s, some of the paranoia of recent years, concerning the Japanese 'economic miracle' seems to be fading. There are an increasing number of press reports (cf. Rafferty, 1994) and some academic studies which suggest that the Japanese economy itself is now in trouble. More specifically, in relation to the concerns of this chapter, there are also reports that to date Japanese investments in Hollywood have not, on the whole, been profitable (cf. Reed and Rafferty, 1994), as the Hollywood acquisitions have mainly functioned to drain cash out of the Japanese parent companies. The resignation, in November 1994, of Sony's inspirational chairman, Akio Morita, has been interpreted by many as induced by the financial strain put on the company by the string of flops produced by Columbia Pictures since its takeover by Sony. However, even as Japan's star is seen to fade, other stars rise in the West's imaginative firmament of the East: now all the talk is of the threat posed to the West not so much by Japan itself, but by the startling economic growth-rates of its symbolic offspring – the 'Four Tigers' of South-East Asia – Taiwan, Hong Kong, South Korea and Singapore.

9

THE POLITICS OF SILENCE
The meaning of community and the uses of media

A group is a collection of people who are resolved to keep silent about the same thing: a thing that then becomes a secret. This 'point of silence' holds the group together, sustains it, and even structures it. To violate it is to violate a taboo, to re-open a great wound. It is to risk driving the group to despair because it has absorbed and digested this silence to ensure its very survival.

(Daniel Sibony, 1993)

The media industries have been assigned a leading role in the cultural community of Europe: they are supposed to articulate the 'deep solidarity' of our collective consciousness and our common culture; and, at the same time, they are asked to reflect the rich variety and diversity of the European nations and regions. There is the belief, or hope, that this cultural project will help to create the sense of community necessary for Europe to confront the new world order. But in as much as Europe can imagine itself as a community, it seems that it is an unimaginable community that is being imagined.

Over the past ten years or so, there has been a concerted series of initiatives across Europe, aimed at the transformation of the broadcasting and media industries. A new media order is being shaped, and what the politicians and the bureaucrats who are its architects are hoping is that media industries and technologies will support and sustain the project for European integration and unity. With the implementation of the EC Television Directive in October 1991, they took a big step in the elaboration of a legislative programme designed to extend the organisation and regulation of broadcasting beyond the confines of national boundaries. 'Television without frontiers' is about creating a broadcasting industry and culture that will serve the needs of the European Community into the next century.

What is at issue is the question of media and community. It has been frequently observed that mass communications have played a fundamental part in the historical development of national cultures and identities. Print

174

and then broadcast media brought into being mass publics who began to imagine the community of the nation and nationalism. On the basis of this historical experience, it is now being widely assumed that the media are destined to play an equally significant part in the development of European culture and identity. The inference is that transnational media will give rise to transnational publics, who will then begin to imagine the new community of Europe. What the politicians and bureaucrats believe is that, in creating the economic community of the single market, they are at the same time creating the basis for a future political and cultural community at a European scale.

We want to question these inferences and assumptions about what the media can do for the European project. If we look at contemporary developments, particularly in the period since the idealism of '1992' has been exploded by the realities of 1989, the prospects for building a transnational community look bleak. If there are tendencies towards integration at the economic level, what we are seeing in the political and cultural life of the continent are dynamics of fragmentation and division. Europe is 'caught in the clash between two opposing forces: the logic of economics and interdependence that spells community, and the logic of ethnicity and nationality that demands separation' (Joffe, 1993: 43). The great danger is that, as it is caught between these contradictory logics, Europe lacks the political resources to address the problems that confront it. 'We now have an essentially economic vision of the state and an essentially cultural vision of society', Alain Touraine observes, and 'we have a great need for properly political categories to mediate between the world of the economy and the world of cultures' (Thibaud and Touraine, 1993: 28–9). It is this political silence, this crisis of political will, that forecloses any meaningful sense of post-national community in the new Europe.

This is the context in which a new media order is being evolved in Europe, and in which expectations are being raised about its capacity to promote integration and cohesion. We shall argue that these expectations of the politicians, the bureaucrats and whoever, cannot be met: the media will not be the means to create the imagined community of Europe. We are inclined to agree with Philip Schlesinger when he argues that the case of Europe in fact 'illuminates the *limitations* of what we may expect a communications policy to do and causes us to think again about the relations between the social and the communicative' (1993: 7). What we are now seeing is the inability to achieve any congruence between the economic space of the large market and the political and cultural spaces of European community. Particularly disturbing is the difficulty of building a political public sphere across national boundaries.

These limitations in the development of a European media culture reflect the broader tensions and contradictions in the European project, but there are also limitations that derive from the changing nature of the

175

broadcast media themselves. François Brune (1993a: 4) has argued that the contemporary media have brought about a kind of devalorisation of reality, a 'dispossession of the real', which serves to disorientate viewers and to inhibit their access to political consciousness. What they do is to 'make us purely spectators, that is to say powerless . . . . In the face of what is presented as the order of things, we can only listen, watch and keep silent'. We want to pursue this line of enquiry. What is it in the nature of the media that inhibits the development of transnational community?

MEDIA AND COMMUNITY

What we are seeing in the European media industries is the emergence of a new supra-national regulatory environment in which the emphasis has shifted dramatically towards questions of economic, industrial and competition policy, and away from the political concerns that characterised the old public service system. Now the emphasis is on the creation of a large European audiovisual market that will eliminate barriers to the buying and selling of programmes and to their transmission and reception in the Community. New media technologies and markets seem to make a mockery of borders and frontiers; the order of the day is the 'free circulation' of media products and services. In the broadcasting industry, it is felt, 'the continuation of national barriers and of the fragmentation they cause prevents European producers from taking up the challenge presented by external competitors. They are a major handicap for Europe's industry and cultural identity' (Commission of the European Communities, 1986: 6). European media must move rapidly from their old state of fragmentation to a new condition of integration and cohesion.

This is associated with the transition from a model of regulation which required broadcasters to provide a diverse and balanced range of programmes (education, information and entertainment) for citizen viewers, to a successor model in which the imperative is to maximise the competitive position of European media businesses aiming to satisfy the needs of consumers in global markets. That is to offer a stark, and therefore somewhat reductionist, account of the changes we are seeing in European broadcasting, and we shall qualify it shortly. The stark version has the merit, however, of highlighting the economistic logic that is such a powerful force in the project of European transformation. J. G. A. Pocock describes the new European order as an 'empire of the market'. What is being constructed, he argues, is an economic community based on

a set of arrangements for ensuring the surrender by states of their power to control the movement of economic forces which exercise

176

the ultimate authority in human affairs. The institutions jointly operated, and/or obeyed, by member states would then not be political institutions bringing about a redistribution of sovereignty, but administrative or entrepreneurial institutions designed to ensure that no sovereign authority can interfere with the omnipotence of a market exercising 'sovereignty' in a metaphorical because non-political sense.

(1991: 9)

This might mean that Europe can only aspire to be an economic-administrative union, committed to the inhibition and containment of the political forces that perpetually threaten its fragmentation or dissolution. It is no doubt possible, though deeply problematical, to go further and maintain that the hegemony of the economic and technocratic is essential in the immediate future to create the cohesion and integration that would, in the longer term, sustain a supra-national community that is more than economic. Whichever, the present reality is that the political is subordinated to the economic. In the sphere of broadcasting, the present reality is that the cause of private media and advertisers prevails over concerns of public service and media democracy.

Of course, it is all a great deal more difficult, and constructing an empire of the market cannot be just an economic matter. Culture and politics insist on complicating the Euro-media business; the creation of a European media market inevitably comes up against the problem of cultural preferences, tastes and desires. Some twenty years ago, Thomas Guback identified an economic logic struggling to express itself through the European project. The creation of an economically integrated Europe, he argued, 'favours the enlargement of firms to international stature, with concomitant trends toward standardisation, at the expense of small enterprises and a great deal of variety'. And if this is the case, he went on,

> then it is obvious that the major emphasis is not upon *preserving* a variety of cultural heritages, but rather upon drawing up a new one which will be in tune with supranational economic considerations. In that case, we had better forget about the past and concentrate upon seeing the creation – or fabrication – of a new economic European consumer whose needs will be catered to – if not formed – by international companies probably operating with American management and advertising techniques.
>
> (Guback, 1974: 10–11)

This logic is still at work. There is still the belief, or maybe hope, that it will be possible to fabricate the new model European consumer who will consume new model European programmes.

177

If it is an economic logic that drives this project, it is also the case that it carries with it a certain 'vision' through the expectation that the single market in broadcasting will help to promote the reimagination of community and identity in Europe. As the free circulation of programmes throughout the Community reinforces Europe's production and trans-mission capacity, it is argued, so will it come to promote the ideals of the 'Europe of culture' and the 'citizens' Europe'. For the vision of 'tele-vision without frontiers' to become a reality, there must be congruence between the economic space of the Community and its cultural space. 'Programmes intended, from the beginning, for all of Europe', the Commission believes, 'could count on an audience and resources that would never be available at a national level; they would help to strengthen the feeling of belonging to a Community of countries at once different and deeply united' (Commission of the European Communities, 1986: 9). Pan-European television will help in improving mutual knowledge among the peoples of Europe and will increase their consciousness of the values and the destiny they have in common. It is a deeply problematical vision, but its existence seems to have some kind of neces-sity. It constitutes an ideal of a sort for the future of European culture, perhaps the only sort of ideal that a market technocracy is capable of producing.

What the European Community is struggling to create is, in fact, an expanded version of the national broadcasting model; one that seeks to maintain, at a higher level, the congruence between economic and cultural spaces of broadcasting. It aims to persuade us that a European audience might come to enjoy the imagined community and solidarity of some kind of supra-national identification. In the era of public service broadcasting, coherence and integrity were conserved over decades, in the face of both regionalist and internationalist pressures, through the national compro-mise. The possibility that this could now be succeeded by the similar coher-ence of a European compromise seems unlikely even while the idea is still on the drawing board. It was the correspondence of economic, political and cultural spaces that gave national broadcasting its resonance and vitality. This is difficult to replicate at the larger, continental scale. But, above all, the processes of globalisation have stirred up forces that now seem to make such correspondence ever more difficult to sustain at any level.

What is also problematical about this European media project is that it is based on a very thin and abstract condition of unity. It risks the contempt of a reality whose complexities are indifferent and resistant to such imaginings. The integrity of this European cultural area is threat-ened by forces both outside and within it. From without, the challenge to Europe's fragile integrity comes from those who take very seriously the idea of 'free circulation' – so seriously that they believe products and programmes should be flowing freely on a global scale. For them, the idea of constructing a European cultural area, based as it must be on cultural protectionism and defensiveness, is an anachronism and an absurdity. 'Is the culture in any of these European countries so flimsily anchored that European consumers must be caged and blinded else their links with their past, like an exploding star, vanish?', asks Jack Valenti, President of the Motion Picture Association of America (quoted in Cate, 1990: 4). These interests aim to use what they see as their GATT rights to make sure that 'television without frontiers' means a great deal more than the small European affair that the European Community intends.

Inside Europe, this ideal of unity is contested by those who assert a contrary ideal, one that celebrates the diversity and difference of identities in Europe. Against the principle of a cultural melting pot, the advocates of European nationalism and regionalism struggle to sustain the image of a continent that is really and essentially a cultural mosaic. Here the emphasis is precisely on the preservation of a variety of cultural heritages, both national and regional. The evidence from audience behaviour suggests that television remains very much a national medium, and that national television cultures remain a force to be reckoned with. It is difficult, at the present time, to see what other kind of identification there is to compete, and hard to see why national cultures of television will not continue as the fundamental points of reference well into the future. There is at the same time an excitement about the possibilities opened up by broadcasting at the sub-national and small national scale. For the protagonists of this cause, these possibilities are about the revitalisation of identity and community in the face of those forces that are seen to have promoted centralisation and homogenization. Regional and local media are seen as fundamental resources of both democracy and identity. We have here an appeal to the kind of situated meaning and emotional belonging that seem to have been eroded by the forces of internationalisation and globalisation. What is invoked in the rich diversity of a 'Europe of the regions and small nations' is a new particularism for our times.

In the evolution of EC broadcasting policy both integrationist and particularist strategies have figured. In the 1980s, what prevailed was the strategy to create a large audiovisual market, which could sustain an equally large audiovisual industry, competitive on a global scale with US and Japanese interests. Here, as Richard Collins argues, 'unity through a common European television channel and common European programming . . . was advocated for the integrative effects on European culture and consciousness it promised' (1992: 10–14). More recently, however, there has been an apparently contrasting emphasis on diversity over unity, for example in the European Community's MEDIA programme. In this case, the emphasis has been on the need for recognition of, and

179

sensitivity towards, cultural difference. 'We have no interest in promoting a melting pot', as one EC policy-maker recently put it, 'we want to preserve European identities'. And, of course, this question of diversity and differences is mixed up with the still significant and salient question of national broadcasting industries and policies. In the view of a French observer, 'aesthetic and cultural differences, which make up the richness of European nations, are incompatible with cultural unification . . . . Culture, and particularly audiovisual culture, touches the very heart of nationalism' (Cluzel, 1992: 46).

What seems necessary is some kind of accommodation between the aspirations for a common European culture and the more comfortable certainties of national or regional attachments. In the formulation of EC audiovisual and communications policy, a 'Cultural Europe' is being fashioned, or rather refashioned, for us to belong to and identify with:

> Europe's cultural dimension is there in the collective consciousness of its people: their values are a joint cultural asset, characterised by a pluralist humanism based on democracy, justice and liberty . . . .
> It also involves new kinds of solidarity based on belonging to European culture and greater participation of the people in cultural life, as well as new possibilities for exchange and cooperation which enrich the diversity of our local, regional and national culture.
>
> (Commission of the European Communities, 1988b: 3)

What is being asserted is the continuing relevance and vitality of the European idea. It is the idea of a historical continent which is sufficient to itself, but which contains within itself rich and varied resources of belonging and identity; to be European now is to enjoy a complexity and plurality of allegiances.

There are two observations that should be made here about this association of media and community in the new Europe. The first is that what is presented in terms of richness, complexity and choice might better be seen in terms of tension and stress in identities. To be within an integrated Europe seems desirable, and yet such a way of belonging is also rather abstract and is associated with fears that something about who we are is being lost or damaged in the process. And if the alternative of cultural nationalism represents a way of reasserting that something, there is also sufficient awareness of the limitations of parochial and restrictive attachments. What we see is, in fact, a condition of suspension between identities in which none of the alternatives seems entirely satisfactory. This, as Julia Kristeva argues, can easily translate into an identity crisis 'where people no longer know what their values are, what their future can be, and refuse all projects of community which they consider threatening' (1992a: 1). What is there of this complexity in the European broadcasting directives, or in the Maastricht Treaty with its commitment to 'contribute to the flowering of the cultures of the Member States'?

The second observation is that the emphasis of EC broadcasting policy is on questions of cultural community at the expense of those of political community. Under the old public service regimes in Europe, broadcasting assumed a dual political role, serving as the focus of national or nationalist culture, and as the basis for the political public sphere and democratic politics of the nation state. How successfully or unsuccessfully this was accomplished is a matter of opinion and debate: the point is that within the national compromise both functions were, in principle at least, held together at the same territorial scale. In the context of the new European media this kind of accommodation looks highly problematical. The European Community has so far failed to develop an adequate political culture or a basis for European citizenship (Barret-Kriegel, 1992). The emphasis on cultural community in Europe then compensates for, and deflects attention from, this political absence. The danger is that, within the European audiovisual space, the compensations of cultural identification will prevail over the political objectives of public debate and citizen rights.

COMMUNITY IN THE NEW EUROPE

Historically, the mass media have played a fundamental part in the political life of modern Europe. Not only were the media born with the bourgeois democracies, but they have been inseparable from them and have evolved in concert with them. These democracies have developed on the basis of the political legitimacy of the nation state and the political space of national cultures. In the post-war period particularly, it has been broadcasting that has played the most powerful integrative role, becoming one of the paramount institutions through which social collectivities have constituted and considered themselves as national. Broadcasting has functioned as the space in which the *imaginaire* of a national community is reflected and shaped, and as the pre-eminent forum through which the democratic life of the nation state has been represented.

In the context of increasing European integration, however, important issues are being raised about the future role of the media in the constitution of political and cultural community. If it has been suggested that the new media will help to construct a democratic public sphere on a European scale, there is as yet little sense of what political community might mean on this transnational basis. The 'official' policy of the European Community in effect represents the transposition of the national conception of broadcasting to the supra-national level. 'This', as Philip Schlesinger observes, 'immediately raises questions about its

181

plausibility in circumstances where no single politico-cultural community is confronted by television, but rather that television faces cultural, linguistic, and political diversity' (1993: 10). To understand the contribution of broadcasting to the reconstruction of European identity, to consider whether European broadcasting can come to terms with this diversity, we must first understand something of the nature of the community that is being constructed.

It is through some sense of community that people have felt they can belong to, and identify with, a particular territory. Community has been about social integration, about achieving a sense of coherence and cohesion within a social group; it should be seen as a kind of compromise, a way of holding conflicting forces in tension. In modern societies, of course, the scale and complexity of social processes ensure that the meaning of community is no straightforward matter. Eileen and Stephen Yeo (1988) have distinguished competing meanings of community. At one level, they suggest, community is a positive quality of relationship, 'the characteristic of holding something in common, a feeling of common identity and, most positively of all, a quality of mutual caring in human relations' (ibid.: 230–1). It is 'community made *by* people *for* themselves'. At another level, community is associated with state and nation. In this area of meaning, 'the community *already exists*, has perhaps existed from time out of mind. It certainly pre-dates and does not depend upon the activity of the inhabitants for whom it is supplied, from above; it is made for people, not by them' (ibid.). Here it is a formal and abstract relationship, a social contract which, at its most democratic, reflects public opinion and is concerned with the public good (but which, of course, is not always democratic).

The nature and the scope of community have, over the past century and a half, been contested around these competing meanings. It has been a contestation between 'community from below' and 'community from above': the struggle between a more particular and localised sense of community, a sense of community created from inside, with its more ethical and human relations, and the more abstract and transcendent sense of community associated with system integration across the extended territory of modern societies. What is significant, however, is the success which national communities have had in holding these contrary dynamics in tension. As the Yeos put it, there has been an aim 'to fuse or to confuse the two opposites and to attach warm feelings about mutuality and fellowship to unequal social relationships which are structured from above and which often involve the state' (ibid.). In modern societies, social integration and cohesion have been most effective when there has been a complementary, or perhaps compensatory, balance of power between the enchantment of mutuality and the more formal and contractual relations of the enlarged political community.

It is, of course, at the level of the nation state that this compromise between mutualist and contractual senses of community has been held in tension. Through its sovereign state, the national community has, in principle at least, disposed of the political resources both to represent the collective interests of its citizens and to act as arbitrator or regulator in the event of conflicts of interest. Through the mechanisms of the nation state, internal conflicts have been managed and external conflicts and threats have been absorbed or deflected. But more than this, the nation has been the 'place' in which its citizens feel they have their roots. It evinces a direct and even visceral experience of belonging. In Slavoj Žižek's psychoanalytical terminology, the nation has functioned as 'our Thing':

> as something accessible only to us, as something 'they', the others, cannot grasp, but which is nonetheless constantly menaced by 'them'. It appears as what gives plentitude and vivacity to our life. . . . If we are asked how we can recognise the presence of this Thing, the only consistent answer is that the Thing is present in that elusive entity called 'our way of life'.
>
> (Žižek, 1990: 52)

The national 'Thing' is about the unique way a community 'organises its enjoyment'. Or, in Edgar Morin's terms, nationalism represents the 'projection onto the national of infantile feelings that were once felt towards the family'; the nation is the 'homeland', the 'motherland' or 'fatherland' (1990: 30). The national community in this sense is about the way a community organises its collective need for both affirmation and security.

It seems now, however, that something has happened, or is happening, to the enjoyment and security of members of national communities. There is the feeling that we are in a period when the authority of the nation state is being undermined, when the state can no longer guarantee economic and political integration, and when the idea of a 'national community of fate' is problematical. Eric Hobsbawm makes the point in its strongest form when he argues that the nation state is in retreat, and that any future history of the world

> will inevitably have to be written as the history of a world which can no longer be contained within the limits of 'nations' and 'nation-states' as these used to be defined, either politically, or economically, or culturally, or even linguistically. It will see 'nation-states' and 'nations' or ethnic/linguistic groups primarily as retreating before, resisting, adapting to, being absorbed or dislocated by, the new supranational restructuring of the globe.
>
> (1990: 182)

This process of change can be seen as a reflection of the forces of globalisation that are overcoming national boundaries, undermining national states, and, it is said, creating a new kind of global civil society. 'At the end of the twentieth century', argues Ronnie Lipschutz, 'we are seeing the leaking away of sovereignty from the state both upwards, to supra-national institutions, and downwards, to subnational ones' (1992: 399), and in the process we are seeing the growth of a 'global civil society [which] represents an ongoing project of civil society to reconstruct, re-imagine, or re-map world politics' (ibid.: 391). This global civil society mirrors the type of supra-national society that existed before the seventeenth century, Lipschutz suggests, when 'prior to the Treaty of Westphalia and the emergence of the state system, there existed a relatively vibrant trans-European civil society, linked to territories but not restricted to territory' (ibid.: 400).

Does this period of transformation then mark the beginning of the end for the 'Westphalian model' of sovereign state power? Does the idea of Europe and European community represent a next, and a more cosmopolitan, stage in the political and cultural life of this continent? When we look at the aspirations and the inspirations of the politicians and the bureaucrats we are likely to doubt this. What we are in fact seeing in the project to construct a European Community seems to be more about trying to recreate the conditions of national community at a higher order – the construction of a kind of European nation state. Europe is invoked as a new basis for integrating and unifying contradictory and conflicting forces. The expectation is that the relation between mutuality and political community might be renegotiated and held in compromise at this higher level. We see, then, a kind of transfer or displacement of nationalisms to bring into existence a new and enlarged community, with the same objective and aspiration as the national community of achieving correspondence between state, people and territory.

But if Europe has begun to emerge as a market and as a power bloc, it is more difficult to see the construction of a common and unitary political culture comparable to that which was historically achieved by the nation state. Whatever else we might say about it, the nation state was able to hold in balance the mutualist and political senses of community, and thereby to achieve some compromise between cultural belonging and political life. What is problematical at the scale of Europe is to combine community as mutuality with community as democratic state; to reconcile the ideal of a 'community of culture' with that of 'political community'. As a consequence, what appears to be happening is that questions of citizenship and questions of identity are becoming dissociated.

Most critical, in the light of what is happening to the powers of the nation state, is the question of political culture and citizenship at the European level. In a discussion of what it might mean to move from a national to a continental political space and public sphere, Stig Hjarvard recognises that 'at the European level there is no public with the ability to perform a critical function or represent alternative interpretations or definitions of the political agenda' (1993: 90). The deficiencies of the European public sphere, he goes on, are 'the effect of an unequal development in which the internationalisation of capital and formation of a supra-state administration and regulation have grown rapidly but have not been accompanied by a parallel development of public knowledge'. Hjarvard seems to imply that the 'democratic deficit' in Europe can be corrected. As yet, he suggests, 'a European public sphere is only in its beginning', and we still have some way to go in elaborating the appropriate mechanisms for effective publicity and debate across the continent.

But is it just a question of the appropriate mechanisms? Or are there more profound obstacles to the development of a European political culture? We must be concerned, Etienne Balibar suggests, with 'what the state is tending to become, how it is behaving, and what functions it is fulfilling in the European space . . . a space which, in particular, cannot simply be reduced to the figure of a "territory"' (1991: 16). The problem he identifies is the apparent inability to develop a political culture and citizenship appropriate to times of transnational community. Europe is caught between the limits of the nation state and non-existence of a supranational alternative. If the European Community has developed certain administrative (and repressive) apparatuses – that is, a certain kind of *statism* – it has not managed to constitute itself as a *Rechtstaat*, a state through which Europeans are represented as citizens. Under this reign of 'statism without a true state', all the conditions are in place, Balibar argues, 'for a collective sense of *identity panic* to be produced and maintained. For individuals fear the state . . . but they fear still more its disappearance and decomposition' (ibid.: 17). This points to a crisis of politics and of the political in contemporary Europe.

If the European Community is in one respect an attempt to create the conditions of national community at a higher level, it might also turn out to be a mechanism for sustaining nations and nationalisms in a world that is increasingly shaped by the forces of globalisation. We could see the Community as offering a way for member states to pool certain aspects of their sovereignty in order to hold on to others which have greater significance real or symbolic – for them. We might, for example, see the principle of subsidiarity as a mechanism for the 'renationalisation' of what has been achieved through the existence of the Community. But it is not just a question of the preservation of the European nation states. We are also seeing the proliferation of a whole array of new nationalist, regionalist and ethnic aspirations. This reflects the persistent appeal of nationalist sentiments and attachments in a Europe that is being reshaped within the new world order. 'Why', asks Tom Nairn, 'has the End of History carried us forward into a more nationalist world?' (1993: 6). Even as he argues for the declining historical significance of nationalism, Hobsbawm (1990), too, has to recognise that it is still a prominent force in the world, and that there is still as much of it in the world as there ever was. (See also Hobsbawm (1994) for an even more pessimistic assessment of the resurgence of nationalism in Europe in the post-Communist period.) Nationalist sentiments and attachments are set to play a significant role in the future of European life – but they will do so in an altered context, a context in which our relation to the national community is different.

This resurgent spirit of nationalism is a complex and a contradictory phenomenon. In one respect, it can be seen as an expression of the revitalisation of civil society, an assertion of more meaningful collective identities against the bureaucratic and technocratic vision of Europe emanating from Brussels. Julia Kristeva points to the search for new forms of democratic participation, and suggests that these new kinds of particularistic attachment represent 'attempts to close the gap between government and the man in the street, between politics and the hands-on exercise of responsibility' (1992a: 1). But there can also be a dangerously narrow and parochial quality in these attachments. They mobilise warm feelings of mutuality and ideals of community created from within and sustaining familial or kinship relations. The danger in this neo-nationalism is that questions of identity eclipse those of citizenship and democracy. Jonathan Friedman observes:

> the weakening of former national identities and the emergence of new identities, especially the dissolution of a kind of membership known as 'citizenship' in the abstract meaning of membership in territorially defined, state-governed society, and its replacement by an identity based on 'primordial loyalties', ethnicity, 'race', local community, language and other culturally concrete forms.
>
> (1989: 61–2)

Where people once turned to the state to represent their interests and guarantee their rights, the danger is that they will now turn to group solidarities for protection. The weakening of political life at the local level opens the way for cultural identity to become both refuge and solace. At this level, too, the compromise between the political and cultural aspects of community is destabilised.

What is at issue is the question of community in Europe now. We have suggested that there are contradictory strategies at work in the continent: on the one hand, there is the project to create the supra-national entity of the European Community; on the other, there is the reassertion of the particularistic and emotional communities of the European nations and regions. The resolution – which is in fact a perpetual deferral or quasi-resolution – appears to be the acceptance of some kind of schizophrenic compromise between the conditions of integration and fragmentation. The problem is that neither in itself seems to represent an acceptable or a meaningful choice. Jacques Derrida identifies the acute dilemma: on the one hand, the European cultural entity 'cannot and must not accept the capital of a centralising authority', and yet, on the other, it 'cannot and must not be dispersed into a myriad of provinces' (1992: 39). 'Neither monopoly nor dispersion, therefore. This is, of course, an aporia', Derrida observes (ibid.: 41). This is what makes the experience of community both frustrating and discomforting.

In one sense, the issue is about how Europe might move beyond the Westphalian model of sovereign power. This model 'depicts the development of a world community consisting of sovereign states which settle their differences privately and often by force; which engage in diplomatic relations but otherwise demonstrate minimal cooperation; [and] which seek to place their own national interests above all others' (Held, 1993: 17). Within this perspective, the political culture of citizenship is concerned almost exclusively with domestic issues – 'our' community – and citizens are not concerned with, or involved in, the foreign affairs that go on beyond the boundaries of their sovereign state. The national community includes 'our' people, over whom 'our' state has jurisdiction, and at the same time it excludes strangers and aliens, from whom we differentiate ourselves, and towards whom we have minimal responsibilities and obligations. What is now called for, and indeed what is recognised in the more ambitious expressions of Europeanism, is the need to come to terms with other cultures, communities and nations. In the context of the changing world order, there is the need to recognise that a community's obligations extend beyond itself; that a community can no longer simply follow the self-interest of its own members, but must acknowledge the increasing interdependence of cultures and the consequent obligations to 'foreign' citizens, both beyond and within its frontiers (Brown and Shue, 1981). If the European project is to mean anything, if the Westphalian model is ever to be replaced by a more open and ecumenical political culture, then these obligations must find expression in and through the creation of political and cultural institutions.

What is currently happening in Europe, however, is a far cry from this aspiration. We see, in the resurgence of nationalist sentiments and in the apparent inability to imagine Europe as anything other than a national community writ large, the powerful hold that the Westphalian model has in European culture. In the face of uncertainties and instabilities, the spontaneous political culture of Europe – both the European Community and the national communities – is one of closure and introversion. In Europe now, 'the great temptation is that of withdrawal, whether it be at the local, regional, national or continental level, and whether it assumes an economic, political, religious or racial aspect'. The most general problem is that of 'the contrast between the search for economic progress and the fear of insecurity, between the opening up of frontiers and nostalgia for closed and stable communities' (Hassner, 1991: 20). Rather than the displacement of the Westphalian model, what we are seeing is more like its modification and reconfiguration to suit the conditions of the new order. 'After the inequality in law which opposes nationals against foreigners', observes René Gallissot, 'we now have, with the closure of the frontiers of the European economic community, the distinction in nature between those of "European stock" and those who are non-Europeans'. 'It isn't a question of a return', he argues, 'but of an enlargement or transposition of the xenophobic and racist discrimination that was previously – and still remains, of course – national in its form' (Gallissot, 1992: 12).

At issue is the question of community in the new context of globalisation, a new world order, and all the anxieties provoked by such a challenge to old certainties. In such circumstances, there are dilemmas about which kind of community can provide greatest stability and security. Can national communities be sustained? Is it the case that local communities might be more viable in the new global context? Or is more to be gained through the creation of a European-wide community? What is not called into doubt, however, is the value of community and of communitarian belonging. For Iris Young, the ideal of community 'expresses a desire for social wholeness, symmetry, a security and solid identity which is objectified because affirmed by others unambiguously' (1990: 232). Also: 'The impulse to community often coincides with a desire to preserve identity and in practice excludes others who threaten that sense of identity' (ibid.: 12). This being the case, there will always be a certain intolerance towards the outsider. By their very existence, outsiders threaten to expose the imaginary basis of our identity: strangers do not have the same inclination to suspend their disbelief about the imaginary contract by which we claim membership of our community. In Europe now, the struggle to sustain the principles of community involves the struggle to adapt the principles of national community – which have most fulfilled the desire for wholeness and security – to the new order. It is a struggle that is being waged in the context of a world in which it is increasingly impossible to avoid strangers; a world in which the fiction of 'our' community is therefore always going to be exposed and vulnerable.

COMMUNITY AND INHIBITION

The principle, or the aspiration, at work in the formation of national communities has been that of homogeneity – ethnic, religious, linguistic, cultural, territorial. Monolithic and inward-looking, the unitary nation

188

state has seemed to be the realisation of a desire for coherence and integrity (though we might suspect that, rather than being the realisation of this desire, it was the *Realpolitik* of nation-building that created the conditions of possibility for such a desire, or such a kind of desire, to be imagined). And, in so far as it has sought to eliminate difference and complexity, the formation of a national community and culture has involved the extrusion or the marginalisation of elements that have seemed to compromise the clarity of national being. As Zygmunt Bauman (1992: 678–9) argues, the 'promotion of homogeneity had to be comple- mented by the effort to brand, segregate and evict the "aliens"'. As such, this kind of nationalist identity 'is perpetually under conditions of a besieged fortress. . . . Identity stands and falls by the security of its borders, and the borders are ineffective unless guarded' (ibid.). Whatever coherence and integrity is achieved, it is at the cost of a perpetual vigilance in maintaining the boundary between natives and strangers. It is this identitarian logic, with its anxious, self-enclosed way of being and of belonging, that has come to seem the natural and unavoidable mode of identification in modern times.

It is this kind of identity-thinking that, at a higher order, is now shaping the present attempts to construct a sense of European community. It is the promotion of homogeneity at this higher level that seems to fulfil our expectations of community, culture and identity. What is being created, then, through the transference or the aggregation of nationalist sentiments, is the unity of a unitary continent. The language of official Euro-culture is significant: it is the language of cohesion, integration, unity, community, security. The new European order is being constructed in terms of an idealised wholeness and plentitude, and European iden- tity is conceived in terms of boundedness and containment. At this higher level, what still seems to be needed is the clear distinction between natives and aliens. Imagined in this sense, of course, it is likely to be as precarious and fearful as the national communities described by Bauman. Its desired coherence and integrity will always have to be sustained and defended against the forces of disintegration and dissolution at work in the world.

In the new European Community, the matter of territorial coherence and integrity is paramount. As economic frontiers have been lifted within the Community to create the single market, the security of Europe's external borders has become, all the more, a fundamental issue. If, for most of this century, the 'Communist bloc' defined a 'natural' boundary to the east, the end of the Cold War has brought this convenient state of affairs to an end. Once again the Eastern Question is on the agenda; along its eastern and south-eastern edges, Europe is now seeking to renegotiate its territorial limits as an economic and political entity. Recall the comments of J. G. A. Pocock (1991), quoted on pages 176–7.

Yet it is not simply a matter of economic or even political criteria for inclusion and exclusion. What is at issue along these eastern and southern margins is also very much about the culture and identity of Europe. What is at stake can be inferred from Lord Owen's observation in an interview with *Newsweek* (6 August 1990: 54): 'You have to have clarity about where the boundaries of Europe are and the boundaries of Europe are not on the Turkish-Iran border'. This desire for clarity, this need to be sure about where Europe ends, is about the construction of a symbolic geography that will separate the insiders from the outsiders, those who belong to the Community from the strangers that threaten to disturb its unity and coherence. Through the same process by which it is creating itself, then, this small, white and Western European community is also creating the aliens that will always seem to haunt its hopes and ideals. Already we see how fears are turning to resentment against immigrants, refugees, terrorists, drug-dealers, asylum-seekers – all those who symbolise disrespect for Europe's frontiers. And we see, too, how machinations of defence are increasingly being mobilised against these intruders and marginal figures. As Jonathan Eyal (1993) observes, Western Europe is building up 'a set of defences, often imperceptible but much more efficient than the Berlin Wall. From an airline clerk to a Hungarian border guard, everyone is working to prevent people coming [into] the West'.

The nature and scale of transformation across the continent is such, however, that those who are considered to be aliens and strangers – the 'new barbarians' – will be increasingly in the midst of the European Community. Europeans will not be able to avoid them. The fundamental question, then, is whether they have the resources to live with them. As Alain Touraine argues, the great issue for society now is 'to teach people to live together, to respect their differences whilst searching for elements of unity' (Thibaud and Touraine, 1993: 32). If Europeans are to address this issue, then they will have to struggle towards some better accommodation between their own needs and desires to belong and the obligation they surely have to be open to the needs of Others. They will have to find some way of bridging national and cosmopolitan values.

In the 1990s, in the context of the emerging New World Order, whatever it may be, Europe is faced with enormous and daunting problems. It would be foolish to deny the scale of the difficulties presented to Europe by the collapse of the Soviet Union or by the wave of migration from east and south. What we are arguing is that those difficulties, which have to be faced in one way or another, are exacerbated by the mentality of the European Community itself. It is with Europe as an imaginary institution that we shall have to come to terms. It is a certain idea and ideal of Europe that now stands in the way of the broader geo-political and geo-cultural changes that are called for.

We hear a great deal about the idea and ideals of European community, about the transcendence of frontiers, about a diversity and plurality of cultures which still has a fundamental unity. Günter Grass makes an ironic observation on these lofty ideals when he writes about the gypsy population of Europe: 'They could teach us how meaningless frontiers are: careless of boundaries, Romanies and Sinti are at home all over Europe. They are what we claim to be: born Europeans!' (1992: 108). And yet it seems that Europe is afraid of gypsies. There is no place for them in the European Community: 'Because they are different. Because they steal, are restless, roam, have the evil eye and that stunning beauty that makes us ugly to ourselves. Because their mere existence puts our values into question' (ibid.: 107). What they expose is what is lacking in us and in our project for European unity. This should give us great cause for concern. How are we to comprehend this disparity between the ideals of European Community and what the real Europe is turning out to be? And how are we to explain our seeming incapacity – our refusal or resistance – to deal with this disparity and all its unthinkable consequences?

We need to come to terms with the nature of our identity desires. Julia Kristeva (1992b) has described the 'psychic violence' at work in contemporary modes of identification. 'We are attracted to this violence', she argues, 'so the great moral work which grapples with the problem of identity also grapples with this contemporary experience of death, violence and hate' (ibid.: 106). This violence is rooted in the fears and anxieties that are being provoked by the enormous upheaval and change that is shaking the European continent. Fears are associated with – that is to say projected onto – the Other, and the perceived threat from that Other then mobilises feelings of hatred and violence. Jacques Rancière has argued that the fundamental issue we must confront is 'the question of the other as a figure of identification for the object of fear . . . I would say that identity is first about fear: the fear of the other, the fear of nothing, which finds on the body of the other its object' (1992: 63–4). It is this fear that stands in the way of the European ideal. What concerns Rancière is whether Europe has the means, and the will, to 'civilise' that fear.

Fear and anxiety are always present, and are always likely to give rise to violent and aggressive forms of behaviour. What is needed is some mechanism that will contain and defuse these feelings. As Paul Hoggett argues, this must 'constitute some kind of bounded space within which both meaning and anxiety can be held and therefore worked upon'. Such a space, he suggests, is crucial for 'the development of a subject which can face its own fear without visiting this upon the Other' (Hoggett, 1992: 349). Forms of collective association and community can constitute precisely such containing spaces. And in so far as in much of Europe, and for most of the time, overt violence at least is managed and contained, we might assume that appropriate mechanisms are in place to deal with our fears and anxieties.

What we want to argue, however, is that this is not the case. If it were, we might expect to see some release of our tensions, some modification of our behaviour, some greater acceptance of the Other. What we see, however, is a condition in which violence is held in check but in which our fears are never worked through and civilised. Communities can function to partially contain our fears but to inhibit our ability to deal with them properly. Isabel Menzies has described how communities of a different order function as a means of social defence against anxiety:

> The characteristic feature of the social defence system . . . is its orientation to helping the individual avoid the experience of anxiety, guilt, doubt, and uncertainty. As far as possible, this is done by eliminating situations, events, tasks, activities and relationships that cause anxiety or, more correctly, evoke anxieties connected with primitive psychological remnants in the personality.
>
> (1960: 109)

In so far as it fulfils this expectation, the institution tends to become idealised. At the same time, however, there is always the fear that its function as a container of anxieties will break down and there is always a sense of impending crisis. 'The social defence system represents', according to Menzies, 'the institutionalisation of very primitive psychic defence mechanisms, a main characteristic of which is that they facilitate the evasion of anxiety, but contribute little to its true modification' (ibid.: 117). There is a striking resemblance between this strategy of coping and that which is mobilised by the organisation of community at both a national and a European level.

We organise ourselves into communities in such a way as to accommodate fears and anxieties without having to come to terms with, and therefore modify, them. Community then becomes resistant to change and development. There is a fear of change, a fear of being changed, a fear of being incapable of changing. Community becomes organised around the mechanisms of inhibition. In order to preserve certain features of their way of 'existence', writes Daniel Sibony,

> people are sometimes obliged literally to sacrifice certain avenues of thought. They do it because they fear breakdown, which they think they do not have the means to deal with. And as time passes, it becomes true that they do not have the means. And then they brandish their impotence as an *objective* fact, a given reality, that was not caused by anybody.
>
> (1993)

The capacity to think and act is inhibited. The community that is organised to evade anxiety is also organised to avoid thinking and learning.

THE SILENCE OF POLITICS

The silence of the masses is also in a sense obscene. For the masses are also made of this useless hyper information which claims to enlighten them, when all it does is clutter up the space of the representable and annul itself in a silent equivalent.

(Jean Baudrillard, 1985a)

We want now to raise some final questions about the media in the light of this broader discussion of community and identity in Europe. There are many issues that could be covered, for example the way in which the media relate to fear, anxiety and violent emotions. Here we want to consider particularly how the media are implicated in the mechanisms of defence and evasion of anxiety that we have just been discussing. The question of media and community, which has been the central concern of this chapter, is usually discussed in terms of the positive sense of community, those evoked by the Yeos (1988): imagined community is about feelings of shared culture and identity in common. But there is another aspect to community, that in which it is held together not by what it avows as its collective values, but by what it collectively disavows. Community can function as a social defence system, serving partially to contain or to avoid fear and anxiety, but also to inhibit the real working through or modification of those feelings. The institution of community then serves as a mechanism of closure, driven by the compulsion to avoid the painful experience of change and development. What are crucial are the processes of inhibition that militate against thinking and against acting in the light of clear thought.

As we pointed out at the beginning of this chapter, the media are now being seen, at least by the politicians and the bureaucrats, as fundamental to the creation of European union and an imagined community of Europe. Through the media, it is anticipated, it will be possible to construct a European cultural and political public sphere. We have already referred to Stig Hjarvard's observation that, as yet, there is no meaningful public or public sphere at the European level. Hjarvard believes that this is because the process of Europeanisation is still at an early stage. He does, however, acknowledge some of the difficulties that must be confronted. For one thing, there is the 'unclarified legitimacy' of European political institutions. And there is also the problem of the enormous scale of the European political space, and the question of the sheer number of interests that will seek representation at the European level. To these difficulties can be added the problem of demarcation caused by the changing size and character of the European Community. What is clear is that 'a European political sphere cannot have the same character as its national counterpart' (Hjarvard, 1993: 89–90). There is the need for a new kind of media system, and to create such a system will require both effort and imagination.

We must all, surely, hope that the media can be made to support the development of a European public sphere and political culture. The media could clearly play a significant part in the development of a transnational civil society, and also in mediating between that civil society and the supra-national institutions of the European Community. But if this is to be the case, we must take account of difficulties other than those raised by Hjarvard; difficulties of a different order, associated not with questions of implementation, but with the nature of contemporary media and media culture. Here we will make just two points. First, we want to draw attention to the fact that the media can actually lend themselves to the processes of evasion and inhibition that we described above; there is the possibility that the media may function to support the mechanisms of collusive interaction and agreement associated with social defensiveness and closure. And, second, we want to argue that there have been recent developments in media systems and practices that work against the creation of a mature and critical political culture, and may even work in favour of depoliticisation and privatism.

The assumption in most discussions about the public sphere is that media audiences have a desire for knowledge and information, which then become the basis for political reflection and debate. But what if there are also other processes at work? The psychoanalyst Wilfred Bion paid great attention to the desire to not know. Thinking, he argued, is discomforting and disturbing. In thinking 'you have to take the risk of finding out something you don't want to know', and, consequently, 'most people want to closure off what they don't want to see or hear' (Bion, 1978: 8–9). There is a fear of knowing the truth which can make people desire to limit their freedom of thought and thinking.

Jean Baudrillard (1985a) has made a strangely similar observation in the context precisely of media and political culture. We believe that what he says should be taken very seriously. 'The deepest desire', he suggests, 'is perhaps to give the responsibility for one's desire to someone else. . . . Nothing is more seductive to the other consciousness (the unconscious?) . . . than not to know what it wants, to be relieved of choice and diverted from its own objective will'. And now, he argues, the masses have come to recognise 'that they do not have to make a decision about themselves and the world, that they do not have to wish, that they do not have to know, that they do not have to desire' (ibid.: 585). In this case, though it is not how Baudrillard himself interprets it, we can see the inhibition on knowledge and action manifesting itself in a collective form as a social pathology.

Even if one is reluctant to go along with Baudrillard in seeing this as some kind of challenge by the masses, one must surely acknowledge that he has identified a significant shift in political communication and culture. What he identifies is 'the disappearance from the public space, from the scene of politics, of public opinion in a form at once theatrical and representative as it was enacted in earlier epochs' (ibid.: 579). Others have also drawn attention to this degradation of political life and to the functioning of the media as public sphere. There is sometimes the feeling that politics has now become merely a television spectacle, but we should realise that politics has always functioned as a spectacle. The point, as Paolo Carpignano and his colleagues stress,

> is not so much that politics has become a spectacle, but that *the spectacle form itself is in crisis*. Put in a different way, the crisis of representational politics could be read as the crisis of a communicative model based on the principle of propaganda and persuasion.
>
> (Carpignano *et al.*, 1990: 35, our emphasis)

What has been undermined is the very ideal of public opinion, the belief that public knowledge can, and should, inform and shape political life.

This demise of the age of public opinion is associated with significant transformations in the functioning of mass-media systems and practices. Carpignano *et al.* describe this in terms of 'a crisis of legitimacy of the news as a social institution in its role of dissemination and interpretation of events', and of the development of new social relationships of communication which, they argue, have made the talk show the pre-eminent expression of the 'public mind' in the new age of television (ibid.). Ignacio Ramonet (1991) has also drawn attention to the undermining of the media as a source of authoritative knowledge. He, too, sees the decline of news coverage as central to understanding the changes in process, arguing that, as the role of journalists and presenters has been undermined, 'it is the force of the image that now prevails': 'the objective is not to make us understand a situation, but to make us take part in an event'. For Ramonet, this abandonment to the immediacy of the image has an enormous social cost. 'Becoming informed is tiring', he argues, 'but this is the price of democracy' (ibid.: 12). The mode of information now works against the principles of informed understanding and political action.

What is at issue in this decline of civic and political culture? How are we to understand how changes in the media system are implicated in this development? Without claiming to give a full answer to these questions, we would suggest that the mechanisms of social defence systems must be taken into account. One factor, at least, in the crisis of politics may well be the desire to not know, to not act. And it may be that television, particularly, functions to support the processes of inhibition and evasion of anxiety. New media systems claim to bring us more information and more direct access to events, and yet, as argued earlier (see chapter 7), at the same time, it would seem that they also enable detachment and screening from the reality of what is seen. It may be that the rise of the talk show in fact represents a response to the tensions and stresses of contemporary individuals (and individualism); that talk shows and 'reality shows' are the 'therapy' of those who feel socially excluded (Ehrenberg, 1993). Through this form of television the excluded and the powerless are compensated by the sense that they are at least living this experience collectively.

Perhaps this will suffice in a culture where public life seems increasingly inhibited. In this culture, as Baudrillard says, 'people are at the same time told to constitute themselves as autonomous subjects, responsible, free, and conscious, and to constitute themselves as submissive subjects, inert, obedient and conformist'. They are caught in a double bind, 'exactly that of children in their relationship to the demands of the adult world' (Baudrillard, 1985a: 588). In the viewers and consumers within this culture a schizophrenic feeling is created. 'You cannot', comments François Brune, 'at the same time, be treated as a marketing target and be respected as an active political subject'. What happens is that the child withdraws into a kind of autism; the child develops an 'inner silence', what Brune calls 'the silence of the target' (1993b: 157).

* * *

> And I'm neither left or right
> I'm just staying home tonight,
> getting lost in that hopeless little screen.
> (Leonard Cohen, 'Democracy')

Historically the media have played a central part in the imagination of national communities; it is probably the case that the creation of a culture and identity in common would have been impossible without the contribution of print and subsequently broadcast media. As Stuart Hall puts it in the case of the BBC and the British nation:

> Far from the BBC merely 'reflecting' the complex make-up of a nation which pre-existed it, it was an instrument, an apparatus, a 'machine' through which the nation was constituted. It *produced* the nation which it addressed: it constructed its audience by the ways in which it represented them.
>
> (1993: 32)

The expectation in many quarters is that the construction of a European media system will now make it possible to construct a Europe-wide imagined community out of the different and often conflicting cultures in the

196

continent. The objective of the politicians and the bureaucrats appears to be 'to project public service broadcasting onto a European level, by allowing it to act as an integrative, homogenising force, producing an informed community, conscious of its shared history and traditions' (Davis and Levy, 1992: 476). The media industries are expected to be a catalyst for the construction of a European community.

There must be considerable scepticism about such a possibility. If there was a moment when it seemed possible that the media might contribute to the reimagination of community, recent developments in Europe have served to make clear the profound difficulties that stand in the way of such a project. The contradictions that beset the project of the European Community have become increasingly clear. If there has been considerable success in creating the economic space of the enlarged market, the development of political institutions and a public sphere at a continental level remains problematical. And if the ideal of pan-Europeanism has made some advances, it is also the case that we have seen the resurgence of particularistic attachments which may threaten disintegration and fragmentation. It is difficult to see how any communications or cultural policy can really come to terms with these complex and contradictory logics. Philip Schlesinger (1993) is right to argue that the case of European media policy is likely to reveal the limitations of a rationalist approach to cultural management on a transnational basis. The question of political culture and of a European public sphere seems particularly fraught with difficulties, and the belief that the old public service model can be aggregated to a European level seems wishful at best.

The contribution of the media to the declared ideals of the European Community, then, is questionable. But what must also be taken into account is their involvement in the more unconscious processes of community. We have described a certain kind of closure that is characteristic of both national and European ways of belonging, seeking to understand this in terms of psycho-geography. Community, at whatever level, may function as a mechanism for social defence and the evasion of anxieties and fears. This is the aspect of its coherence and cohesion about which a group conspires to remain silent. Community is then likely to function to inhibit the processes of knowing, understanding and the modification of behaviour. The media, which we assume to be working in the cause of public knowledge and understanding, may come to function in accordance with these mechanisms of inhibition. Recent developments in media systems and practices would seem to confirm this functioning. Fears attached to knowing may be something we have to take into account in considering the depoliticisation of media culture. The issue, then, is the geography of anxiety and fear in the new Europe, and the implication of the media in this psycho-geography.

10

THE END OF WHAT?

Postmodernism, history and the West

The travellers could describe the phonograph as a new and improved portable god, and call upon the native kings to obey it. A god capable of speaking, and even of carrying on a conversation, in the presence of swarms of listeners could be something entirely new in Central Africa, where the local gods are constructed of billets of wood, and are hopelessly dumb. There is not a Central African who would dare refuse to obey the phonograph god.

(*New York Times*, 19 January 1885)

No one speaks English, and everything's broken . . . .

(Tom Waits, 'Tom Trambert's Blues')

In response to contemporary arguments that 'we' have now entered some notionally 'postmodern' era, Cornel West argues for the need to 'pluralise and contextualise the postmodernism debate' (1991: 3), and specifically to 'note the degree to which postmodernism is an American phenomenon' (ibid.: 5). However, when he says 'American', there is a certain slippage between the terms 'European', 'American' and 'Western'. West goes on to argue that 'postmodernism . . . is a set of responses . . . to the decentring of Europe – of living in a world that no longer rests upon [that] European hegemony which began in 1492' (ibid.: 6). Of course, if Europe discovered America in 1492, five hundred years later, leading world-power status had unquestionably passed from Europe to America itself, in the wake of the exhaustion of the European powers in the twentieth century's two major wars. None the less it can also be argued that the 'American Century', envisaged by Henry Luce at the end of the Second World War, in fact only lasted until 1973. In the wake of the oil crisis of that year, the dollar was symbolically disenthroned in the world currency market and, it can be argued, the postmodern era proper began – a period characterised, not least, by waning American confidence and increasing competition for world dominance from the burgeoning Pacific powers.

The question is, what did end in that moment in 1973? One possible answer would be that it was the end of the untroubled hegemony of the

198

classic tradition of 'Western civilisation', initiated in Europe, but then transposed across the Atlantic. As West notes, that tradition was always perceived (under the continuing influence of Matthew Arnold and T. S. Eliot) as one in which 'the best of Europe was modelled on Periclean Athens, Elizabethan England and . . . early imperial Rome' (West, 1991: 8). The problem has always been the threat posed to this 'civilisation' by the 'barbarians' surrounding it on all sides.

Towards the end of his account of Los Angeles as the *Capital of the Third World*, Philip Rieff recounts what was, for him, a troubling conversation with Nathan Gardels, editor of the LA-based political journal *New Perspectives Quarterly*, during which Gardels argued that LA's (and by implication the whole of the western USA's) 'European period' is ending:

> 'I don't really know . . . maybe it was after the defeat in Vietnam, or earlier, after the 1965 immigration reform. It's hard to say, but what I do know is that every time I go to Europe nowadays, there is a moment when I think to myself very little of what I'm seeing here has all that much to do with the future of Southern California . . . .'
>
> (Rieff, 1993: 258)

Writing in 1956, Christopher Dawson noted that, when Lord Acton had been planning the *Cambridge Modern History*, he had conceived it as a universal history – a study of universal historical forces, and yet simply took it for granted that this history would be a European one, and that 'it was only, or primarily, in Europe and its colonies that the movement of world history was to be found' (Dawson, 1956: 606, cf. also Mackinder, 1904). The presumption implicit in Lord Acton's conception of history has, of course, contemporary parallels. The television series shown in Japan under the title of *Some Aspects of Western Civilisation*, made and presented by the British art historian, Sir Kenneth Clark, had originally been shown in Europe (and in America) under the simpler, but rather more presumptuous, title of *Civilisation*.

As Eric Wolf notes, the term 'history' is often used as a synonym for a particular, retrospectively constructed, genealogy of the West,

> according to which ancient Greece begat Rome, Rome begat Christian Europe, Christian Europe begat the Renaissance, the Renaissance the Enlightenment, the Enlightenment political democracy and the industrial revolution. Industry, crossed with democracy, in turn yielded the United States, embodying the right to life, and the pursuit of happiness.
>
> (Wolf, 1982: 5)

As Wolf argues, the basic problem with this kind of post-hoc teleological narrative, is that it turns history into a moral success story, in which the winners prove that they are virtuous and good by winning, and ancient

Greece, for example, rather than representing a significant historical reality in its own right, becomes a 'prehistoric Miss Liberty, holding aloft the torch of moral purpose in the barbarian night' (ibid.).

At stake here is the overweening self-confidence of a notion of 'Europe' ('with and without the "North America" whose addition turns it from "Europe" into "Western civilisation"' (Pocock, 1991: 10)) which is seen as being 'formed by . . . the community of nations which are largely characterised by the inherited civilisation whose most important sources are the Judaeo-Christian religion, Hellenistic ideas of government, philosophy, arts and science and Roman views concerning law' (Pieterse, 1991: 3). Put the other way round, what this means, of course, is that a contemporary entity, such as the European Community, can be seen to have rather old historical roots – as a 'neo-Carolingian construct: a regrouping of Neustria, Franconia, Burgundy and Lombardy, in the areas defined by the treaty of Verdun in the ninth century . . . a regrouping of the lands of west Latin culture, as modified by the Enlightenment' (Pocock, 1991: 7).

The problem, though, is that while it is illuminating to trace the internal historical roots of the development of contemporary Europe in this way, this is still too self-regarding a story, from which certain crucial threads are absent. Thus Pieterse notes that, while official EC rhetoric speaks of an era of the transcendence of all narrow nationalisms, still this culture,

> reproduced in textbooks, declarations and media programmes, continues to be the culture of imperial Europe . . . its self image, its dominant culture, is still that of an Old World. . . . Certain key experiences are missing from this European culture: the experience of decolonisation, of migrations, post-imperial ('we are here because you were there') and otherwise, and of globalisation.
>
> (1991: 4)

THE END OF HISTORY?

In the context of these arguments, Francis Fukuyama's 'The End of History' (originally published as an essay in *The National Interest* in 1989, reissued in extended form as *The End of History and The Last Man*, 1992) is worthy of comment, in three different respects. The first concerns the question of cognitive relativism and the issue of the 'decidability' of anything in history; the second concerns the question of the type of history which Fukuyama attempts to offer; while the third concerns the adequacy (or otherwise) of the particular historical arguments which Fukuyama offers to account for the developments with which he is concerned. He defends the currently unfashionable Enlightenment Rationalist Fundamentalist claims that history is a coherent or intelligible process, and that human life is philosophically intelligible (cf. Fukuyama, 1992: xiii).

This approach flies in the face of the current intellectual tendencies towards incredulity in relation to all meta-narratives (which Lyotard (1987) takes as a defining feature of our 'postmodern condition'), and also in the face of the widespread cognitive relativism, which Gellner (1992: 29) characterises as a 'kind of hysteria of subjectivity', in which it is increasingly held that 'everything in the world is fragmented and multi-form, nothing really resembles anything else, and no one can know another' (ibid.: 45) and which Geertz (1988) decries as a form of episte-mological (and moral) hypochondria. Thus far, we would want to support Fukuyama's intervention, and would agree with Fish (1989) that, for example, the recognition of the textual status of history, in the work of the 'New Historicists' (cf. Veeser, 1989), while in itself opening up inter-esting lines of enquiry, offers no intellectual barrier to the making of historical assertions. These two activities (the development of general theories of knowledge and the practice of history) are logically indepen-dent (cf. Fish, 1989: 305–8), and see Norris (1991) for a similar analysis of Derrida, in which the recognition that philosophy has a rhetorical dimension is distinguished from the presumption that philosophy is there-fore nothing but a form of rhetoric.

In the face of postmodern presumptions, concerning the supposed 'incoherence' of the contemporary world, Comaroff and Comaroff invoke the anthropological tradition of writers such as Edmund Leach, who, they argue,

> would have scorned any postmodern suggestion that, because the world was experienced as ambiguous and incoherent, it must there-fore lack all systematicity; that because social life seems episodic and inconsistent, it can have no regularity; that, because we do not see its invisible forms, society is formless; that nothing lies behind its broken, multi-facetted surfaces. The very idea would have struck [Leach] as a lamentable failure of the analytic imagination. . . . We require good grounds for claiming the non-existence of a system or a structure – the fact that we are unable to discern one at first glance is hardly proof that it is not there. . . . Absence and disconnection, incoherence and disorder, have actually to be demonstrated. They can neither be presumed, nor posited by negative induction.
>
> (1992: 23–4)

The politics of this 'new sceptism', about the very possibilities of any form of coherent knowledge of the world, have provided the occasion for acid comment by some of those who have always felt disqualified from the position of subject, rather than object, of knowledge. Thus Mascia-Lees et al. (1989: 15; quoted in Massey, 1991b: 33) observe that 'when Western white males – who traditionally have controlled the production of knowledge – can no longer define the truth . . . their response is to conclude that there is not a truth to be discovered'. The issue, as formulated by Nancy Hartsock (1989) is that

> it seems highly suspicious that it is at this moment in history, when so many groups are engaged in 'nationalisms', which involve redefinitions of the marginalised Others, that doubt arises in the academy about the possibility of a general theory which can describe the world, about historical 'progress'. Why is it, exactly at the moment when so many of us, who have been silenced, begin to demand the right to name ourselves, to act as subjects rather than objects of history, that just then, the concept of subjecthood becomes problematic . . . (that) just when we are forming our own theories about the world, uncertainty emerges about whether the world can be adequately theorised.
>
> (Hartsock, quoted in Massey, 1991b: 33)

In a similar vein, Linda Nicholson (1990: 6) raises the possibility that postmodernism may be 'a theory whose time has come for men, but not for women', and goes on to note that Di Stefano (1990) raises the possibility that

> since men have had their Enlightenment, they can afford a sense of decentred self and a humbleness regarding the coherence and truth of their claims. On the other hand, for women to take on such a position is to weaken what is not yet strong.
>
> (Nicholson, 1990: 6)

THE FICTION OF THE GENERAL AMELIORATION OF THE WORLD

For Enlightenment thinkers, such as Condorcet or Turgot, history was understood as a linear progression of humanity towards a condition of perfection, ultimately embracing the whole of mankind, based on the principles of reason. As Whitton remarks, such a rationalist conception of history allowed Enlightenment commentators to 'demean or deride those cultures, past or present, which lacked consciousness of the principles of Enlightened Reason. Such cultures tended to be seen as lesser stages in the development towards this enlightened perfect end' (1988: 15), and it was their good fortune that they would be able to acquire the rational principles of the Enlightenment, direct from those societies who had acquired such 'simple truths and infallible methods . . . only . . . after long error' (Condorcet, quoted in ibid.: 150).

It was against the arrogant presumptions of such perspectives that the late-eighteenth-century social philosopher Gottfried van Herder developed his critique of the manner in which abstract Enlightenment philosophy might legitimise the stifling of different cultural communities all over the world, in favour of an externally imposed, European ideal. Thus Herder ironically notes that this idealised conception of Enlightenment society, with its

> general, philosophical philanthropic tone . . . wishes to extend our own idea of virtue and happiness to each distant nation, to even the remotest age of history. . . . [It] has taken greater sophistication for virtue, Enlightenment for happiness, and in this way, invented the fiction of the general amelioration of the world.
>
> (Herder, quoted in ibid.: 154)

The question for us is whether Fukuyama's own argument ends up inventing a fiction of a similar kind. In fact, his argument has been widely misunderstood, and some part of the criticism which it has received has been quite misinformed. As he notes in the introduction to the extended version of his argument, 'what I suggested had come to an end was *not* the occurrence of events, evolutionary processes' (Fukuyama, 1992: xiii). In this, he takes his cue from Kant's 1784 essay 'An idea for a universal history', in which Kant argued that history did have a final purpose, the realisation of human freedom, implied in human potentiality, the achievement of which was the goal towards which progress ran, which was what made the whole of history intelligible. In his *Philosophy of History*, Hegel (1956) converts Kant's argument into the more concrete proposition that the creation of the Liberal State constitutes (literally) the practical achievement of human freedom. Fukuyama's contribution, is, in one sense, simply to shift the date at which the Liberal State is declared universally victorious – from 1806 and the Napoleonic conquest of Prussia (Hegel's chosen date) to 1989 – with the collapse of Communism, and the 'victorious' emergence of the USA from the Cold War.

Fukuyama recognises that, as an evolutionary scheme, this kind of history, much like that of classical marxism, has its roots in Christian ideas of history – as the gradual working out of God's will on earth, leading to the Day of Judgement, which would usher in the kingdom of heaven on earth – as the final end of man, which would, retrospectively, make all previous events intelligible. However, Fukuyama does not seem to grasp the extent to which, in so far as his own evolutionary scheme replicates the model of 'the Judaeo-Christian tradition [in which] Time has been conceived of as the medium of a sacred history' (Fabian, 1983: 2), his argument is a fundamentally regressive one, in which faith in salvation is simply replaced by 'faith in progress and industry', as the meaning and motor of history. As Fabian notes, this kind of evolutionary history has a close counterpart in the Christian-medieval conception of 'sacred time' – time as the medium of salvation, the vehicle of a continuous, meaningful story. This was the very conception of time against which Enlightenment thought was initially pitched, in the attempt to break with this conception of time, in terms of a history of (potential) salvation, and to introduce a secularised conception of time – as natural history, a conceptual space of geological and palaeontological record, of potentially 'uneventful' data, rather than the medium in which some pre-ordained, evolutionary purpose was gradually 'achieved' (ibid.: 17).

Ultimately, Fukuyama's analysis represents an attempt to revamp the 'modernisation' theories of post-Second World War American sociology (see Rostow, 1960; Lerner, 1964), in which it is presumed that industrial development necessarily follows a universal pattern – that set by the leading capitalist economies of the West – a process which would 'guarantee' an 'increasing homogenisation of all human societies, regardless of their historical origins or cultural inheritances' (Fukuyama, 1992: xiv). In this model, it is 'the logic of modern natural science' (the presumed motor of economic development) which replaces the will of God (or the human spirit, or the class struggle) as the motor force of evolution, and which, according to Fukuyama, 'would seem to dictate a universal evolution in the direction of Capitalism' (ibid.: xv). This is held to be the case in so far as only the social arrangements of liberal capitalism are deemed capable of providing an adequate framework for the full realisation of the potential for growth provided by science and technology – at least in Fukuyama's view. Thus, he claims,

> all countries undergoing economic modernisation must increasingly resemble one another: they must unify nationally, on the basis of a centralised state, urbanise, replace traditional forms of social organisation (like tribe, sect and family) with economically rational ones, based on function and efficiency, and provide for a universal education of their citizens.
>
> (ibid.: xv)

At the risk of flippancy, it could be suggested that Fukuyama's grasp of the relations of cause and effect, in this analysis, is of the same order as that of any other cargo-cult devotee, who builds an airstrip, and then waits for good things to arrive from the sky. As Wolf notes in his critique of modernisation theories, the fundamental problem of this model is that societies are seen as endowed 'with the qualities of internally homogeneous, externally distinctive, bounded objects' (1982: 6), but are not understood in their relations to one another. In this model, there is the 'modern' West, the East only recently delivered from Communism ('a disease of modernisation' – Rostow, quoted in ibid.: 7), and the Third World of 'underdeveloped' societies, whose modernisation can only be achieved if ways can be found to help them break free of the stranglehold of 'tradition' (see Lerner, 1964).

The missing term, in Fukuyama's analysis, is the concept of imperialism. We shall never understand the relative positions of, say, Britain and India, if we imagine that it is simply a matter of Britain having been 'more successful' in the world economy, and displaying traits which India must emulate, if it wants to 'catch up'. The theory of imperialism would suggest that, rather than the 'facts' of Britain's 'development' and India's 'under-development' being incidental to each other, the former is, in large part, a consequence of the latter, and vice versa. That is the point of Rodney's (1972) work on *How Europe Underdeveloped Africa*, and of Prebisch's (1950) and Gunder Frank's (1969) work on 'the development of under-development' in Latin America. As Wallerstein (forthcoming: 5) puts it, 'underdevelopment is not undevelopment, a primordial, or pre-capitalist, or pre-modern state of being, but rather the consequence of the historic process of world-wide development through the linked formation of core and periphery'. In this dynamic, the colonies of the periphery, supplying raw materials to the 'core' industrial nations, are, on the whole, locked into a vicious cycle of low productivity, and a long-term decline in their terms of trade, which continually works to reinforce the advantage of the already 'developed' nations.

Contrary to Fukuyama's 'evolutionist' scheme, Braudel (1988) argues that we are far too inclined to think of 'modes of production' as following each other, like some cortège or procession, in successive historical periods. Rather, he argues, 'the different modes of production are all attached to each other. The most advanced are dependent on the most backward, and vice-versa: development is the reverse side of underde-velopment' (ibid.: 70).

Maurice Godelier concludes the argument of his 'Is the West the model for humankind?' with a biting rejoinder to Fukuyama's celebration of the 'end of history', as represented by the final embodiment of Western reason, the US government and its 'victory' in the Cold War. As Godelier puts it, in this situation, what should our response be? What should we do?

> Must we join in the applause or tip-toe off the stage? Leaving aside the people of the Third World, why should silence be required of those in the West who continue to believe that Christianity is not the only true religion, and that there is indeed no true reli-gion; those who see that political democracy does exist, and welcome it, but know there is much to be done to extend social democracy, and that nearly everything remains to be done to ensure that the economy and the wealth produced by capitalism, or appropriated by it, are shared out more fairly, in the West and elsewhere? Why should we refuse to see these bad aspects, which are there and do affect our lives? What reason could there be

for putting up with them? Could it really be because the end of history has arrived and we are at last living in the best of all possible worlds?

(1991: 339)

FROM THE END OF HISTORY TO THE END OF ETHNOCENTRISM

Fukuyama proclaims the 'end of history'; various authors have spoken of a crisis (or even an end) of representation; Lyotard, some time ago, pronounced our entry into the 'postmodern condition'. In all of this, the question has to be raised as to the degree to which this is, in fact, a deeply ethnocentric perception of whatever changes are at stake. It is by no means clear that 'postmodernism' is a global (as opposed to a specifically Western, or even American) 'condition'. Stuart Hall suggests that postmodernism is, on the one hand, 'about how the world dreams itself to be "American"' (1986: 46) and, on the other, simply 'another version of that historical amnesia, characteristic of American culture – the tyranny of the new' (ibid.: 47). As he goes on to argue, many of the grander claims made in respect of any 'global postmodernism' can readily be seen to be ideological:

> what it says is, *this* is the end of the world. History stops with us. But whenever it is said that *this* is the last thing that will ever happen in History, that is the sign of the functioning, in the narrow sense, of the ideological – what Marx called the 'ideological' effect.
>
> (ibid.)

As Hall notes, the fundamental issue concerns the fact that 'since most of the world has not yet properly entered the modern era, who is it exactly who "has no future left"? And how long will this "no future" last into the future?' (ibid.) or again, in relation to Baudrillard's claims, concerning the 'implosion of the real', what significance does all this have when, as Hall puts it, 'three quarters of the human race have not yet entered the era of what we are pleased to call the "real"' (ibid.: 46)?

In a similar vein, Paul Gilroy (1989) has insisted that ideas of 'postmodernism', despite their grandiose claims, can usefully be seen as having their origins in, and being symptoms of, a more localised, rather narrower, crisis – the crisis of the downwardly mobile white intellectuals of Western Europe, working in the decaying public sector of those economies, during the period of the long slump that began with the oil crisis of 1973. Craig Owens (1985: 57) speaks of a crisis 'specifically of the authority vested in Western European culture and its institutions'. Cornel West openly mocks Lyotard's tendency to uncritically generalise from local perceptions:

when you actually look at [Lyotard's idea of] 'increasing incredulity towards master narratives' and see the religious and ideological and national revivals in Eastern Europe and the Soviet Union . . . you say . . . 'Who is he talking about, in terms of increasing incredulity towards master narratives? He and his friends hanging out on the left bank? Whom does he have in mind?'

(1991: 5)

As Julien and Mercer (1989) suggest, it is the ethnocentrism of much of the debate around postmodernism and the 'end of history' which is most worthy of comment. In all of this, of course, Fukuyama, Lyotard, and others, are simply heirs to the long tradition which, as Robert Young (1990: 2–3) remarks, begins with Hegel and is continued by Marx – the development of a universalising narrative of the unfolding of a 'rational system' of World History, which amounts to nothing more or less than a negative form of the history of European imperialism – a form of knowledge which continually expropriates and incorporates its 'Others', in a conceptual mimicry of the geographical and economic absorption of the non-European world by the West.

As Foucault (1980) suggests, in this connection, it could well be that claims as to the universal validity of Western culture and rationality are no more than a mirage associated with economic domination and political hegemony. Certainly, as Said (1978) has argued, Western forms of Orientalism and historicism have often produced a kind of essentialist universalism, what Levinas (1983) calls a form of 'ontological imperialism', in which human history is seen from the viewpoint of (and/or as culminating in) Europe and the West – providing narcissistic forms of self-centred knowledge – philosophy as 'egology', as Levinas puts it (quoted in R. Young, 1990: 17).

It is this equation of 'knowledge', as such, with its Occidental forms; this 'Europeanisation' (or perhaps now 'Westernisation') of world culture, which is the object of much of Derrida's critique. As Derrida notes, we still live in a situation in which 'the white man takes his own Indo-European mythology, his own *logos* . . . the myths of his own idiom, for the universal form of that which he must still wish to call reason' (1971: 213). As Robert Young (1990) points out, the logocentrism which is the object of Derrida's critique is described by Derrida as 'nothing but the most original and powerful ethnocentrism in the process of imposing itself on the world' (Derrida, 1974: 3) and, to that extent, as Young notes, Derrida's own deconstructionist project can be understood as a deconstructing 'of the concept, the authority and the assumed primacy of the category of "the West"' (R. Young, 1990: 19) – much in the spirit of Toynbee's objection to the 'Late Modern Western convention of identifying a parvenu and provincial Western society's history with "History"' writ large' (ibid.: 19). To remark on this recurrent slippage is also to insist on the explication of the centrality of the idea of 'whiteness' – as the usually unstated ethnic/mythic dimension of Enlightenment civilisation (cf. Amin, 1989: 89–91 and Malcomson, 1991, for an excellent summary analysis of the process through which 'Western' history projects the source of its supposedly unique rationality back onto a mythical Greek 'classical civilisation', whose actual African and Oriental roots are then denied. Cf. also Bernal, 1987).

QUESTIONS OF PERIODISATION AND SPATIALISATION: MODERNISM AND IMPERIALISM

Quite apart from the critique of the ethnocentrism of 'Western history', there remains, as we argued earlier, the need to historicise contemporary debates about postmodernism or the 'end of history'. One way of approaching this debate is, in fact, to pose the question of how the significance of the 'postmodern' is transformed, depending on how the 'modern' period (which it is presumed to supersede) is dated. One possibility (which seems implicitly to underlie Fukuyama's argument) is to equate the 'end of history' with the end of Communism, and to focus on Communist 'modernism' as a 'blind alley' into which part of the 'West' blundered in 1917: in that case, postmodernism represents the victory of Liberalism over Communism. Another strategy is to read the modern period back to 1789 and the French Revolution – in which case postmodernism is effectively the end of Enlightenment thought (this seems to be the Lyotard/Baudrillard position), and of its ideas of Reason and Progress in human affairs. However, in either case, these are stories in which the West's development is seen as *sui generis* (characterised by the march of Reason, from the Greeks, through the Dark Ages, to the Renaissance, the Enlightenment and the Liberal State). Here, the story of the West is told as a dynamic of forces internal to itself – even if it is sometimes recognised that the 'West' is a historical rather than a geographical construct, including some societies (e.g. Japan) manifestly in the East, and excluding others (e.g. Mexico or Chile) which are about as far West as you can get.

Against all this, it can be argued (cf. Hall, 1992) that the rise of the West needs, in fact, to be understood as part of a global story, in which Western development has always to be posed in the context of the West's relation with the Others who were, variously, discovered, explored and colonised by the West. In that case, we can perhaps more usefully date the beginning of the 'modern' period from the time of the first Portuguese voyages of discovery in the fifteenth century, or perhaps, for convenience, from the 'discovery' of the 'New World' in 1492.

If Marshall McLuhan (1964) imagined that the 'global village' was a new thing, in the 1960s, it is worth remembering that, as the work of Braudel (1988) and Wallerstein (1974) amply demonstrates, there has been some form of effective 'world system' or global economy, with an initial base in north-western Europe, at least since the fifteenth century, if not before. Even that periodisation is itself questionably ethnocentric: there is considerable evidence of fairly systematic Chinese trade with India and East Africa well before that date. However, it is also necessary to note that any attempt to understand the intersections of history and geography must deal carefully with questions of periodisation. Braudel (1988: 39) calls for a 'discriminatory geography' which recognises that, social developments being unevenly distributed in geographical space, there are always 'areas into which world history does not reach, zones of silence and undisturbed ignorance' (ibid.: 18), which remain 'outside world-time' (ibid.: 42). We should not make the mistake of presuming that it is the same 'time' everywhere (what we might call the 'Do they know it's Christmas?' mistake), and certainly not in relation to any fixed scheme of evolutionary development.

TELLING HISTORY: THE STORY OF THE WEST?

The first questions, necessarily, are 'who speaks, of whom?'; 'who is empowered to tell what kind of stories about who else?'; and 'who speaks and who is spoken of, but silent?' In the preface to his study of *The Writing of History* Michel de Certeau (1988) offers an analysis of Jan Van der Straat's famous allegorical etching of the explorer Amerigo Vespucci encountering 'America', represented by a nude woman, reclining in a hammock, on the sea-shore, where Vespucci has just landed. De Certeau's argument is, in general terms, that all of historiography has arisen from the European encounter with the unknown Other. As he puts it:

> the conqueror will write the body of the other and trace there his own history. From her, he will make a 'historied' body. . . . She will be 'Latin' America . . . . she is a *nuova terra*, not yet existing on maps – an unknown body, destined to bear the name, *Amerigo*, of its inventor. But what is really initiated here is a colonisation of the body by the discourse of power. This is writing that conquers. It will transform the space of the other . . . this writing fabricates Western History.
>
> (ibid.: xxv–xxvi)

As de Certeau puts it, 'the past is the fiction of the present' (ibid.: 10) and, as Wright (1985) argues, the shaping of the story of the past always plays a crucial role in the determining of the historical present. Indeed, we have argued elsewhere that control over the franchise on the representation of the past is always a powerful resource in the construction of identities, and in the mobilisation of resources in the struggle over the direction of the future. The question at issue is, of course, one of power. As de Certeau notes, 'historiography takes the position of the subject of action – of the prince, whose objective is to "make history"' (ibid.: 17). Pocock develops this theme more fully, focusing on the association between sovereignty and historiography: 'a community writes its own history when it has the autonomous political structure needed if it is to command its own present, and typically, the history it makes will be the history of that structure' (1991: 8). Pocock questions whether historiography would exist without this connection to state and power, given the intrinsic connection between having a voice in controlling one's present, and in controlling the story of one's past. As he argues, without sovereignty, no historiography; without historiography, no identity.

These questions of power over the telling of history are, of course, in essence, the same questions at the centre of contemporary debates about cultural imperialism – which likewise centre on the question of who has the right (or the power – often a different matter) to tell the story of contemporary events – in the form of the flow of world news – or the power to control the dominant fictions of our age. To the extent that this parallel holds, we argue that the analyses offered (see below) by scholars such as Greenblatt (1992) and Todorov (1984), of the historical process through which the West has represented its Others, have much to offer the narrower debates, about contemporary forms of cultural imperialism, within media studies. However, before attempting to develop that argument, we want first to turn the matter round, and address the rather less well-worked (but possibly even more instructive) question of how those 'Others' have perceived the West, even if they have not had the power (or even, sometimes, the desire) to impose their visions on the West, in the same way that the West has systematically imposed its own visions on them.

EUROPEANS AS EXOTICA

From the point of view of contemporary presumptions of Western superiority in relation to other peoples, it is interesting to note that the Arab historian Ibn Khaldun, in his *Prologomena* (written in Tunis in the fourteenth century), when contrasting 'us Westerners' with 'Easterners' elsewhere, actually refers to the contrast between the Western (Maghreb) and the Eastern parts of the Arab world (Khaldun, 1987: 5). While he offers interesting comments on the cultures of important groups – such as those of the Jews and the Persians (ibid.: ch. 2) – he does not find Europeans, of any sort, worthy of comment. This should not, in fact, be so surprising, given the self-evident superiority of the Arab world over what we call the 'West' at the time. This is no simple matter of Arab ethnocentrism. Certainly Roberts (1990: 326) notes that the Arabs of the time 'regarded the civilisations of the "cold lands of the north" as a meagre, unsophisticated affair' and spoke of Europe, dismissively, as the 'land of the Franks', on the far edge of the western seas – where 'Franks', roughly translates as 'barbarians', and the western seas are, self-evidently, of less interest to the Arabs than the Red Sea and the Indian Ocean, given the access those routes offer to the East and its treasures. Moreover, this perception was shared by others, as well as the Arabs themselves. Roberts also notes that the superiority of Arab goods to those of Europe was so obvious to the inhabitants of Calicut that when Vasco da Gama showed them what he had brought from Portugal to give to their king, they laughed at him – as he had nothing to offer which could compare with what Arab traders already brought to India from other parts of Asia (ibid.: 588).

Watanabe (1991) tells the story of three Portuguese men, shipwrecked off the coast of Japan in 1543, being simply referred to by the Japanese as 'men of barbaric race from the South West'. This term, 'Southern Barbarians', was then used indiscriminately to lump together other foreigners, from other Western nations, with people from other parts of South East Asia. In this context, the differences between being Portuguese and being Dutch, or Indian or Indonesian, were immaterial to the Japanese: the barbarousness of such people, from the Japanese perspective, consisted simply in their non-Japaneseness.

Kramer (1993) offers a parallel analysis of the perception of the first European colonists by Africans (cf. also DeLiss, 1991). Kramer argues that the first Europeans in Africa were by no means perceived by Africans to be unique, incomparable beings, as they liked to regard themselves. Kramer notes:

A way of thought to which the category of the new is unknown, recognising in its place solely the return of that which has always been, could not avoid likening the curious appearance of the European with that which was already familiar, placing it in a relationship to the self which had been established at the dawn of time. The familiar, of which the European was seen as one variation, was the opposite to the cultivated person, and European culture was purely and simply the 'other' to the native culture in question. Where the epitome of the 'other' was the wilderness, void of man, the European seemed to be a part of what we call 'nature'; and where the 'other' was epitomised by a neighbouring people, the European seemed to be a representative of some other people, a stranger or barbarian. In other words, Europeans were for Africans as Africans were for Europeans: primarily, one further sort of savage, among other savages.

(Kramer, 1993: x)

211

Compare this analysis with Todorov and Greenblatt, discussed below, on native Americans' difficulties in recognising the invading Spaniards as a form of human life.

However, beyond these conceptual difficulties, the 'white man' largely posed more practical questions, for many native populations. As an Apache Indian put it:

> The biggest of all Indian problems is the Whiteman. Who can understand the Whiteman? What makes him tick? How does he think and why does he think the way he does? Why does he talk so much? Why does he say one thing and do the opposite? Most important of all, how do you deal with him? Obviously, he is here to stay. Sometimes it seems like a hopeless task.
>
> (quoted in DeLiss, 1991: 7; see also Basso, 1979)

WESTERN VISIONS: MANIFEST DESTINY?

Hobsbawm (1992) noted that 1492 was not only the date of Columbus' discovery of the New World – it was also the date of the Spanish 'reconquest' of Granada. This represented the final repulse of the Moors, who had long colonised what we now know as Spain. Moreover, this year – the date of the defeat of the Infidels – was also the date of the final expulsion of the Jews from Spain. Indeed, it can be argued that these two latter events constituted a kind of 'inner purification, as a prerequisite to external conquest' (Stuart Hall Lecture, 'Mapping the futures' Conference, Tate Gallery, London, 20 November 1992). Columbus' own understanding of his journey to the New World was, of course, as an approach to the court of Kublai Khan, in order to raise funding for the reconquest of Jerusalem. Thus, Todorov notes that 1492 symbolises a 'double movement' in which Spain expels its 'interior Others' (the Moors, the Jews) and discovers the 'exterior Other – that whole America which will become Latin' (Todorov, 1984: 50).

As Hobsbawm puts it, '1492 marks the beginning of Eurocentric world history, of a conviction that a few Western and Central European countries were destined to conquer and rule the globe, a form of Euromegalomania' (1992: 15). This was, of course, not simply a matter of material power, as the basis of invasion and conquest, but also of symbolic forms of power and domination, in which the 'New Worlds' were to be subordinated and incorporated, within the representational terms of European language. In this 'colonising of the marvellous' (cf. Greenblatt 1992: 25), it was the coloniser's power to incorporate and represent the Other, in their own terms, which constituted the (unrepresented) ground of the exercise of colonial power.

In understanding the significance of the 'discovery of the New World' we can draw on the parallel work of Todorov and Greenblatt. Todorov argues that it is

> the conquest of America that heralds and establishes our present identity; even if every date that permits us to separate any two periods is arbitrary, none is more suitable, in order to mark the beginning of the modern era, than the year 1492. Since 1492 we are, as Las Casas (*Historia de Las Indias*) has said, in that time so new and like to no other.
>
> (1992: 5)

Todorov argues that, alongside the 'coincidence' of the victory over the Moors, the exile of the Jews, and the discovery of America, the year 1492 is also significant in that it sees the publication of the first grammar of a modern European language – the Spanish grammar of Antonia de Nebrija – who, notes Todorov, 'writes, in his Introduction, these decisive words: "Language has always been the *companion* of empire"' (ibid.: 123). The significance of the linguistic dimension of imperial power is also of concern to Greenblatt, who notes that

> the founding action of Christian imperialism is christening. Such a christening [such as Columbus' first act of (re)naming Guanahani as San Salvador] entails the cancellation of the native name – the erasure of the alien, perhaps demonic, identity – and hence a kind of 'making new'; it is, at once, an exorcism, an appropriation and a gift . . . the taking of possession [and] the conferral of identity are fused, in a moment of pure linguistic formalising.
>
> (1992: 83)

Although Greenblatt differentiates his own analysis from Todorov's by somewhat downplaying the latter's emphasis on the importance of the conquistadores' 'literal advantage' over the Indians (in having at their disposal a superior technology of representation – writing) as the key explanation of the Aztecs' failure to mount effective resistance to the Spanish invasion, he none the less recognises the force of Todorov's analysis. Todorov's argument is that the crucial cultural difference between the European and American peoples was that the latter had no effective form of writing, and the most important consequence of this, he argues, was a fatal 'loss of manipulative power' in their dealings with the Spaniards. As Greenblatt puts it, summarising Todorov's argument,

> the absence of writing determined the predominance of ritual over improvisation, and cyclical time over linear time, characteristics that led, in turn, to disastrous misperceptions, and miscalculations in the face of the conquistadores (the Aztecs misinterpreted the Spaniards as Gods, whose arrival represented the long-delayed fulfilment of an

213

Aztec religious prophecy: since their arrival and conquest had been foretold as inevitable, resistance was pointless). The unlettered peoples of the New World could not bring the strangers into focus: conceptual inadequacy initially precluded an accurate perception of the other. The culture that possessed writing could accurately represent to itself (and hence strategically manipulate) the culture without writing, but the reverse was not true. For, in possessing the ability to write, the Europeans possessed an unmistakably superior representational technology.

(ibid.: 11)

As Greenblatt notes, Europeans of the time felt powerfully superior to virtually all the peoples they encountered. Quite apart from their developed and mobile technologies of power, they were also armed with an immense confidence in the centrality of their own culture:

such was the confidence of this culture that it expected perfect strangers – the Arawaks of the Caribbean, for example – to abandon their own beliefs, preferably immediately, and embrace those of Europe, as luminously and self-evidently true. A failure to do so provoked impatience, contempt and even murderous rage.

(ibid.: 9)

Greenblatt argues that the Spaniards' commitment to a form of 'Christian Universalism' – 'the conviction that [their] principal symbols and narratives are suitable for the entire population of the world' – commits them to imposing the 'unrestrained circulation of [their own] mimetic capital' (ibid.: 186, n. 2). More prosaically, Todorov simply notes that Columbus, a deeply pious man, 'who for this very reason regards himself as . . . charged with a divine mission', was principally animated by the desire to achieve nothing less than 'the universal victory of Christianity' (1992: 10).

However, this proved a frustrating task, for the Indians did not immediately respond, which both puzzled and infuriated the conquistadores: 'when taught the mysteries of our religion, they say that these things may suit Castilians, but not them, and they do not wish to change their customs' (Ortiz, quoted in ibid.: 151). This seemingly wilful 'blindness', on the part of the Indians, then becomes the justification for imposing Christian 'salvation' on them, by force, for

although these barbarians are not altogther mad . . . yet they are not far from being so. They are not, or are no longer, capable of governing themselves, any more than madmen or even wild beasts or animals. Their stupidity is much greater than that of children and madmen in other countries.

(Vitoria, quoted in ibid.: 15)

214

The Spaniards' overwhelming and absolutist confidence in their own culture (which contrasts markedly with the implicitly relativist position of the Indians, whose rejection of Christianity – even if it might 'suit Castilians' – so disappointed Ortiz, quoted above) is perhaps most brutally displayed in Columbus' description of his intentions of taking a number of captured Indians back to Spain: 'Our Lord pleasing, at the time of my departure, I will take six of them from here to Your Highnesses, that they may learn to speak' (quoted in Greenblatt, 1992: 171, n. 46). Not to be able to speak Spanish is to be deemed unable 'to speak'. None the less, such conceptual errors, when supported by material power, have profound consequences. Todorov reports that, when the Spaniards first landed on the peninsula which we now know as Yucatan, they asked, in Spanish, for the name of the place. The Mayas answered '*Ma c'ubah than*', which means 'we do not understand you'. The Spanish transliterated the sounds they heard as 'Yucatan', and presumed that this was the name of the place. Ever since, the place has been, of course, known as Yucatan (1992: 98–9).

As Todorov notes elsewhere, the first spontaneous reaction to a 'stranger' is to imagine that his difference, from our own 'normality', necessarily takes the form of inferiority – that he is not really human or, if human, represents a savage or barbarian form of humanity. If he does not speak our language, perhaps that is because he speaks none at all, or cannot 'speak' (cf. Columbus' letter, quoted above). It is, Todorov argues, precisely

> in this fashion that European Slavs call their German neighbours *nemec*, 'mutes', the Mayas . . . call the Toltec *nunob*, 'mutes' . . . and the Aztecs . . . call those who do not speak Nahuatl *tenime*, 'barbarians' or *popoloca*, 'savages', because they share the scorn of all peoples for their neighbours.
>
> (ibid.: 76)

The notion of 'barbarism' is, of course, inherently relative: each of us is the Other's barbarian (ibid.: 190). To become such a thing, one need only speak a language of which the Other is ignorant – which is then merely 'babble' to his ears. Thus, Montaigne notes, 'we call barbarous anything that is contrary to our own habits. Indeed we seem to have no other criterion of truth and reason than the type and kind of options and customs current in the land where we live' (1990: 108–9). Late in his life, Las Casas, disillusioned with the imperial project in which he was initially complicit, comes to recognise that

> a man will be called a barbarian in comparison with another man because he is strange in his ways of speaking and because he pronounces the other's language badly. According to Strabo, Book

215

XIV, this was the main reason the Greeks called other peoples barbarians . . . because they pronounced the Greek language improperly. But from this point of view, there is no man or race which is not barbarian in relation to another man or race. As Saint Paul says . . . 'There are so many kinds of voices in the world' [but cf. McBride, 1980, on this point] and none of them is without significance. Therefore, if I know not the meaning of the voice, I shall be unto him that speaketh a barbarian, and he that speaketh shall be a barbarian unto me . . . . Thus, just as we consider the peoples of the Indies barbarians, they judge us to be the same, because they do not understand us.

(Las Casas, quoted in Todorov, 1992: 191)

In fact, as noted above, the peoples of the Indies actually made the logically complementary, but practically fatal, error of classifying the Spaniards as gods, rather than as barbarians.

However, not all Greeks behaved as Strabo speculated – we can still learn from the principled stance taken by Herodotus on these matters. Herodotus 'did not deny the existence of the gods of foreigners. However barbarous and grotesque the foreigner's conception of his gods may be, it never seems to occur [to Herodotus] to doubt their objective existence. Furthermore, he never makes derogatory remarks or disparaging comments about them. He never once evinces the belief that there are no gods but the gods of the Greeks nor even that the gods of the Greeks are superior to the gods of other peoples. He follows his own principle, that none but a fool will laugh at the customs of strangers (Linforth, 1926, quoted in Greenblatt, 1992: 187, n. 6).

None the less, as noted earlier, in relation to the naming of Yucatan, 'by mistake', fools are often powerful for their foolishness. As Todorov puts it, ever since 1492, Western Europe has attempted to 'assimilate the other, to do away with an exterior alterity, and has in great part succeeded. Its way of life and its values have spread around the world; as Columbus wished, the colonised peoples have adopted our customs, and have put on clothes' (1992: 248). Nowadays, one might add, they can all drink Coca-Cola while watching CNN on television. And so we pass from 1492 to 1992, via Umberto Eco's conceit of the televising of 'The Discovery of America':

DAN: Good evening, folks. Here it's 7pm on the 11th of October 1492, and we're linked directly with the flagship of the Columbus expedition. As of now, in a joint effort, all our TV networks will be transmitting round the clock, twenty five hours. We're linked with the telecamera installed on the flagship, the *Santa Maria* . . . First a word from Jim, Jim?

JIM: Well, Dan. . . . It's the beginning of a new age, which some

216

commentators have already suggested calling The Modern Era. . . .
But I'd like to hear from Alastair Cook, who has just arrived from
London, especially to take part in this historic broadcast. Alastair?
Can you hear me? . . .

ALASTAIR: I didn't hear very well . . . . One of the engineers says
it must have been interference. This apparently happens a lot in the
New World . . . . But . . . there we are! Admiral Columbus is about
to speak!

COLOMBUS: A small step for a sailor, a giant step for His Catholic
Majesty.

(Eco, 1993: 135–45)

The Cherokee (or, as he would prefer it, Ani Yunh Wiya) artist Jimmie
Durham makes the point that

colonisation is not simply the language of some political rhetoric of
past decades. Europe may be passing through a post-colonial time,
but we in the Americas still live in a colonial period. Our countries
were invaded, genocide was and is committeed against us, and our
lands and lives are taken over for the profit of the coloniser.

(Durham, 1993: 172)

Or, as he puts it, more forthrightly, in one of his poems.

Look, cousins, you made the wrong turn . . . .
This is not New Jersey and this is not the New World.
You need to get your bearings straight.
We live here and you are scaring the fish.

(ibid.: 141)

POSTMODERNISM: NEW TO YOU?

As Doreen Massey (1992) has noted, contemporary writing on the question
of postmodernity makes much of the fact that this period involves some
supposedly new sense of dislocation, of hybridity, of displacement. The
problem which Massey raises is the sense in which this perception is, in
fact, very much a First World perspective. As she notes, the assumption
which runs through much of the literature on postmodernity, is that this
is quite a ncw and remarkable situation.

Massey's basic point is that, for the inhabitants of all the countries
around the world colonised by the West, the experience of immediate,
destabilising contact with other alien cultures has a very long historical
resonance. What is new is simply that this experience of dislocation has
now returned, through patterns of immigration, from the peripheries, to
the metropolis. Ulf Hannerz puts it another way, when he remarks that

217

'it may well be that the First World has been present in the consciousness of many Third World people a great deal longer than the Third World has been on the minds of most First World people' (1991: 110). In a similar sense, Anthony King remarks that

the culture, society and space of early twentieth century Calcutta or Singapore prefigured the future in a much more accurate way than did that of London or New York. 'Modernity' was not born in Paris but rather in Rio. With this interpretation, Euro-American paradigms of so called 'postmodernism' have neither much meaning, nor salience, outside the narrow geographical confines of Euro-America, where they developed.

(1991: 8)

Again, as, Ien Ang puts it,

the peripheries of the world, those at the receiving end of the forces of globalisation, where capitalist modernisation has been an imposed impulse, rather than an internal development, as was the case in the West, are potentially more truly postmodern than the West itself, because in those contexts the eclectic juxtaposition and amalgamation of 'global' and 'local' cultural influences is a necessity, and therefore an integrated mode of survival, rather than a question of aesthetics.

(1991: 7)

Or, in the words of Salman Rushdie (1982), 'those of us who have been forced by cultural displacement to accept the provisional nature of all truths, all certainties, have perhaps had modernism forced upon us'.

For these reasons, as Massey notes, to characterise 'time–space compression', and the consequent sense of dislocation, as a problematically new and dramatic development is very much a Western, colonialist view, in so far as this sense of dislocation, as she puts it, 'must have been felt for centuries, though from a very different point of view, by colonised peoples all over the world, as they watched the importation, maybe even used, the products of the . . . European [and later American] colonisation' (1991a: 24).

There is also a further set of questions which we must address, which concern the tendency of theories of postmodernity to fall into a kind of formalist, post-structuralist rhetoric, which overgeneralises its account of 'the' experience of postmodernity, so as to decontextualise and flatten out all the significant differences between the experiences of people in different situations, who are members of different social and cultural groups, with access to different forms and quantities of economic and cultural capital. The point is simply that 'we' are *not* all nomadic or fragmented subjectivities, living in the same 'postmodern' universe. For some categories

218

of people (differentiated by gender, race and ethnicity, as much as by class) the new technologies of symbolic and physical communications and transport (from aeroplanes to faxes) offer significant opportunities for interconnectedness. For those people, there may well be a new sense of 'wider', postmodern opportunities. However, at the same time, for other categories of people, without access to such forms of communications and transport, horizons may simultaneously be narrowing. Many writers have referred to the contemporary dynamic of simultaneous globalisation and localisation. However, for some people, the globalising aspect of that dynamic is the dominant one, while for others it is very much the localising aspect which is increasingly operative, as their life-chances are gradually reduced, and they increasingly remain stuck in the micro-territories in which they were born. To give but one example, John Singleton's film *Boyz N the Hood* (1991) dramatises the sense in which, for many of the most deprived Blacks and Latin Americans, locality is in fact destiny, where the horizon, far from being global, extends only as far as the boundary of 'the Hood'. Indeed, the militant adoption of the position of the 'home-boy' can readily be seen as a defensive reaction to the absence of any other choices.

All of this is to suggest that we must be very cautious when applying any abstracted notion of postmodernity, and must resist the temptation to generalise our theories, in such a way as to ignore the continuing, significant differences in the experience of this era, by people in different social and geographical locations. However, there remains the fundamental claim that there definitely is something significantly new about this period. While not wanting to deny such significant changes as have, and are, occurring it would seem that we should be cautious in accepting, too readily, any claims that our contemporary experience is so significantly new and different from all that has gone before. Some of the claims that have recently been made for the distinctiveness of postmodernity are not, in fact, so very new. We refer, in particular, to the claims that the era of postmodernity is distinctively characterised by an increasing tendency to the 'mediation' and 'global interconnectedness' of social experience.

The first claim, concerning 'mediation', is largely associated with the work of Jean Baudrillard (1988). However, it can in fact, readily be argued that Baudrillard's work depends on, and draws on, in an unacknowledged way, a rather older tradition in American social psychology. As long ago as the mid-1950s, the American social psychologists Horton and Wohl (1956) were arguing that our social experience is increasingly subsumed, and indeed supplanted, by forms of para-social relationships, which media viewers develop with the characters they watch on the screen. Indeed, it is Horton and Wohl, not Baudrillard, who originate the concept of the 'simulacrum' and its key place within the field of contemporary social relations.

219

The second claim, that postmodernity is characterised by an increasing sense of global interconnectedness, can equally be seen to have quite long historical roots. As noted earlier, it was thirty years ago that Marshall McLuhan was already claiming that the effects of modern communications technologies were such as to lead to a position in which effectively we all live in a 'global village' (McLuhan, 1964). It is this second claim which will be the key concern here. The issue on which we will focus concerns the extent to which the 'global village' is, in fact (and despite Japan's growing challenges to American predominance in the cultural industries) an American Village. We shall insist that the tendencies towards globalisation, stressed by theorists of postmodernity, cannot in fact be understood outside of the long history of American cultural imperialism. In the first instance, it is also well worth reminding ourselves of the extent to which a strategy of cultural imperialism has, in fact, been a perfectly conscious and explicit matter of American foreign policy in the period at least since the Second World War, if not since the 1920s.

THE MEDIA ARE (STILL MAINLY) AMERICAN

One of the fundamental facts of our postmodern era, as Jeremy Tunstall (1977) noted some time ago, is that, of course, the media are American. Someone, somewhere, is watching a Hollywood film every minute of the day and night. These days, the American media dominate, not just in film, but in television and in telecommunications as well. Again, this contemporary dominance has long historical roots. In the 1920s, as President of the Board of Trade, Herbert Hoover was quick to notice the potential of the American motion picture industry, as a form of export-led advertising for American consumer products, and for the American 'way of life'. To that extent, the American government was involved, from a very early period, in subsidising and encouraging the export of American movies, and the American movie subsequently became, according to the claims of the Motion Picture Association of America, 'the most desired commodity in the world' (Guback, 1979). The contemporary American dominance of the international media runs on tracks established many years ago, in America's early dominance of the international film business, not only in terms of its dominance in production, but also in terms of control of finance and distribution systems. However, it was during the period following the Second World War, when the European powers were exhausted, that the American government came to see the full potential of media export policies, as a way of furthering American foreign policy interests in the world at large.

In his book *The American Century* Henry Luce, one-time editor of the American magazine *Life*, argued that we must accept wholeheartedly our duty and our opportunity, as the most powerful and vital nation in the world, to exert upon the world the full impact of our influence, for such purposes as we see fit, and by such means as we see fit . . . it now becomes our time to be the powerhouse from which ideas spread throughout the world.

(1941: 3)

Herbert Schiller claims that Luce, as the controller of one of the most powerful communication complexes in thc United States (the *Time*, *Life*, *Fortune* magazine conglomerate) understood, earlier than many people, that 'the fusion of economic strength and information control, image making and public opinion formation was the new quintessence of power, international and domestic' (Schiller, 1969: 1). That is to say that Luce understood that thc very availability of a developed international communication system, which the USA had at the close of the Second World War, was a unique instrument of power, and one which had simply not been available to would-be expansionist states in previous eras. American governmental strategy, in this connection, developed fast. The strategy was founded on a combination of economic and communications power, in the furtherance of what was understood as the project of 'the American Century'. Thus we find President Truman, in 1947, proclaiming 'we are the new giant of the economic world. Whether we like it or not, the future pattern of economic relations depends on us. The world is waiting to see what we do. The choice is ours' (quoted in ibid.: 6).

American strategy depended on the defence and expansion of 'freedom' – crucially, freedom of trade and freedom of speech. The problem, of course, is that, in a free or unregulated exchange between the strong and the weak, the strong tend to do better and to become even stronger. Thus, in Schiller's view, freedom of speech has, in fact, meant the opportunity of the American mass media to disseminate their message throughout the world arena. As he puts it, if free trade is the mechanism by which a powerful economy penetrates and dominates a weaker one, then the free flow of information is the channel through which the life-styles and the values of America have been imposed on poor and vulnerable societies. Schiller demonstrates, quite simply, the extent to which these were matters of conscious American policy, at key points in the post-war period. Thus, he quotes from the Congressional committee, set up in 1967 to consider modern communications and foreign policy. The committee produced a paper called 'Winning the Cold War: the American ideological offensive', which argued that

to a significant degree, what America does will shape the emerging international communications system . . . to a very large degree, other countries will imitate our experience and will attach them-selves to the institutions and systems we create. . . . Given our information technology and information resources, the USA clearly could be the hub of the world communication systems.

(ibid.: 9)

This was also, straightforwardly, a matter of military concern. America had taken over the main role of 'world policeman', and the American military desperately needed effective international communications to co-ordinate their forces.

Out of this conjuncture emerged the very strong links which Schiller points to (and which still persist) between the American military and the big American communication companies. However, beyond this concern with with their own international communication needs (to co-ordinate military forces abroad), the same committee also saw, very clearly, the potential use of international communications as a means of influencing foreign populations:

> Certain foreign policy objectives can be best pursued by dealing directly with the people of foreign countries, rather than with their governments. Through the use of modern instruments and technologies of communications, it is possible today to reach large and influential sections of national populations – to inform them, to influence their attitudes . . . to motivate them to particular courses of actions. These groups, in turn, are capable of exerting, noticeable, even decisive, pressure on their governments.
>
> (Committee on Foreign Affairs, 1964: 6–7)

The crucial issue here is the ability to by-pass the control of national governments. At this point, the committee recognised that the very status of communications had changed, so that telecommunications had progressed from being an essential 'support' of international activities, to being itself a direct instrument of foreign policy.

Schiller argues that the contemporary situation exhibits two particular features of significance. In the first place, he argues, we see a significant move towards a situation in which information itself becomes a commodity for sale, and towards a position in which the communications and information industries serve as the dynamo of contemporary economic development. In this context, communication ceases to be a merely secondary adjunct, facilitating business, and communication itself becomes 'big business'. In this connection, he quotes the Director of the Pentagon's 'Information Processing and Techniques Office' who claimed that 'the nation that dominates this information processing field will possess the keys to world leadership in the twenty-first century' (Schiller, 1985: 18). The second development to which Schiller calls attention is the extent to which this new 'heartland' of communication and information technology is itself now increasingly controlled by a very small

222

number of powerful transnational corporations, which may be based (as indeed a large number of them are) in the USA, but which operate, simultaneously in many different countries around the world, on a global scale. In Schiller's view, the problem here is that the activities of these transnational corporations depend precisely on the overcoming of national boundaries, and the opening up of the 'free flow' of information, across a world market. The concerns of national governments, to regulate communications in their own countries, therefore present an obstacle to the transnational corporations, and these transnational corporations are increasingly concerned (and increasingly able) to override national government policies, to the extent, perhaps, of posing a threat to the very sovereignty of individual nations. Thus, Schiller argues, we see contemporaneously, a 'vast extension in cultural control and domination . . . a new global system of authority, on the basis of information control . . . in which the transnational communications companies now bypass traditional forms of national political authority' (ibid.).

There are many dimensions to the question of media or cultural imperialism. As far as the world pattern of international television flow is concerned, the USA is indisputably the world's number one television exporter. The USA continues to export a far greater quantity of television programmes to the rest of the world than all other nations combined manage to do, while, at the same time, America imports only one or two per cent of its own television broadcast output. Moreover, this pattern of American dominance is even more prevalent in such crucial areas of television programming as prime-time fictional and news programming. To take the second of those examples, to this day, 'world news' is largely supplied by a very small number of press and news agencies, all of which are Anglo-American (cf. Smith, 1980). These agencies clearly shape the international political agenda by the way in which they define values. To this extent, in almost all cases, the flow of world news is mainly one-way, and in most cases Anglo-American video news agencies provide the core of broadcast television news. To that extent, it is in fact difficult to exaggerate either the direct presence or the indirect influence of Anglo-American materials and styles on television news throughout the world.

However, it is not simply a question of the export of American programmes, as such. The influence of the American media extends far beyond that. In particular, its influence can be seen in the extent to which the media of other countries throughout the world have either franchised from, or literally copied, American TV formats. There are, for example, national 'versions' of the television programme *Blind Date* in many different countries of the world. It is not simply that America exports a lot of television programmes – beyond that, America has written the 'grammar' of international television – the formats of television, developed in America, have literally 'set the frame' for the production of television, in most other countries.

DOES THE SUBALTERN LISTEN?

In recent years, the cultural imperialism (or media imperialism) thesis has, in fact, come under substantial criticism, and a number of revisions of the basic thesis have been advanced. These criticisms are various, but among them there is the point that the media imperialism thesis was originally developed, at the height of American cultural hegemony, in the late 1960s. This was a peak of predominance from which America has most certainly since declined. In the same sense, the original thesis tends to focus exclusively on the pattern of American television exports, without paying sufficient attention to non-American forms of cultural imperialism, involving, for instance, the continuing export of cultural materials by British and French agencies to ex-colonies in Africa, or in another context, the strength of Mexico as a television exporter to other Latin American countries, or the position of Brazil, and its export of telenovelas back to the Catholic countries of southern Europe. All of these factors must of course be taken into account in any adequate version of the thesis of media imperialism (cf. Mattelart, Delcourt and Mattelart, 1984).

Most fundamentally, critics of the cultural imperialism thesis argue that the thesis presumes a hypodermic model of media effects. That is to say, it assumes that the effects of viewing American televisual material on audiences across the world can be automatically predicted. The issue here is that such empirical work as has been done in this field demonstrates not so much the direct effects of America media material, as the capacity of audiences in different situations to reinterpret the American-produced material which they view in a way which is influenced by their local circumstances. Mattelart and his colleagues (ibid.) give the example of the frequency of American-produced series, featuring 'Aryan' heroes, being subject to a process of 'reverse identification', when viewed by Third World populations, who will more often identify with the 'bad guys' in the story. That should not suggest to us that cultural power does not exist, or that the American-dominated international media have no effect whatsoever – rather it should alert us to the complexity of the modes in which cultural power is both exercised and resisted (see Morley 1992, and, Gripsrud, forthcoming, for elaborations of this argument).

CULTURAL IMPERIALISM REVISITED

In 'Not yet the post-imperial era' Schiller (1991) argues that the key change since the date of his original *Mass Communications and American Empire*

224

(1969) is that today 'national (largely American) media-cultural power has been largely (though not fully) subordinated to transnational corporate authority' (1991: 13) so that if 'American *national* power no longer is an exclusive determinant of cultural domination' and if it is 'transnational corporate cultural domination' which is now the key issue, none the less, and against those who celebrate the supposed 'semiotic democracy' of our supposedly postmodern and pluralistic society, that domination still exists and still bears 'a marked American input' (ibid.: 15).

Elsewhere, Schiller argues that American cultural imperialism, dominated by the big US companies, has simply given way to a form of transnational corporate cultural domination – under the sway of the big, 'stateless' transnationals. To that extent, he writes, today's world market economy 'has evolved from, but retains the central characteristics of, the original American pattern', in which what we see is a 'global system with many nationally based transnational corporations employing the communications and cultural practices and processes that originated, and continue to prevail, in the USA' (Schiller, 1992: 39). Thus, Schiller argues that

> Twenty five years ago, U.S. media products flooded the world. Today, there is no diminution of American popular cultural exports. What has changed is that the producers have become huge, integrated, cultural combines . . . [who] . . . offer . . . a total cultural environment . . . to a global . . . market. . . . [But] the cultural conglomerates now are not exclusively American owned. U.S. cultural styles and techniques . . . have . . . become transnationalised.
>
> (ibid.: 12–3)

Schiller's argument is that, while American cultural imperialism is not dead, 'it no longer adequately describes the global cultural condition. Today it is more useful to view transnational corporate culture as the central force' (ibid.: 14–15).

None the less, the Third World's earlier dreams of the possibility of a 'New World Information Order', less dominated by a one-way flow of information from the West, seem little nearer to fruition than they were twenty-five years ago. It is still the case that

> the overwhelming majority of world news flows from the developed to the developing countries, and is generated by four large transnational news agencies – AP, UPI, AFP and Reuters. Moreover, the West dominates the use of satellites, the electromagnetic spectrum, controlling the use of airwaves, telecommunications, micro-electronics, remote-sensing capabilities, direct satellite broadcasting and computer-related transmission.
>
> (Wete, 1988: 139)

SATELLITE TELEVISION: GLOBAL TIME AND THE THEFT OF HISTORY

Annabelle Sreberny-Mohammadi (1992) argues that, in discussion of media effects, what is often omitted, in the focus on the medium's 'contents', is any concern with the effects on our lives of what Cavell (1982) calls the very 'fact of television' – in terms of its impact on cultural orientations, patterns of sociability and modes of perception (cf. Sreberny-Mohammadi, 1992). Wilk offers a useful extension of this argument. Wilk's principal concern is with the transnational media as an 'instrument of global time' (forthcoming: 1). His argument is that critics of media imperialism, in the Third World, have focused too much, in the past, 'on the content of individual programmes and on the developed countries' control of that content' and have failed to realise that 'the greatest impact of television lies not in the content . . . but in the concepts of time and distance carried by the immediacy of the medium' (ibid.).

Wilk's argument returns us to the questions concerning the cultural construction of time and history raised earlier in this chapter. Drawing on Chakrabarty (1992), Wilk reminds us that, just as it can be argued that Western linear models of history grew along with the development of the colonial world system, 'the expansion that turned the rest of the world into "peoples without history" [cf. Wolf, 1982] gave the colonies a master narrative of progress, which left the colonial subject with a historical clock that could only count cultural difference' (Wilk, forthcoming: 7).

He argues that, before the coming of television to the colonies,

time, distance, and culture are almost interchangeable concepts, in explaining and justifying the differences between the colony and the metropole . . . the colony is seen as primitive, backward and under-developed. . . . The ultimate effect . . . is to objectify the concept of tradition, of a kind of culture that is rooted in a distant time and a remote place. The colony is backward because it is dominated by unchanging tradition – timeless, isolated and pervasive. The flow of time, in this context, is the product of colonial agents . . . who collectively represent themselves as agents of 'progress' – a term opposed to 'tradition', that also merges time, distance and culture. Progress implies movement in time, from unchanging past to the dynamic future; in space, from the isolated hinterland to the bustling city; and in culture, from static tradition to fashionable modernity.

(ibid.: 3)

The point here, of course, as Wilk notes, is that, while it is premised on the idea of progress, 'catching up' is never really possible (cf. Sangari, 1987), and while the time lag (or culture lag: measured, for instance, by the number of fashion 'seasons' behind the metropolis the colony is

226

currently running) can get longer or shorter, the 'clock is always set in the metropole . . . and the colonies can never catch up' (Wilk, forthcoming: 3).

In this situation, Wilk notes, the programming of much Third World television (cheap local programmes interspersed with outdated metropolitan cast-offs) seems

> designed as an object lesson in colonial time. The viewer is hardpressed to tell whether the differences between their own experiences and those depicted in *Father Knows Best* [an imported US sitcom] are the result of the passage of time, the geographic distance between their country and the USA, or real cultural differences between themselves and Americans.
>
> (ibid.: 4)

It is this temporal disjunction of social experience which is disrupted by the arrival of satellite television, according to Wilk, because the programmes (and especially the news and sports programmes) broadcast are so immediate:

> There is no lag. The Belizean family, in their rickety house, in a swamp, on the edge of Belize City, is not only watching the same programmes as urban North America, but far more importantly, they are watching them at the same time. What the Belizeans are watching, is happening *now*. . . . Satellite television has removed an essential element from the equation of colonial time. Distance between the metropole and the colony can no longer be reckoned in terms of time. . . . TV time is now a single clock, ticking away a single rhythm, in every place it reaches . . . the direct experience of a flow of events, that was once far away, safely filtered, and only dimly and indirectly perceived.
>
> (ibid.: 5)

In consequence, of course, as Wilk notes,

> We can't just sit back and expect that problems will be solved when Belize 'catches up'. Between Belize and the U.S., the time lag is gone, the distance is closing; what remains are cultural economic and political differences, that require new explanations.
>
> (ibid.: 6)

Ted Turner, head of CNN, has claimed (cf. Dowmunt, 1993: 1) that his company is the 'town-crier' of the 'global village' heralded so long ago by Marshall McLuhan. Certainly, in times of international crisis, CNN can come to play a crucial role. As Ang argues, 'It is largely through the representational practices of Ted Turner's CNN that the Gulf War could be dubbed the Third World War – a war in which the whole world

227

. . . participated, through the electronic collapsing of time and space induced by satellite telecom technology' (1991: 4). For Schiller (1992), the central issue here concerns the control of sources of information. Thus, he argues, 'most of the world's understanding of what was happening in the Gulf, and what it signified, came from practically a single U.S. source – CNN . . . [which] in turn acquired its material essentially from the Pentagon and the White House' (ibid.: 1).

However, there is another dimension to the issue, which takes us beyond the question of the control over the transmission of information. Thus, Caldorola (1992) argues that, in the context of the Gulf War, the very visual immediacy of the medium of satellite television also had the curious effect of denying the viewer any historical perspective on events, submerging the 'real' in a fictionalised narrative, and effectively reinforcing the cultural distance between the rest of the global audience and those on whom the Allies' bombs fell. In this context, it is perhaps incumbent upon us to think a little more carefully about 'who is at the end of history, and how they got there' (Clarke, 1991: 39).

BIBLIOGRAPHY

Abercombie, N., Hill, S. and Turner, B. (1984), *The Dominant Ideology Thesis*, London: Allen & Unwin.

Abish, W. (1983), *How German is it?*, London, Faber & Faber.

Adorno, T. W. (1985), 'On the question: what is German?', *New German Critique*, 36: 121–33.

Aglietta, M. (1979), *A Theory of Capitalist Regulation: The US Experience*, London: New Left Books.

Ahmed, A. (1992a), *Postmodernism and Islam*, London: Routledge.

Ahmed, A. (1992b), 'Palestine revisited', *New Statesman and Society*, 20 November.

Ajzenberg, A. (1988), 'Fonder une nouvelle citoyenneté', *Terminal*, 39/40/41: 71–4.

Aksoy, A. and Robins, K. (1992), 'Hollywood for the 21st century: global competition for critical mass in image markets', *Cambridge Journal of Economics*, 16(1): 1–22.

Al-'Azm, S. J. (1981), 'Orientalism and orientalism in reverse', *Khamsin*, 8: 5–26.

Albertsen, N. (1986), 'Towards post-Fordist localities? An essay on the socio-spatial restructuring process in Denmark'. Paper presented to the XIth World Congress of Sociology, New Delhi, August.

Alger, C. F. (1988), 'Perceiving, analysing and coping with the local–global nexus', *International Social Science Journal*, 117: 321–40.

Alibhai, Y. (1989), 'Community whitewash', *The Guardian*, 23 January.

Althusser, L. (1972), *For Marx*, Harmondsworth: Penguin.

Amin, S. (1989), *Eurocentrism*, London: Zed Books.

Anderson, B. (1983), *Imagined Communities*, London: Verso.

Ang, I. (1985), *Watching Dallas*, London: Methuen.

Ang, I. (1991), 'Global media/local meaning', *Media Information Australia* (62), November: 4–8.

Ang, I. (1992), 'Hegemony-in-trouble', in D. Petrie (ed.) *Screening Europe*, London: British Film Institute.

Ang, I. and Morley, D. (1989), 'Mayonnaise culture and other European follies', *Cultural Studies*, 3: 133–44.

Anzieu, D. (1984), *The Group and the Unconscious*, London: Routledge & Kegan Paul.

Appadurai, A. (1986), 'Theory in anthropology: center and periphery', *Comparative Studies in Society and History*, 28(2): 356–61.

Appadurai, A. (1988), 'Putting hierarchy in its place', *Cultural Anthropology*, 3(1): 36–49.
Appadurai, A. (1990), 'Disjuncture and difference in the global cultural economy', in M. Featherstone (ed.) *Global Culture*, London: Sage.
Arts Council (1988), *An Urban Renaissance*, London: Arts Council of Great Britain.
Ascherson, N. (1988), 'Below stairs in Europe's house', *The Observer*, 11 December.
Ascherson, N. (1989), 'Little nations hang out their flags', *The Observer*, 1 October.
Ascherson, N. (1990), 'Europe 2000', *Marxism Today*, January.
Atkinson, P. (1992), *Understanding Ethnographic Texts*, London: Sage.
Auletta, K. (1993a), 'Raiding the global village', *The New Yorker*, 2 August: 25–30.
Auletta, K. (1993b), 'The last studio in play', *The New Yorker*, 4 October: 77–81.
Balibar, E. (1991), 'Es gibt keinen Staat in Europa: racism and politics in Europe today', *New Left Review*, 186.
Banks, M. and Collins, R. (1989), 'Tradeable information and the transnational market', Research paper, CCIS, London: University of Westminster.
Barraclough, G. (1963), *European Unity in Thought and Action*, Oxford: Basil Blackwell.
Barret-Kriegel, B. (1992), 'La Citoyenneté en Europe', *Raison Présente*, 103.
Barthes, R. (1982), *The Empire of Signs*, New York: Hill and Wong.
Bassand, M. (1988), 'Communication in cultural and regional development', in M. Ernste and C. Jaeger (eds), *Information Society and Spatial Structure*, London: Belhaven.
Bassand, M., Hainard, F., Pedrazzani, Y. and Perrinjaquet, R. (1986), *Innovation et changement social: actions culturelles pour un développement local*, Lausanne: Presses Polytechniques Romandes.
Basso, K. (1979), *Portraits of 'The Whiteman'*, Cambridge: Cambridge University Press.
Baudrillard, J. (1985a), 'The masses: the implosion of the social in the media', *New Literary History*, 16(3).
Baudrillard, J. (1985b), 'The ecstasy of communication', in H. Foster (ed.) *Postmodern Culture*, London: Pluto.
Baudrillard, J. (1988a), *America*, London: Verso.
Baudrillard, J. (1988b), *Selected Writings*, edited by M. Poster, Cambridge: Polity Press.
Bauman, Z. (1992), 'Soil, blood and identity', *Sociological Review*, 40(2).
Bausinger, H. (1984), 'Media, technology and everyday life', *Media, Culture and Society*, 6(4): 343–52.
Beard, S. (1991), 'Blade runner boys', *The Modern Review*, Autumn.
Ben-Dasan, I. (1972), *The Japanese and the Jews*, New York: Wetherhill.
Benedict, R. (1974) [1946], *The Chrysanthemum and the Sword*, New York: Meridian.
Benton, S. (1989), 'Greys and greens', *New Statesmen and Society*, 2 June.
Berger, J. (1990), 'Keeping a rendezvous', *The Guardian*, 22 March.
Berger, P., Berger, B. and Kellner, H. (1974), *The Homeless Mind: Modernism and Consciousness*, Harmondsworth: Penguin.
Berman, M. (1983), *All that is Solid Melts into Air: The Experience of Modernity*, London: Verso.
Bernal, M. (1987), *Black Athena*, London: Free Association Books.
Bhabha, H. (1987), 'Interrogating identity', in L. Appignanesi (ed.) *Postmodernism and the Question of Identity*, London: Institute of Contemporary Arts.

Bhabha, H. (1989), 'Beyond fundamentalism and liberalism', *New Statesman and Society*, 3 March: 34–5.

Bigsby, C. (ed.) (1975), *Superculture: American Popular Culture and Europe*, London: Paul Elek Books.

Billaudot, B. and Gauron, A. (1985), *Croissance et crise: vers une nouvelle croissance*, 2nd edition, Paris: La Découverte.

Bion, W. R. (1978), *Four Discussions with W. R. Bion*, Strath Tay, Perthshire: Clunie Press.

Birgel, F. A. (1986), 'You can go home again: an interview with Edgar Reitz', *Film Quarterly*, Summer.

Bodroghkozy, A. (1992), 'Is this what you mean by color TV?', in L. Spigel and D. Mann (eds) *Private Screenings*, Minneapolis: University of Minnesota Press.

Böll, H. (1961), *Billiards at Half Past Nine*, London: Calder and Boyars.

Booz-Allen, H. (1993), *The Changing Environment for UK Broadcasters and its Economic Implications*, London: ITV Network Association.

Boyer, R. (1986a), *La Théorie de la régulation: une analyse critique*, Paris: La Découverte.

Boyer, R. (1986b), *Capitalismes fin de siècle*, Paris: Presses Universitaires de France.

Braudel, F. (1988), *Civilisation and Capitalism vol. 3: The Perspective of the World*, London: Collins/Fontana.

Brennan, T. (1989), 'Cosmopolitans and celebrities', *Race and Class*, 31(1): 1–19.

Breton, P. and Proulx, S. (1989), *L'Explosion de la communication*, Paris/Montreal: La Découverte/Boréal.

Brown, C. (1989), 'Holston exports', *Broadcast*, 13 October.

Brown, P. G. and Shue, H. (eds) (1981), *Boundaries: National Autonomy and Its Limits*, Totowa, New Jersey: Rowman & Littlefield.

Brune, F. (1993a), 'Néfastes effets de l'idéologie politico-médiatique', *Le Monde diplomatique*, May.

Brune, F. (1993b), *'Les Médias pensent comme moi!': Fragments du discours anonyme*, Paris: L'Harmattan.

Brunsdon, C. (1986), 'Women watching TV', *Medie Kulture*, 4.

Brunsdon, C. and Morley, D. (1978), *Everyday Television: Nationwide*, London: British Film Institute.

Buruma, I. (1989), 'From Hirohito to Heimat', *New York Review of Books*, 26 October.

Buruma, I. (1991a), 'A Euro-flag of many colours', *The Guardian*, 28 September.

Buruma, I. (1991b), 'The pax axis', *New York Review of Books*, 25 April.

Cable Authority (1987), *Cable and the Inner Cities*, London: Cable Authority.

Caldorola, V. (1992), 'Time and the television war', *Public Culture*, 4(2).

Calhoun, C. (1988), 'Communications technology and the transformation of the urban public sphere'. Paper presented to the International Conference on Information, Technology and the New Meaning of Space, International Sociological Association, Research Committee 24, Frankfurt, 15–19 May.

Cardiff, D. and Scannell, P. (1987), 'Broadcasting and national unity', in J. Curran, A. Smith and P. Wingate (eds) *Impacts and Influences: Essays on Media and Power in the Twentieth Century*, London: Methuen.

Carey, J. (1977), 'Mass communication research and cultural studies: an American view', in J. Curran, M. Gurevitch and J. Woollacott (eds) *Mass Communication and Society*, London: Edward Arnold.

Carpignano, P., Andersen, R., Aronowitz, S. and Difazio, W. (1990), 'Chatter in the age of electronic reproduction: talk television and the "public mind"', *Social*

Text, 25/26: 33–55.

Castells, M. (1983), 'Crisis, planning, and the quality of life: managing the new historical relationships between space and society', *Environment and Planning D: Society and Space*, 1(1).

Castoriadis, C. (1990), *Le Monde morcelé*, Paris: Seuil.

Castoriadis, C. (1992), 'Reflections on racism', *Thesis Eleven*, 32.

Cate, F. H. (1990), *The European Broadcasting Directive*, Washington, D.C.: America Bar Association, Communications Committee Monograph Series 1990/1.

Cavell, S. (1982), 'The fact of television', *Daedalus*, 3(4).

Certeau, M. de (1988), *The Writing of History*, New York: Columbia University Press.

Chakrabarty, D. (1992), 'The death of history? Historical consciousness and the culture of late capitalism', *Public Culture*, 4(2).

Chalmers, M. (1984), 'Heimat: approaches to a word and a film', *Framework*, 26–7: 90–101.

Chow, R. (1993), *Writing Diaspora*, Bloomington: Indiana University Press.

Christopherson, S. and Storper, M. (1986), 'The city as studio; the world as back lot: the impact of vertical disintegration on the location of the motion picture industry', *Environment and Planning D: Society and Space*, 4(3): 305–20.

Clarke, J. (1991), *New Times and Old Enemies*, London: HarperCollins.

Clemens, J. (1987), 'What will Europe watch?', *Journal of the Royal Television Society*, 24(6).

Clifford, J. (1986), 'Introduction: partial truths', in J. Clifford and G. Marcus (eds) *Writing Culture*, Berkeley: University of California Press.

Clifford, J. (1988) *The Predicament of Culture: Twentieth Century Ethnography, Literature and Art,* Cambridge, Mass.: Harvard University Press.

Clifford, J. (1992), 'Travelling cultures', in L. Grossberg *et al.* (eds) *Cultural Studies*, London: Routledge.

Clifford, J. and Marcus, G. (eds) (1986), *Writing Culture*, Berkeley: University of California Press.

Cluzel, J. (1992), L'audiovisuel – la veille du marché unique', *Revue politique et parlementaire*, 959.

Coker, C. (1992), 'Post-Modernity and the end of the cold war: has war been disinvented?', *Review of International Studies*, 18(3): 189–98.

Collins, R. (1988), 'National culture: a contradiction in terms?' Paper presented to the International Television Studies Conference, London, 20–22 July.

Collins, R. (1989) 'The peculiarities of English satellite TV in W. Europe', London: University of Westminster, C.C.I.S.

Collins, R. (1992), 'Unity in diversity: the European single market in broadcasting and the audiovisual, 1982–1992'. Paper presented to the PICT National Conference.

Collins, R., Garnham, N. and Locksley, G. (1988), *The Economics of Television: UK Case*, London: Sage.

Comaroff, J. and Comaroff, J. (1992), *Ethnography and the Historical Imagination*, Boulder, Col.: Westview Press.

Commission of the European Communities (CEC) (1983), 'The Community of culture', *European File*, 5/83.

Commission of the European Communities (1984), *Television Without Frontiers*, Brussels: Commission of the European Communities.

Commission of the European Communities (1986), 'Television and the audiovisual sector: towards a European policy', *European File*, 14/86, August–September.

Commission of the European Communities (1987), *A Fresh Boost for Culture in the European Community*, Brussels: Commission of the European Communities.

Commission of the European Communities (1988a), 'Towards a large European audiovisual market', *European File*, 4/88, February.

Commission of the European Communities (1988b), 'The European Community and culture', *European File*, 10/88, May.

Committee on Foreign Affairs (1964), 'Winning the Cold War: the US ideological offensive', 88th USA *Congress House Report*, No. 1352, April 27: 6–7.

Connell, I. (1983), 'Commercial broadcasting and the British Left', *Screen*, 24(6).

Connolly, W. (1989), 'Identity and difference in global politics', in J. Derian and M. Shapiro (eds) *International/Intertextual Relations: Postmodern Readings of World Politics*, Lexington, Mass.: Lexington Books.

Conte-Helm, M. (1989), *Japan and the North East of England: From 1862 to the Present Day*, London: Athlone Press.

Cope, N. (1990), 'Walkman's global stride', *Business*, March.

Corm, G. C. (1989), *L'Europe et L'Orient: de la Balkanisation à la Libanisation – histoire d'une modernité inaccomplie*, Paris: La Découverte.

Cornford, J. and Robins, K. (1995), 'Beyond the last bastion? Industrial restructuring and the labour force in the British television industry', in G. Sussman and J. Lent (eds) *Communication Workers of the World: The New International Division of Labour*, Boulder, Col.: Westview Press.

Courlet, C. and Judet, P. (1986), 'Nouveaux éspaces de production en France et en Italie', *Annales de la recherche urbaine*, 29.

Crookes, P. and Vittet-Philippe, P. (1986), *Local Radio and Regional Development in Europe*, Manchester: European Institute for the Media.

Cumings, B. (1991), 'CIA's Japan 2000 caper', *The Nation*, 30 September.

Curran, J. (1990), 'The "new revisionism" in mass communications research', *European Journal of Communication*, 5(2–3): 135–64.

Curti, L. (1988), 'Imported Utopias', unpublished paper, Instituto Orientale, Naples.

Dahrendorf, R. (1990), 'Europe's vale of tears', *Marxism Today*, May.

Dale, P. N. (1987), *The Myth of Japanese Uniqueness*, London: Routledge.

Davidson, I. (1990), 'Old European ghosts return to haunt Germany', *Financial Times*, 22 March.

Davis, H. and Levy, C. (1992), 'The regulation and deregulation of television: a British/West European comparison', *Economy and Society*, 21(4).

Dawson, C. (1956), 'The relevance of European history', *History Today*, 6(9).

DeLillo, D. (1985), *White Noise*, London: Picador.

DeLiss, C. (1991), *Exotic Europeans*, London: South Bank Centre Publications.

deMause, L. (1990), 'The Gulf War as mental disorder', *The Nation*, 11 March: 301–8.

Derrida, J. (1971), 'White mythology', reprinted (1982) in J. Derrida, *Margins of Philosophy*, Chicago: Chicago University Press.

Derrida, J. (1974), *Of Grammatology*, Baltimore: Johns Hopkins University Press.

Derrida, J. (1992), *The Other Heading*, Bloomington: Indiana University Press.

Dickson, M. (1993), 'Tremors on the television', *Financial Times*, 15 October.

Donald, J. (1988), 'How English is it? Popular literature and national culture', *New Formations*, (6): 31–47.

Donzelot, J. (1979), *The Policing of Families*, London: Hutchinson.

Dowmunt, T. (ed.) (1993), *Channels of Resistance*, London: British Film Institute.

Drakulić, S. (1993a), *Balkan Express: Fragments from the Other Side of War*, London: Hutchinson.

Drakulić, S. (1993b), *How We Survived Communism and Even Laughed*, London: Vintage.

Dufour, Y. R. and Dufour-Gompers, N. (1985), 'Journalists, anxiety and media as an intra-psychic screen', *Israel Journal of Psychiatry and Related Sciences*, 22(4): 315–24.

Duncan, S., and Goodwin, M. (1988), *The Local State and Uneven Development: Behind the Local Government Crisis*, Cambridge: Polity Press.

Dupuy, G. (1988), 'L'Eurovision ou le conflit de réseau et des territoires', in H. Bakis (ed.) *Information et organisation spatiale*, Caen: Paradigme.

Durham, J. (1993), *A Certain Lack of Coherence: Writings on Art and Cultural Politics*, London: Kala Press.

Eco, U. (1985), 'Innovation and repetition: between modern and post-modern aesthetics', *Daedalus*, 114(4): 161–84.

Eco, U. (1992), 'Chaosmos: the return of the Middle Ages', in R. Kearney (ed.) *Visions of Europe*, Dublin: Wolfhound Press.

Eco, U. (1993), 'The discovery of America' [original, 1968], in *Misreadings*, London: Jonathan Cape.

Ehrenberg, A. (1993), 'La vie en direct ou les shows de l'authenticité', *Esprit*, January.

Eliot, T. S. (1948), *Notes Towards the Definition of Culture*, London: Faber & Faber.

Ellis, J. (1982), *Visible Fictions*, London: Routledge.

Elsaesser, T. (1985), 'Germany's imaginary America: Wim Wenders and Peter Handke', in S. Haywood (ed.) *European Cinema*, Birmingham: Aston University, Modern Languages Department.

Elsaesser, T. (1988), 'National cinema and international television', in C. Schneider and B. Wallis (eds) *Global Television*, New York: Wedge Press.

Elsaesser, T. (1989), *New German Cinema: A History*, London: British Film Institute/Macmillan.

Emberley, P. (1989), 'Places and stories: the challenge of technology', *Social Research*, 56 (3).

Enzensberger, H. M. (1992), quoted in B. Ruys, 'Crossborder', *The Guardian*, 24 November.

Eyal, J. (1993), 'All subterfuge, no refuge', *The Guardian*, 15 February.

Fabian, J. (1983), *Time and the Other: How Anthropology makes its Object*, New York: Columbia University Press.

Fabian, J. (1990), 'Presence and representation: the other and anthropological writing', *Critical Inquiry*, 16: 753–72.

Fallows, J. (1989a), 'Containing Japan', *Atlantic Monthly*, May.

Fallows, J. (1989b), *More Like Us*, Boston: Houghton Mifflin.

Fallows, J. (1991a), 'The crucial difference', *Times Literary Supplement*, 27 September.

Fallows, J. (1991b), 'Is Japan the enemy?', *New York Review of Books*, 30 May.

Feraud-Royer, R. M. (1987), 'Conversations publiques', *Annales de la recherche urbaine*, 34: 15–22.

Ferro, M. (1993), 'Médias et intelligence du monde', *Le Monde diplomatique*, January: 32.

Fish, S. (1989), 'Commentary: the young and the restless', in H. Veeser (ed.) *The New Historicism*, London: Routledge.

Flores, E. (1988), 'Mass media and the cultural identity of the Puerto Rican people'. Paper presented to the Conference of the International Association for Mass Communications Research, Barcelona, July.

Fontaine, J. (1988), 'Public or private? The constitution of the family in anthro-pological perspective', *International Journal of Moral and Social Studies*, 33.
Foster, H. (ed.) (1985), *Postmodern Culture*, London: Pluto Press.
Foucault, M. (1980), 'Georges Canguilhem: philosopher of error', *Ideology and Consciousness*, 7.
Frampton, K. (1985), 'Towards a critical regionalism: six points for an architec-ture of resistance', in H. Foster (ed.) *Postmodern Culture*, London: Pluto.
Franklin Lytle, P. (1992), 'US policy toward the demise of Yugoslavia: the "virus of nationalism"', *East European Politics and Societies*, 6(3): 303–18.
Fraser, N. (1989), 'Keeping the world covered', *The Observer*, 12 November.
Frèches, José (1986), *La Guerre des images*, Paris: Denoël.
Friedman, G. and LeBard, M. (1991), *The Coming War with Japan*, New York: St Martin's.
Friedman, J. (1989), 'Culture, identity and world process', *Review*, 12(1).
Frith, S. (1983), 'The pleasures of the hearth', in V. Burgin, J. Donald and C. Kaplan (eds) *Formations of Pleasure*, London: Routledge.
Fukuyama, F. (1992), *The End of History and the Last Man*, Harmondsworth: Penguin.
Fusco, C. (1989), 'About locating ourselves and our representations', *Framework*, 36.
Gabler, N. (1988), *An Empire of their Own: How the Jews invented Hollywood*, London: W. H. Allen.
Galleano, E. (1993), Interview with Miguel Bonasso, in *The Last Café*, transmit-ted Channel 4, London, 12 April.
Gallissot, R. (1992), 'Dépasser le nationalisme sinon les nationalismes nous dépassent', *L'Homme et la société*, 103.
Garitaonandia, C. (1993), 'Regional television in Europe', *European Journal of Communication*, 9(3): 277–94.
Garnham, N. (1983), 'Public service versus the market', *Screen*, 24 (3): 6–27.
Garnham, N. (1986), 'Concepts of culture: public policy and the cultural indus-tries', *Cultural Studies*, 1(1): 23–38.
Garnier, J.-P. (1987), 'L'éspace médiatique ou l'utopie localisée', *Espaces et sociétés*, 50.
Geertz, C. (1988), *Works and Lives: The Anthropologist as Author*, Cambridge: Polity Press.
Geisler, M. (1985), 'Heimat and the German Left', *New German Critique*, 36: 25–67.
Gellner, E. (1992), *Postmodernism, Reason and Religion*, London: Routledge.
Giddens, A. (1990), *The Consequences of Modernity*, Cambridge: Polity Press.
Gifreu, J. (1986), 'From communication policy to reconstruction of cultural indus-tries', *Cultural Studies*, 1(1).
Gilroy, P. (1986), *There Ain't No Black in the Union Jack*, London: Hutchinson.
Gilroy, P. (1989), Remarks on postmodernism, in discussion at National Film Theatre, London, quoted in I. Ang and D. Morley 'Mayonnaise culture and other European follies', *Cultural Studies*, 3(2): 133–44.
Gitlin, T. (1989), 'Postmodernism: roots and politics', *Dissent*, Winter.
Glenny, M. (1988), 'The rise in spirit: cultural identities in E. Europe', *The Guardian*, 15 December.
Godelier, M. (1991), 'Is the West the model for humankind?', *International Social Science Journal*, 128.
Gorbachev, M. (1987), *Perestroika: New Thinking for our Country and the World*, London: Collins.

Gordon, R. (1989), 'Les entrepreneurs, l'entreprise et les fondements sociaux de l'innovation', *Sociologie du travail*, 30(1): 107–24.

Gramsci, A. (1971), *Prison Notebooks*, London: Lawrence & Wishart.

Grass, G. (1992), 'Losses', *Granta*, 42.

Grassmuck, V. (1991), 'Otaku: Japanese kids colonise the realm of information and media', *Mediamatic*, 5(4).

Greenblatt, S. (1992), *Marvellous Possessions: The Wonder of the New World*, Oxford: Oxford University Press.

Gripsrud, J. (forthcoming), *The 'Dynasty' Years*, London: Routledge.

Grotstein, J. (1981), *Splitting and Projective Identification*, New York: Jason Aronson.

Guback, T. H. (1974), 'Cultural identity and film in the European Economic Community', *Cinema Journal*, 14(1).

Guback, T. H. (1979), 'Film as international business', in A. Mattelart and S. Siegelaub (eds) *Communication and Class Struggle*, vol. 1, Paris/New York: International General.

Gunder Frank, A. (1969), *Latin America: Underdevelopment or Revolution?*, New York: Monthly Review Press.

Gupta, A. and Ferguson, J. (1992), 'Beyond culture: space, identity and the politics of difference', *Cultural Anthropology*, 7: 6–23.

Habermas, J. (1984), *The Theory of Communicative Action, vol. 1: Reason and the Rationalisation of Society*, Cambridge: Polity Press.

Hägerstrand, T. (1986), 'Decentralisation and radio broadcasting: on the "possibility space" of a communication technology', *European Journal of Communication*, 1(1).

Hall, S. (1981), 'Encoding/decoding in TV discourse', in S. Hall, D. Hobson, A. Lowe and P. Willis (eds) *Culture, Media, Language*, London: Hutchinson.

Hall, S. (1986), 'On postmodernism and articulation', *Journal of Communication Inquiry*, 10(2): 45–60.

Hall, S. (1987), 'Minimal selves', in L. Appignanesi (ed.) *Postmodernism and the Question of Identity*, London: Institute of Contemporary Arts.

Hall, S. (1988), 'New ethnicities', in K. Mercer (ed.) *Black Film, British Cinema*, ICA Document No. 7, London: Institute of Contemporary Arts.

Hall, S. (1992a), 'The West and the Rest', in S. Hall and B. Gieben (eds) *Formations of Modernity*, Cambridge: Polity Press.

Hall, S. (1992b), 'European cinema on the verge of a nervous breakdown', in D. Petrie (ed.) *Screening Europe*, London: British Film Institute.

Hall, S. (1993), 'Which public, whose service?', in W. Stevenson (ed.) *All Our Futures: The Changing Role and Purpose of the BBC*, London: British Film Institute.

Hannerz, U. (1991), 'Cosmopolitans and locals in world culture', in M. Featherstone (ed.) *Global Culture*, London: Sage.

Hansen, M. (1985), 'Dossier on Heimat', *New German Critique*, 36: 3–25.

Hartley, J. (1978), 'Invisible fictions', *Textual Practice*, 1(2): 121–38.

Hartmann, C. and Husband, P. (1972), 'Race and the British media', in D. McQuail (ed.) *The Sociology of Mass Communication*, Harmondsworth: Penguin.

Hartsock, N. (1989), 'Rethinking modernism', *Cultural Critique*, 7: 187–206.

Harvey, D. (1985), 'The geopolitics of capitalism', in D. Gregory and J. Urry (eds) *Social Relations and Social Structures*, London: Macmillan.

Harvey, D. (1987), 'Flexible accumulation through urbanisation: reflections on "post-modernism" in the American city', *Antipode*, 19(3): 260–86.

Harvey, D. (1989), *The Condition of Postmodernity*, Oxford: Basil Blackwell.

Hassan, I. (1990), 'The burden of mutual perceptions: Japan and the United States', *Salmagundi*, 85–6.

Hassner, P. (1991), 'L'Europe et le spectre des nationalismes', *Esprit*, October.

Häussermann, H. and Siebel, W. (1987), *Neue Urbanität*, Frankfurt: Suhrkamp.

Hearn, L. (1959), *Japan: An Attempt at Interpretation*, New York: Tuttle Books.

Hebdige, D. (1988a), *Hiding in the Light*, London: Routledge.

Hebdige, D. (1988b), 'Towards a cartography of taste', in D. Hebdige, *Hiding in the Light*, London: Comedia/Routledge.

Hebdige, D. (1990), 'Fax to the future', *Marxism Today*, January.

Hegel, G. W. F. (1956), *The Philosophy of History* [original, 1837], New York: Dover.

Held, D. (1988), 'Farewell nation state', *Marxism Today*, December.

Held, D. (1993), 'By the people, for the people', *Times Higher Education Supplement*, 22 January.

Heller, A. and Feher, F. (1988), *The Postmodern Political Condition*, Cambridge: Polity Press.

Higson, A. (1989), 'The concept of national cinema', *Screen*, 30(4).

Hjarvard, S. (1993), 'Pan-European television news: towards a European political public sphere?', in P. Drummond, R. Paterson and J. Willis (eds) *National Identity and Europe*, London: British Film Institute.

Hobsbawm, E. (1990), *Nations and Nationalism since 1870*, Cambridge: Cambridge University Press.

Hobsbawm, E. (1992), 'Goodbye Columbus', *London Review of Books*, 9 July.

Hobsbawm, E. (1994), *Age of Extremes: The Short Twentieth Century*, London: Michael Joseph.

Hobsbawm, E. and Ranger, T. (eds) (1983), *The Invention of Tradition*, Cambridge: Cambridge University Press.

Hoggart, R. (1958), *The Uses of Literacy*, Harmondsworth: Penguin.

Hoggett, P. (1992), 'A place for experience: a psychoanalytical perspective on boundary, identity and culture', *Environment and Planning D: Society and Space*, 10: 345–56.

Holborn, M. (1991), *Beyond Japan*, London: Jonathan Cape.

Home Office (1988), *Broadcasting in the '90s: Competition, Choice and Quality*, Cm 517, London: HMSO.

Hondius, F. W. (1985), 'Freedom of commercial speech in Europe', *Transnational Data Report*, 8(6).

Hood, S. (1988), 'The couthy feeling', *New Statesman and Society*, 12 August: 30–1.

Horton, D. and Wohl, R. R. (1956), 'Mass communication and para-social interaction: observations on intimacy at a distance', *Psychiatry*, 19: 215–29.

Hoskins, C. and R. Mirus (1988), 'Reasons for the US dominance of the international trade in television programmes', *Media, Culture and Society*, 10(4): 499–515.

Hourani, A. (1946), *Syria and Lebanon: A Political Essay*, London: Oxford University Press.

Hourani, A. (1980), *Europe and the Middle East*, London: Macmillan.

Hudson, R. (1988), 'Uneven development in capitalist societies: changing spatial divisions of labour, forms of spatial organisation of production and service provision, and their impacts on localities', *Transactions of the Institute of British Geographers*, NS 13: 484–96.

Huey, J. (1990), 'America's hottest export: pop culture', *Fortune*, 31 December.

Hutton, W. (1993), 'New tribalism threatens to infect us all', *The Guardian*, 1 February.

Huyssen, A. (1988), 'Mass culture as woman: modernism's other', in T. Modleski (ed.) *Studies in Entertainment*, Bloomington: Indiana University Press.

Innis, H. A. (1950), *Empire and Communications*, Oxford: Clarendon Press.

Ishihara, S. (1991), *The Japan That Can Say No: Why Japan Will Be First Among Equals*, New York: Simon & Schuster.

Isozaki, A. (1991), 'Wayo style: the Japanisation mechanism', *Visions of Japan*, London: Victoria and Albert Museum.

Jameson, F. (1985), 'Postmodernism and consumer society', in H. Foster (ed.) *Postmodern Culture*, London: Pluto.

Januszczak, W. (1990a), *Sayonara Michelangelo: The Sistine Chapel Restored and Repackaged*, Reading, Mass.: Addison-Wesley.

Januszczak, W. (1990b), 'The new Jews', *The Guardian*, 29 December.

Joffe, J. (1993), 'The new Europe: yesterday's ghosts', *Foreign Affairs*, 72(1).

Johnson, S. (1988), *The Japanese through American Eyes*, Stanford: Stanford University Press.

Jouanny, Robert (1988), 'Espaces et identités francophones', *Acta geographica*, 73.

Julien, I. and K. Mercer (1989), 'De margin and De centre', *Screen*, 30(1): 2–11.

Kaes, A. (1989), *From Hitler to Heimat*, Cambridge, Mass.: Harvard University Press.

Kant, I. (1968), 'An idea for a universal history' [original, 1784], in I. Kant, *On History*, Indianapolis: Bobbs-Merrill.

Kaplan, C. (1986), 'The culture crossover', *New Socialist*, 41(9).

Kato, H. (1991), 'The machine cult', *Visions of Japan*, London: Victoria and Albert Museum.

Keane, J. (1989), 'Identikit Europe', *Marxism Today*, April.

Kearney, R. (1988a), *The Wake of Imagination*, London: Hutchinson.

Kearney, R. (1988b), *Transitions: Narratives in Modern Irish Culture*, Dublin: Wolfhound Press.

Kearney, R. (ed.) (1992), *Visions of Europe*, Dublin: Wolfhound Press.

Khaldun, I. (1987), *An Arab Philosophy of History: Selections from the Prologomena of Ibn Khaldun (1332–1406)*, trans. and arranged by C. Issawi, Princeton, New Jersey: Darwin Press.

King, A. (1991), 'Introduction', in A. King (ed.) *Culture, Globalisation and the World System*, London: Macmillan.

Knightley, P. (1991), 'Spider's web across the ocean', *The Guardian Weekly*, 17 March.

Kramer, F. (1993), *The Red Fez: Art and Spirit Possession in Africa*, London: Verso.

Kreutzner, G. (1989), 'On doing cultural studies in Western Germany', *Cultural Studies*, 3(2): 240–9.

Kristeva, J. (1991), *Strangers to Ourselves*, New York: Harvester Wheatsheaf.

Kristeva, J. (1992a), 'Le temps de la dépression', *Le Monde des débats*, October.

Kristeva, J. (1992b), 'Strangers to ourselves: the hope of the singular', in R. Kearney (ed.) *Visions of Europe*, Dublin: Wolfhound Press.

Kundera, M. (1984), 'A kidnapped west or culture bows out', *Granta*, 11: 93–118.

Kureishi, H. (1989), 'England, your England', *New Statesman and Society*, 21 July.

Lash, S. and Urry, J. (1987), *The End of Organised Capitalism*, Cambridge: Polity Press.

Leadbeater, C. (1991), 'Masters of the interior universe', *Financial Times*, 3 September.

Leith, W. (1993), 'The kind of violence lovers hate', *The Independent on Sunday*, 3 January.

Lerner, D. (1964), *The Passing of Traditional Society*, Glencoe, Ill.: Free Press.

Levin, T. (1985), 'Nationalities of language', *New German Critique*, 36: 111–21.
Levinas, E. (1983), 'Beyond intentionality', in A. Montefiore (ed.) *Philosophy in France Today*, Cambridge: Cambridge University Press.
Levitt, T. (1983), *The Marketing Imagination*, London: Collier-Macmillan.
Ley, D. (1989), 'Modernism, post-modernism, and the struggle for place', in J. A. Agnew and J. S. Duncan (eds) *The Power of Place*, Boston: Unwin Hyman.
Liebes, T. and Katz, E. (1989), 'On the critical ability of TV viewers', in E. Seiter, H. Borchers, G. Kreutzner and E.-M. Warth (eds) *Remote Control*, London: Routledge.
Liebes, T. and Katz, E. (1991), *The Export of Meaning: Cross-Cultural Readings of Dallas*, Oxford: Oxford University Press.
Lincoln, E. J. (1994), *Japan's New Global Role*, Washington, D. C.: The Brookings Institution.
Linforth, I. (1926), 'Greek gods and foreign gods in Herodotus', University of California Publications in Classical Philosophy.
Lipietz, Alain (1987), *Mirages and Miracles: The Crises of Global Fordism*, London: Verso.
Lipschutz, R. (1992), 'Reconstructing world politics: the emergence of global civil society', *Millenium: Journal of International Studies*, 21(3).
Lockwood, D. (1954), 'Social integration and system integration' in G. K. Zollschan and W. Hirsch (eds) *Explorations in Social Change*, London: Routledge & Kegan Paul.
Logica (1987), *Television Broadcasting in Europe: Towards the 1990s*, London: Logica Consultancy Ltd.
Luce, H. (1941), *The American Century*, New York: Farrar & Rhinehart Inc.
Lummis, C. (1984), 'Japanese critiques of technological society', *Canadian Journal of Political and Social Theory*, 8(3).
Lyotard, H. A. (ed.) (1987), *The Postmodern Condition*, Manchester: Manchester University Press.
McBride, S. (1980), *Many Voices One World*, Paris: UNESCO.
MacCabe, Colin (1988), 'Those golden years', *Marxism Today*, 32(4).
McGrane, B. (1989), *Beyond Anthropology: Society and the Other*, New York: Columbia University Press.
Mackinder, H. J. (1904), 'Europe: the geographical pivot of history', *The Geographical Journal*, 23(4): 434–7.
McLuhan, M. (1964), *Understanding Media*, London: Routledge & Kegan Paul.
Magas, B. (1992), 'The destruction of Bosnia-Herzegovina', *New Left Review*, 196: 102–12.
Magris, C. (1990), *Danube*, London: Collins-Harvill.
Malcolm, D. (1990), 'Hollywood is the enemy', *The Guardian*, 29 November.
Malcomson, S. (1991), 'Heart of whiteness: Europe goes for the globe', *Voice Literary Supplement*, March 1991.
Mandel, R. (1989), 'Turkish headscarves and the "foreigner problem": constructing difference through emblems of identity', *New German Critique*, 46.
Mani, L. and Frankenburg, R. (1985), 'The challenge of orientalism', *Economy and Society*, 14 (2).
Marcus, G. and Fischer, M. (1986), *Anthropology as Cultural Critique*, Chicago: University of Chicago Press.
Martin-Barbero, J. (1988), 'Communication from culture: the crisis of the nations and the emergence of the popular', *Media Culture and Society*, 10: 447–65.
Mascia-Lees, F. E., Sharpe, P. and Cohen, C. B. (1989), 'The post-modernist turn in anthropology: cautions from a feminist perspective', *Signs*, 15(1): 7–33.

SPACES OF IDENTITY

Massey, D. (1984), *Spatial Divisions of Labour: Social Structures and the Geography of Production*, London: Macmillan.
Massey, D. (1991a), 'A global sense of place', *Marxism Today*, June 1991.
Massey, D. (1991b), 'Flexible sexism', *Environment and Planning D: Society and Space*, 9(1): 31–57.
Massey, D. (1992), 'A place called home', *New Formations*, 17: 3–15.
Mattelart, A. (1979), 'For a class analysis of communications', in A. Mattelart and S. Sieglaub (eds) *Communication and Class Struggle*, vol. 1, New York: International General.
Mattelart, A. and Piemme, J.-M. (1983), 'New technologies, decentralisation and public service'; in A. Mattelart and S. Siegelaub (eds) *Communication and Class Struggle*, vol. 2, New York: International General.
Mattelart, A., Delcourt, X. and Mattelart, M. (1984), *International Image Markets*, London: Comedia.
Mayer, M. (1989), 'Local politics: from administration to management'. Paper presented to the Conference on Regulation, Innovation and Spatial Development, Cardiff, 13–15 September.
Melot, M. (1987/8), 'Questioning Japanism', *Block*, 13.
Melucci, A. (1989), *Nomads of the Present: Social Movements and Individual Needs in Contemporary Society*, London: Hutchinson Radius.
Menzies, I. E. P. (1960), 'A case-study in the functioning of social systems as a defence against anxiety', *Human Relations*, 13(2).
Mercer, K. (1990), 'Welcome to the jungle', in J. Rutherford (ed.) *Identity: Community, Culture, Difference*, London: Lawrence & Wishart.
Meyrowitz, J. (1985), *No Sense of Place*, Oxford: Oxford University Press.
Meyrowitz, J. (1989), 'The generalised elsewhere', *Critical Studies in Mass Communication*, 6 (3): 326–34.
Michaels, E. (1988), 'Hollywood iconography: a Warlpiri reading', in P. Drummond and R. Paterson (eds) *Television and its Audience*, London: British Film Institute.
Miller, D. (1992), 'The Young and the Restless in Trinidad: a case of the local and the global in mass consumption', in R. Silverstone and E. Hirsch (eds), *Consuming Technologies*, London: Routledge.
Mills, P. (1985), 'An international audience?', *Media, Culture and Society*, 7.
Minear, R. H. (1980), 'Orientalism and the study of Japan', *Journal of Asian Studies*, 39 (3).
Miner, E. (1958), *The Japanese Tradition in British and American Literature*, Princeton: Princeton University Press.
Minh-Ha, Trinh T. (1989), *Woman, Native, Other*, Bloomington: Indiana University Press.
Mitsuhiro, Y. (1989), 'The postmodern and mass images in Japan', *Public Culture*, 1(2).
Miyoshi, M. and Harootunian, H. D. (1988), 'Introduction', *South Atlantic Quarterly*, 87(3): 387–401.
Montaigne, M. (1990), 'On cannibals' [original, 1578], in M. Montaigne, *Essays*, Harmondsworth: Penguin.
Moragas Spa, M. de (1988), 'Cultural identity, communication spaces and democratic participation'. Paper presented to the XVI International Congress of the International Association for Mass Communications Research, Barcelona, 24–28 July.
Morin, E. (1990), 'Formation et composantes du sentiment national', *Cosmopolitiques*, 16.

Morley, D. (1992), *Television, Audiences and Cultural Studies*, London: Routledge.

Morris, M. (1987), 'Asleep at the wheel?', *New Statesman*, 26 June.

Mortimer, E. (1990), 'Is this our frontier', *Financial Times*, 3 April.

Mulgan, G. (1989), 'A thousand beams of light', *Marxism Today*, April.

Mulgan, G. and Worpole, K. (1985), *Saturday Night or Sunday Morning*, London: Comedia.

Nairn, T. (1993), 'Demonising nationalism', *London Review of Books*, 25 February.

Neale, S. (1981), 'Art cinema as institution', *Screen*, 22(1).

Nicholson, L. (ed.) (1990), *Feminism/Postmodernism*, London: Routledge.

Nora, P. (1989), 'Between memory and history: les lieux de mémoire', *Representations*, 26.

Norris, C. (1991), *Deconstruction: Theory and Practice*, revised edition, London: Routledge.

Ohmae, K. (1989), 'Managing in a borderless world', *Harvard Business Review*, 67(3).

Owens, C. (1985), 'The discourse of others: feminists and postmodernism', in H. Foster (ed.) *Postmodern Culture*, London: Pluto.

Page, I. (1986), 'Tourism promotion in Bradford', *The Planner*, February.

Parekh, B. (1989), 'Between holy text and moral void', *New Statesman and Society*, 24 March.

Paterson, R. (1980), 'The art of the TV schedule', *Screen Education*, 35: 79–86.

Peet, R. (1982), 'International capital, international culture', in M. J. Taylor and N. J. Thrift (eds) *The Geography of the Multinationals*, London: Croom Helm.

Peet, R. (1986), 'The destruction of regional cultures', in R. J. Johnston and P. J. Taylor (eds) *A World in Crisis? Geographical Perspectives*, Oxford: Basil Blackwell.

Pickering, M. and Robins, K. (1984), '"A revolutionary materialist with a leg free": the autobiographical novels of Jack Common', in J. Hawthorn (ed.) *The British Working Class Novel in the Twentieth Century*, London: Edward Arnold.

Pickering, M. and Robins, K. (1989), 'Dangerous desires: youth, class and sexuality in the work of Sid Chaplin', *Ideas and Production*, 9–10.

Pieterse, P. (1991), 'Fictions of Europe', *Race and Class*, 32.

Pietz, W. (1987), 'The phonograph in Africa: international phonocentrism from Stanley to Sarnoff', in D. Attridge et al. (eds) *Post-structuralism and the Question of History*, Cambridge: Cambridge University Press.

Piore, M. and Sabel, C. (1984), *The Second Industrial Divide: Possibilities for Prosperity*, New York: Basic Books.

Pocock, J. G. A. (1991), 'Deconstructing Europe', *London Review of Books*, 19 December.

Poole, T. (1993), 'Star in the east heralds TV revolution', *The Independent on Sunday*, 18 April.

Powell, E. (1989), 'Sovereignty we won't surrender', *The Guardian*, 17 April.

Powell, N. (1993), 'French redskins take on the cowboys', *The Observer*, 19 September.

Prebisch, R. (1950), *The Economic Development of Latin America, and its Principal Problems*, New York: United Nations.

Rabinow, P. (1986), 'Representations are social facts', in J. Clifford and G. Marcus (eds) *Writing Culture*, Berkeley: University of California Press.

Rafferty, K. (1994), 'Sun sets on Japanese miracle', *The Guardian*, 15 January.

Ramonet, I. (1991), 'L'ère du soupçon', *Le Monde diplomatique*, May.

Rancière, J. (1992), 'Politics, identification and subjectivisation', *October*, 62: 58–64.

Ranvaud, D. (1985), 'Edgar Reitz at Venice', *Sight and Sound*, 54(2): 124–8.

Rath, C.-D. (1985), 'The invisible network', in P. Drummond and R. Paterson (eds) *Television in Transition*, London: British Film Institute.

Rath, C.-D. (1988), 'Live/life: TV as generator of events in everyday life', in P. Drummond and R. Paterson (eds) *Television and its Audience*, London: British Film Institute.

Rath, C.-D. (1989), 'Live television and its audiences', in E. Seiter, H. Borchers, G. Kreutzner and E.-M. Warth (eds) *Remote Control*, London: Routledge.

Ravlich, R. (1989), 'City limits', *Meanjin*, 47(3): 468–82.

Reed, C. and Rafferty, K. (1994), 'Dangerous yen for Hollywood', *The Guardian*, 1 December.

Reich, J. (1990), 'Germany – a binary poison', *New Left Review*, 179.

Reich, R. (1987), 'The rise of techno-nationalism', *Atlantic Monthly*, May: 63–9.

Reich, R. (1990), 'Who is us?', *Harvard Business Review*, January–February: 53–65.

Richards, B. (1989), *Images of Freud: Cultural Responses to Psychoanalysis*, London: Dent.

Ricoeur, P. (1965), 'Civilisation and national cultures', in *History and Truth*, Evanston, Ill.: North-Western University Press.

Ricoeur, P. (1992), 'Universality and the power of difference', in R. Kearney (ed.) *Visions of Europe*, Dublin: Wolfhound Press.

Rieff, D. (1993), *Los Angeles: Capital of the Third World*, London: Phoenix/Orion Books.

Roberts, J. (1990), *The History of the World*, London: Penguin.

Robertson, R. (1991), 'Japan and the USA: the interpretation of national identities and the debate about orientalism', in N. Abercombie *et al.* (eds) *Dominant Ideologies*, London: Unwin Hyman.

Robins, K. (1993), 'The war, the screen, the crazy dog and poor mankind', *Media, Culture and Society*, 15(2): 321–7.

Robins, K. and Cornford, J. (1994), 'Local and regional broadcasting in the new media order', in A. Amin and N. Thrift (eds) *Globalisation, Institutions and Regional Development in Europe*, Oxford: Oxford University Press.

Robins, K. and Gillespie, A. (1988), 'Beyond Fordism?' Paper to International Conference on Information Technology and the Meaning of Space, Frankfurt, May 1988.

Robins, K. and Hepworth, M. (1988), 'Electronic spaces: new technologies and the future of cities', *Futures*, 20(2).

Robins, K. and Webster, F. (1989), *The Technical Fix*, London: Macmillan.

Robins, K. and Webster, F. (1990), 'Broadcasting politics: communications and consumption,' in M. Alvarado and J. O. Thompson (eds) *The Media Reader*, London: British Film Institute.

Rodney, W. (1972), *How Europe Underdeveloped Africa*, London: Bogle-L'Ouverture Publications.

Roud, R. (1971), *Straub*, London: Secker & Warburg.

Rorty, Richard (1985), 'Solidarity or objectivity?', in J. Rajchman and C. West (eds) *Post-Analytic Philosophy*, New York: Columbia University Press.

Ross, S. (1990), 'Worldview address', delivered at the Edinburgh International Television Festival, 26 August.

Rostow, W. (1960), *The Stages of Economic Growth*, Cambridge: Cambridge University Press.

Rushdie, S. (1982), 'Imaginary homelands', *London Review of Books*, 7–20 October.

Rushdie, S. (1990), 'In good faith', *The Independent on Sunday*, 4 February.

Rustin, M. (1987), 'Place and time in socialist theory', *Radical Philosophy*, 147.

Rustin, M. (1989), 'Post-Kleinian psychoanalysis and the post-modern', *New Left Review*, 173: 109–28.
Said, E. (1978), *Orientalism*, Harmondsworth: Penguin.
Said, E. (1984), 'Reflections on exile', *Granta*, 13: 157–72.
Said, E. (1988), 'Identity, negation and violence', *New Left Review*, 171: 46–60.
Said, E. (1989), 'Representing the colonised: anthropology's interlocutors', *Critical Inquiry*, 15(2): 205–25.
Said, E. (1992), 'Europe and its others: an Arab perspective', in R. Kearney (ed.) *Visions of Europe*, Dublin: Wolfhound Press.
Sakai, N. (1988), 'Modernity and its critique', *South Atlantic Quarterly*, 87(3): 475–505.
Samuel, R. (1988), 'Little Englandism today', *New Statesman and Society*, 21 October.
Samuel, R. (1989), 'Introduction: exciting to be English', in R. Samuel (ed.) *Patriotism: The Making and Unmaking of British National Identity*, London: Routledge.
Sangari, K. (1987), 'The politics of the possible', *Cultural Critique*, Fall.
Sanger, D. E. (1990), 'Politics and multi-national movies', *New York Times*, 27 November.
Sassen-Koob, S. (1987), 'Issues of core and periphery: labour migration and global restructuring', in J. Henderson and M. Castells (eds) *Global Restructuring and Territorial Development*, London: Sage.
Saussure, F. de (1974), *Course in General Linguistics*, London: Fontana.
Scannell, P. (1988), 'Radio times', in P. Drummond and R. Paterson (eds) *Television and its Audience*, London: British Film Institute.
Scannell, P. (1989), 'Public service broadcasting and modern public life', *Media, Culture and Society*, 11(2): 135–66.
Schiller, H. I. (1969), *Mass Communications and American Empire*, New York: Beacon Press.
Schiller, H. I. (1985), 'Electronic information flows: new basis for global domination', in P. Drummond and R. Paterson (eds) *Television in Transition*, London: British Film Institute.
Schiller, H. I. (1990), 'Sayonara MCA', *The Nation*, 31 December.
Schiller, H. (1991), 'Not yet the post-imperialist era', *Critical Studies in Mass Communication*, 8: 13–28.
Schiller, H. (1992), *Mass Communications and American Empire*, 2nd edition, updated, Boulder, Col.: Westview Press.
Schlesinger, P. (1986), 'Any chance of fabricating Eurofiction?', *Media, Culture and Society*, 8.
Schlesinger, P. (1987), 'On national identity: some conceptions and misconceptions criticised', *Social Science Information*, 26(2): 219–64.
Schlesinger, P. (1989), 'Cold sore for minimalists and maximalists', *Times Higher Education Supplement*, 13 January.
Schlesinger, P. (1993), 'Wishful thinking: cultural politics, media and collective identities in Europe', *Journal of Communication*, 43(2).
Scholte, R. (1987), 'The literary turn in contemporary anthropology', *Critique of Anthropology*, 7(1): 33–47.
Schudson, M. (1994), 'Culture and the integration of national societies', *International Social Science Journal*, 139.
Scobie, W. (1988), 'Carlo, suitor to La Grande Dame', *The Observer*, 14 February.
Sennett, R. (1971), *The Uses of Disorder*, Harmondsworth: Penguin.
Shamoon, S. (1989), 'Mickey the Euro mouse', *The Observer*, 17 September.

Shibusawa, M., Ahmad, Z. H. and Bridges, B. (1991), *Pacific Asia in the 1990s*, London: Routledge.

Shillony, B.-A. (1991), *The Jews and the Japanese: The Successful Outsiders*, Rutland, Vermont, and Tokyo: Tuttle & Co.

Sibley, D. (1988), 'Purification of space', *Environment and Planning D: Society and Space*, 6(4).

Sibony, D. (1993), 'Bosnie: le point de silence', *Libération*, 7 June.

Silva, M. and Sjögren, B. (1990), *Europe 1992 and the New World Power Game*, New York: John Wiley.

Sivanandan, A. (1988), 'The new racism', *New Statesman and Society*, 4 November.

Sivanandan, A. (1989), 'Rules of engagement', *New Statesman and Society*, 28 April.

Smith, A. (1980), *The Geo-Politics of Information: How Western Culture Dominates the World*, London: Faber & Faber.

Smith, N. (1988), 'The region is dead! Long live the region!', *Political Geography Quarterly*, 7(2).

Snoddy, R. (1993), 'The film that can erase itself', *Financial Times*, supplement on 'Cable TV and satellite broadcasting', 6 October.

Soja, E. J. (1985), 'Regions in context: spatiality, periodicity and the historical geography of the regional question', *Environment and Planning D: Society and Space*, 3(2): 175–90.

Soja, E. (1989), *Postmodern Geographies: The Reassertion of Space in Critical Social Theory*, London: Verso.

Sontag, S. (1979), *On Photography*, Harmondsworth: Penguin.

Sontag, S. (1989), 'L'idée d'Europe (une élégie de plus)', *Les Temps modernes*, 510.

Sreberny-Mohammadi, A. (1992), 'The global and the local in international communications', in J. Curran and M. Gurevitch (eds) *Mass Media and Society*, London: Edward Arnold.

Stam, R. (1983), 'Television news and its spectator', in E. Kaplan (ed.) *Regarding Television*, vol. 2, New York: American Film Institute.

Stefano, C. di (1990), 'Dilemmas of difference: feminism, modernity and postmodernism', in L. Nicholson (ed.) *Feminism/Postmodernism*, London: Routledge.

Stephanson, A. (1987), 'Regarding postmodernism – a conversation with Fredric Jameson', *Social Text*, 17.

Stiegler, B. (1987), 'Réseaux et communauté', *Annales de la recherche urbaine*, 34: 5–14.

Storper, M. and Christopherson, S. (1987), 'Flexible specialisation and regional industrial agglomerations: the case of the U.S. motion picture industry', *Annals of the Association of American Geographers*, 77(1): 104–17.

Suhr, H. (1989), 'Ausländerliteratur: minority literature in the Federal Republic of Germany', *New German Critique*, 46.

Taguieff, P.-A. (1992), 'Nationalisme, réactions identitaires et communauté imaginée', *Hommes et Migrations*, 1154.

Thackara, J. (1989), 'Seeing is disbelieving', *The Listener*, 23 March.

Thibaud, P. and Touraine, A. (1993), 'Républicans ou démocrates? Débat entre Paul Thibaud et Alain Touraine', *Projet*, 233.

Thrift, N. (1987), 'The geography of the late twentieth century class formation', in N. Thrift and P. Williams (eds) *Class and Space: The Making of Urban Society*, London: Routledge & Kegan Paul.

Todorov, T. (1984), *The Conquest of America: the Question of the Other*, New

York: Harper & Row.

Tracey, M. (1988), 'Popular culture and the economics of global television', *Intermedia*, 16 (2): 9–25.

Tran, M. (1990), 'Hollywood rides into the rising sun', *The Guardian*, 30 November.

Tunstall, J. (1977), *The Media are American*, London: Constable.

Tydeman, J. and Kelm, E. J. (1986), *New Media in Europe: Satellites, Cable, VCRs and Videotex*, London: McGraw-Hill.

Veeser, H. (ed.) (1989), *The New Historicism*, London: Routledge.

Virilio, P. (1987), 'The overexposed city', *Zone*, 1/2: 14–31.

Walker, M. (1988a), 'Fortress vision of market future', *The Guardian*, 14 November.

Walker, M. (1988b), 'A pigsty without frontiers', *The Guardian*, 15 November.

Walker, M. (1988c), 'The boom across borders', *The Guardian*, 17 November.

Wallerstein, I. (1974) *The Modern World System*, San Diego,: Academic Press.

Wallerstein, I. (forthcoming), 'Periphery', in *The New Palgrave: A Dictionary of Economic Theory and Doctrine*, New York: Macmillan.

Wallraff, G. (1988), *Lowest of the Low*, London: Pluto.

Wark, M. (1988), 'On technological time: Virilio's overexposed city', *Arena*, 83.

Wark, M. (1991), 'The tyranny of difference: from Fordism to Sonyism', *New Formations*, 15: 43–54.

Watanabe, T. (1991), 'Southern barbarians or the red haired people: the Japanese view of exotic Europeans', in C. DeLiss (ed.) *Exotic Europeans*, London: South Bank Centre Publications.

Waterman, D. (1988), 'World television trade: the economic effects of privatisation and new technology', *Telecommunications Policy*, 12(2): 141–51.

Webster, D. (1988), *Looka Yonder! The Imaginary America of Populist Culture*, London: Routledge.

Webster, D. (1989), 'Coca-colonisation and national cultures', *Overhere*, 9(2): 64–75.

Wendelbo, H. A. (1986), 'What audience for European television?' Paper presented to the International Television Studies Conference, London, 10–12 July.

Wenders, W. (1989), *Emotion Pictures*, London: Faber & Faber.

West, C. (1991), 'Decentring Europe', *Critical Quarterly*, 33(1).

Wete, F. (1988), 'The new world information order', in C. Schneider and B. Wallis (eds) *Global Television*, New York: Wedge Press.

Whelan, J. (1989), 'Destination Newcastle', *Intercity*, November.

Whitton, B. (1988), 'Herder's critique of the Enlightenment: cultural community versus cosmopolitan rationalism', *History and Theory*, 27.

Wilk, R. (forthcoming), 'Colonial time and TV time: television and temporality in Belize', *Visual Anthropology Review*.

Wilkinson, E. (1983), *Japan Versus the West: A History of Misunderstanding*, Harmondsworth: Penguin.

Williams, R. (1983), *Towards 2000*, London: Chatto & Windus/Hogarth Press.

Williams, R. (1989), *Resources of Hope: Culture, Democracy, Socialism*, London: Verso.

Williamson, J. (1990), 'Butch Ridley and the sunrise kids', *The Guardian*, 1 March.

Williamson, J. (1991), 'Mad bad Saddam', *The Guardian*, 31 January.

Winram, S. (1984), 'The opportunity for world brands', *International Journal of Advertising*, 3(1): 17–26.

Wolf, E. (1982), *Europe and the People Without History*, Berkeley: University of California Press.

Wolferen, K. van (1988), 'The Japan problem revisited', *Foreign Affairs*, 69(4).

Wolferen, K. van (1989), *The Enigma of Japanese Power*, London: Macmillan.

Worpole, K. (1983), *Dockers and Detectives*, London: Verso.

Wright, P. (1985), *On Living in an Old Country*, London: Verso.

Wright, P. (1989), 'Re-enchanting the nation: Prince Charles and architecture', *Modern Painters*, 2(3).

Yeo, E. and S. Yeo (1988), 'On the uses of "community": from Owenism to the present', in S. Yeo (ed.) *New Views of Co-operation*, London: Routledge.

Young, I. M. (1990), *Justice and the Politics of Difference*, Princeton: Princeton University Press.

Young, R. (1990), *White Mythologies: Writing, History and the West*, London: Routledge.

Young, R. M. (1989), 'Postmodernism and the subject: pessimism of the will', *Free Associations*, 16.

Zaretsky, E. (1976), *Capitalism, the Family and Personal Life*, London: Pluto Press.

Žižek, S. (1990), 'Eastern Europe's republics of Gilead', *New Left Review*, 183: 50–62.

Žižek, S. (1992), 'Ethnic dance macabre', *The Guardian*, 28 August.

INDEX